THEY BOTH REACHED FOR THE GUN

THEY BOTH REACHED FOR THE GUN

BEULAH ANNAN, MAURINE WATKINS,
AND THE TRIAL THAT BECAME *CHICAGO*

CHARLES H. COSGROVE

Southern Illinois University Press
Carbondale

Southern Illinois University Press
www.siupress.com

Copyright © 2024 by the Board of Trustees,
Southern Illinois University
All rights reserved
Printed in the United States of America

27 26 25 24   4 3 2 1

Cover illustration: Beulah Annan on the witness stand at her trial
(*left*). Chicago Tribune archive photo/TCA. Undated publicity photo
of Maurine Watkins (*right*). Photo by Vandamm Studio © Billy Rose
Theater Division, The New York Public Library for the Performing Arts,
image ID 485274.

ISBN 978-0-8093-3938-9 (paperback)
ISBN 978-0-8093-3939-6 (ebook)

This book has been catalogued with the Library of Congress.

Printed on recycled paper ♻

CONTENTS

FIGURES

PREFACE

Anyone who has read about the history behind the musical *Chicago* and the 2002 blockbuster movie of the same name knows that they are remakes of a 1920s play by Maurine Watkins, who based her comedy on a real Chicago murder case. The case concerned a twenty-four-year-old woman named Beulah Annan, who was tried for fatally shooting her lover Harry Kalsted during a wine-soaked tryst while her husband was at work. During a brief stint as a cub reporter for the *Chicago Tribune*, Watkins happened to cover the Annan case; and the close connection between her play and her reporting was well known when *Chicago* was first produced in 1926. The connection was also pointed out years later by Thomas Pauly in a fresh edition of the play, published in 1997, when *Chicago* the musical was racking up box-office numbers on Broadway.

Since Pauly's book—*Chicago by Maurine Watkins with the Tribune Newspaper Articles That Inspired It*—and the extraordinary success of *Chicago* the movie musical, curiosity about Watkins's play and the history behind it has only grown. In fact, Pauly's book sparked my interest in the relation between the Annan case and *Chicago*. As a historian who has lived nearly my whole life in Chicagoland, I have developed a keen interest in the city's past and have had occasion to write about it. I am also a jazz trombonist, an avocation that made a story set in the Jazz Age especially fascinating for me.

As I explored the original sources for this story, I began to wonder about the degree to which the play reflected fact, as Watkins herself more than once asserted it did in interviews, and what the answer to that question might imply about the nature of the play as a social satire. I discovered that a good deal of information is available for exploring this question but had not been considered by previous analysts of the play. Surviving Chicago police logs, available in the "Homicide in Chicago 1870–1930" database at Northwestern University, make it possible to establish pertinent facts about the way the city dealt with homicide cases, including dynamics of gender in the justice process, the play's topic, as well as dynamics of race, which are nearly invisible in the play. Moreover, three important studies of criminal justice in 1920s Chicago were conducted between 1920 and 1931: *The Negro in Chicago: A Study of Race Relations and a Race Riot*; *The Illinois Crime Survey*; and a series of reports by the National Commission on Law Observance and Enforcement. These period investigations and the data they contain shed further light on the degree to which the play's satirical message was on target.

I also began to question the received account of the Annan case. When I compared previously unexamined documents with the original reporting about the case, I found significant distortions by the press. Among the important pieces of historical evidence that my re-examination of the case brings to light are the transcript of the coroner's inquest, now kept in the archive of the Cook County Medical Examiner's Office, as well as police records and other pieces of information housed in the Fosse/Verdon collection of the Music Division of the Library of Congress. When I analyzed these sources, I discovered that the assumption made by recent re-tellers of Annan's story that her guilt was obvious is not supported by the evidence.

I relied as well on conversations I had with relatives of Beulah Annan, including a number of her first cousins as well as some of their children. A little over a decade after Beulah's death, one of these cousins, Ruth Sherriff, married Perry Stephens Jr., Beulah's only child. Ruth was a valuable source of information about Beulah's first marriage. I conducted some of these interviews in Owensboro, Kentucky, where I also examined records held by the Daviess County Public Library. This research informed my reconstruction of the first eighteen years of Beulah Annan's life in Kentucky and the circumstances that caused her to leave the place of her birth and to seek a life elsewhere, ultimately in Chicago, where she would, unwittingly, inspire a play.

A NOTE ON NAMES

I have given considerable thought to how best to refer to people by name. Since Beulah had family members who shared her last name and since she acquired new last names through multiple marriages, I mostly refer to her by her first name throughout the book to avoid confusion. For the same reason, I use first names for her husbands and family members at points where there might otherwise be confusion. I have also used the first name of her lover Harry Kalsted, when describing him as part of Beulah's biography, so as to avoid the incongruity of calling her by her first name and him by his last name in these parts of the book. Some members of the Kalsted family spelled the name Kalstedt, and this spelling was used by the newspapers in referring to him. But Harry himself signed his name "Kalsted," and I have honored his preference. Finally, Beulah's maiden name was Sheriff, but one branch of her family spelled the name Sherriff. Occasional variations in my spelling of the family name reflect this.

ACKNOWLEDGMENTS

I would like to thank the following persons and institutions for their help in obtaining information for this book: Ruth (née Sherriff) Stephens, Sharon Watts, Bob and Betty Sherriff, Mildred Jenkins, Mary Rafferty, Archie Burton, Anna Price, Nancy Smith, Bill Marksberry, and Josephine Kolaya; staff of the Kentucky Room of the Daviess County Public Library, especially librarians Shelia Heflin and Leslie McCarty; staff of various divisions of the University of Kentucky Libraries; the Research Center of the Chicago History Museum; the Chicago Public Library; Northwestern University Library; Styberg Library and its interlibrary loan service; Susan LaBore, court administrator, Isanti County Government Center (Cambridge, Minnesota); Leo Wiley, court operations supervisor, Criminal Division (Fourth Judicial Circuit, State of Minnesota); the staff at the Beinecke Rare Book and Manuscript Library at Yale University Library, including public services assistant Naomi Saito; librarians of the New York Public Library Performing Arts Center, including Nailah Holmes and John Calhoun; library staff at Dartmouth College; staff at the Cook County Medical Examiner's Office; Elving Felix of the Serial and Government Publications Division of the Library of Congress; the Music Division of the Library of Congress and independent researcher Alicia Kopfstein, who assisted with the Fosse/Verdon collection; and Tony Dudek of the Tribune Content Agency. My wife, Debbie Cosgrove, and my daughter, Katherine Cosgrove, helped with hours-on-end microfilm searches. Very thoughtful copyediting was performed by Robert Brown. I am also indebted to the staff of Southern Illinois University Press for their expert work, including Sarah Jilek, Chelsey Harris, Khara Lukancic, and in particular my editor, Sylvia Frank Rodrigue, for believing in this project and seeing it through with superb guidance.

THEY BOTH REACHED FOR THE GUN

INTRODUCTION

On April 3, 1924, the Chicago police arrested a woman named Beulah Annan for killing a man named Harry Kalsted in her Kenwood apartment on the city's south side. Harry was Beulah's lover, and the two of them had consumed a good deal of wine during their afternoon rendezvous, while Beulah's husband was at work. Police recovered a gun and a blood-stained jazz record.

Beulah's arrest immediately became front-page news in Chicago and across the country. Six weeks later a Chicago jury acquitted her of murder, and the story again made headlines. A young reporter named Maurine Watkins covered Beulah's case for the *Chicago Tribune* and subsequently wrote a play about it. Watkins thought Beulah was guilty and said so. So did her play, *Chicago*, since its plot was widely known to be based on Beulah's case.

The play, which became a Broadway hit, was a satire about the Chicago criminal-justice system, and it carried a social message, namely, that the city's falsely chivalric and sentimental all-male juries were making a mockery of the courts by setting free virtually every woman tried for murder. The play lampooned the press, too, for turning crime news into entertainment.

Watkins's 1926 play was turned into a silent film in 1927, a sound movie starring Ginger Rogers in 1942, and a Bob Fosse musical in the 1970s that was revived to great acclaim in the 1990s and then transformed in 2002 into the Rob Marshall movie *Chicago*, one of the most successful movie musicals of all time. Since Marshall's version, there has been renewed curiosity about the origins of the drama. Besides innumerable webpages, many books have taken up different parts of that history, especially the facts about Beulah Annan. A few have sought to place her in the social context of 1920s Chicago, and some have noted that Maurine Watkins based her play on her reporting on criminal cases involving women, especially the Annan case.

Until now, however, no one has offered a critical examination of the case against Beulah Annan or an exploration of the social assumptions that made the message of *Chicago* plausible in its own time. My aim is to accomplish

1

these things through a fresh retelling of the story of Beulah Annan and the play she inspired.

Watkins's message reflected assumptions influenced by the era in which she lived and the newspaper for which she worked. As she herself once noted in an interview with the *New York World* (January 16, 1927), the *Chicago Tribune*'s stance on criminal cases was always pro-prosecution. As a *Tribune* reporter, Watkins reflected this attitude in her coverage of Annan, and she did the same in her play. *Chicago* portrays its representative police character as an earnest but dumb servant of the law and its representative assistant-state's-attorney character as a shrewd, honest but weary pursuer of truth and justice engaged in a losing battle against dynamics he cannot control—lying defendants, money-grubbing defense attorneys, and misguided jurors who become willing fools whenever they are confronted with a female defendant.

The play's message about the justice system also resonated with the times. For years, Chicagoans had been told that women were committing murder at alarming rates and getting away with it. The papers, usually quoting prosecutors, stoked public anger by citing raw acquittal figures without context, giving the impression that juries were doing nothing to stem the tide of female killers. Many people believed that the jury system had become an ineffective instrument of justice generally, or at least they worried that this might be so.

As noted in a well-regarded 1931 federal study of crime and criminal justice in 1920s Chicago, the "news value" of jury trials had fostered an erroneous popular idea about their role in the criminal-justice system. The public had the false impression that "acquittals by juries constitute the predominant mode or method whereby men accused of crime escape conviction and that the jury trial is the weak spot in the administration [of justice]." These observations explain why the premise of Watkins's play seemed so plausible. The play purported to lay bare all the behind-the-scenes chicanery that was supposedly causing bad jury verdicts in trials of female murder defendants. Similar concerns about juries were prevalent in other cities as well, which gave the play's message a broad appeal. Indeed, theater critics across the country observed that the satire's ridicule of the criminal-justice system in Chicago probably applied to other metropolises, too.[1]

The path of the main character Roxie Hart from arrest to trial to freedom was meant to be typical, and it was widely recognized at the time—from both press coverage of the play and public comments by Watkins herself—that Roxie was modeled on Beulah Annan, whose path through the justice process was supposed to be emblematic. There was even a certain parallel between the way Watkins constructed the plot of the 1926 play and her reporting on the 1924 Annan case.

The opening scene of *Chicago* has Roxie commit cold-blooded murder on stage, thus leaving no doubt about her guilt in the mind of the audience. The "opening scene" of the real-life Annan case was reported in the *Chicago Tribune* on the basis of a confession that Annan had allegedly made to the investigating police and prosecutors. The *Tribune's* first article about the case—unsigned and not necessarily by Watkins—reported this allegation as fact; subsequent signed articles by Watkins took this fact for granted and used it against Annan. Thus, when Annan herself later talked directly to reporters and claimed self-defense, Watkins told her readers that Annan had retracted her confession, implying that she had concocted a phony defense. The plot structure of *Chicago* mirrors this: it presents the facts to the audience right from the start and shows the defendant, who has admitted them, subsequently and outrageously disavowing them. There was, however, an important difference between the real-life case and that of the play. When the actual text of Annan's so-called confession became public at an inquest, it revealed that the prosecutors had misrepresented Annan's words. Watkins's reporting never pointed out this discrepancy; nor did the other papers. Nor have subsequent re-tellers of Annan's story.

Investigating the history of *Chicago* affords a revealing look into ways in which the press, prosecutors, and ultimately even the theater shaped perceptions of crime and criminal justice in 1920s Chicago. In Watkins's opinion and that of George Pierce Baker, her renowned mentor in drama, the play was a piece of biting social critique about a serious subject, a comedy with an earnest message—an *exposé*. The satire was also received by critics as a weighty matter. Yet in reality, the problem it attacked was something of a red herring and not the "weak spot" in the administration of justice in 1920s Chicago. By the same token, the play's singular focus on a minor issue, which it hyped as an outrage, was a sort of misdirection that reinforced what was already a general public obliviousness to more serious conditions in the city's criminal-justice system. When Chicago's corrupt mayor William Hale Thompson told the press that Watkins was "excellently suited to tell the world *all it need know* about the city of Chicago," he had reason to be grateful that her satirical exposé focused on a relatively small matter and seemed to exonerate Chicago's police and prosecutors of any systematically corrupt tendencies. Of course, Watkins was not an investigative reporter, much less a sociologist. Having absorbed prevailing opinions at the *Tribune*, with which she may already have been sympathetic, she mirrored them in the message of her play.[2]

Among the more serious problems with the criminal-justice system in 1920s Chicago were the police's routine use of violence to extort confessions from criminal suspects and the system's pervasive racial bias against African Americans, especially African American men. Roxie Hart was manifestly white, as were all the other characters in *Chicago,* as if the main setting of the dramatic action, the women's wing of Cook County Jail, held no African American women. Yet at one point Roxie complains that she might have to eat "with the wops and the n——s." This was meant to draw guffaws from an audience that was expected to agree with Roxie's white racist sentiments and to find it humorously pretentious that a lowlife like her should be so discriminating about the company she kept in jail. Hence, to the extent that the play carried messages about race, it exploited racism for laughs while insinuating that racism played no role in Chicago's criminal-justice operations, since Chicago juries supposedly let 98 percent of *all* female murderers go free, whatever their race.

Although Watkins was actually not "excellently suited" to offer a behind-the-scenes exposé of criminal justice in Chicago, as an avid newspaper reader and a media insider, she *was* well equipped to comment on newspapers as money-making enterprises. Her play described the methods of the press in turning crime news into lucrative entertainment, and it made fun of so-called sob-sister reporting, the gushingly sympathetic journalism that the tabloids lavished on female defendants. During her days as a reporter, Watkins herself had not been a sob sister. The *Chicago Tribune* did not encourage that sort of reporting by its female staff; and as one of the staider papers, it reported on homicides in matter-of-fact prose. Watkins's articles about Annan mixed matter-of-fact prose with touches of wry wit and light mockery. In this respect, she was something of a trailblazer in women's crime journalism, and her experiments in journalistic tone presaged the satirical approach she used in *Chicago.*

A close look at reporting styles in the news coverage of Annan also turns up another interesting feature of 1920s journalism. Although news editors at papers with strict journalistic standards demanded factual exactitude about the who, what, when, and where of a story, they granted latitude in quotation. It was deemed sufficient for reporters to use their own words in quoting a subject, so long as they succeeded in conveying the "gist" of what someone said. Loose paraphrase was regularly placed between quotation marks, and no one in the news business seems to have had any reservations about this practice.

Even handbooks for would-be reporters written by university professors—academics devoted to raising the standards of journalism—condoned this method of *paraquotation* (my term). As for newspaper readers, they had no way of knowing and probably did not even suspect that many of the quotations they encountered in news articles, across a wide range of topics, were free paraphrases. The possibilities for misrepresentation were rife in paraquotation, and reporters and rewrite staff at certain tabloids felt free to create quotations out of whole cloth.

Creative quotation was certainly practiced by reporters who covered Beulah Annan. To varying degrees, the press fashioned her into a fictionalized character before Watkins turned her into the fictional Roxie Hart. This makes it difficult to pierce the veil to the historical person. Yet the use of critical methods—such as testing quotations against independently established facts, including examples of Annan's own style of speaking, and comparing quotations in different newspaper accounts that claim to report the same interview—makes it possible to discover places in the news coverage where Annan's own voice comes through.

By providing a more accurate and detailed history of Beulah Annan, I may give the impression that my aim is to cultivate sympathy for her and even to vindicate her. As for vindication, I leave it to readers to form conclusions, if any, about whether Annan was guilty or innocent of the crime for which she was tried. Having thoroughly examined the evidence myself, I find grounds for reasonable doubt. Hence, one of my aims is to vindicate the *jury* that tried Annan by showing that the prosecution's case, indeed the evidence as a whole, was insufficient to warrant a conviction.

As for sympathy, Annan's rather sad life history may evoke readers' sympathy at points, unsympathy at other points, indeed a set of mixed feelings overall, along with a good deal of uncertainty about the most crucial thing—whether she killed Harry Kalsted in a drunken rage or in a drunken but genuine fear for her life. I have made every effort to be even-handed in my treatment of her and to proceed similarly with Maurine Watkins, providing context that helps explain each woman's attitudes and decisions. It may be worth mentioning that readers who participated in the review process for this book arrived at contrary opinions about Annan and Watkins, which ranged from encouraging me to go harder on Watkins by emphasizing how she exploited Annan to urging me to treat Watkins more sympathetically while being more severe with Annan.

Beulah Annan would be of little historical importance today had not Watkins's play made a social message out of her, with Watkins claiming that

Chicago was realistic fiction, "real, all through," "all straight, without any idea of exaggeration." In other words, the play was supposed to be an exposé that revealed the truth about Beulah and women like her and, in so doing, presented a scathing behind-the-scenes look at Chicago's criminal-justice system. While the play was also a comedy, its humor derived not from comedic distortion, so Watkins alleged, but from a realistic display of events that were a mockery in themselves, a travesty of justice. These claims deserve critical examination—a thorough historical investigation of all the relevant facts they purport to represent. The chapters to follow take up this task, and in this respect the book offers an assessment of *Chicago* as a social satire, both as Watkins conceived it and as 1920s theater critics received it.

1. BEULAH MAE

Beulah Mae Sheriff was born on a Kentucky farm in 1899 to John and Mary (née Stone) Sheriff. She was the only child of a marriage that did not last.[1]

It cannot have been easy for Beulah's mother to care for a small child and manage a farm wife's heavy load of chores without any female relatives or older children to help. Eventually, an unhappy Mary began urging John to move the family to nearby Owensboro. She was not alone in this wish. "Many a farmer rents his farm," one contemporary observer remarked, "and moves to town on account of his wife and daughters."[2]

But John Sheriff could not imagine moving to the city. He loved country life and did not want to leave his successful farm and the extended Sheriff family to work for an employer in Owensboro at a job he would not enjoy. The couple found themselves at an impasse. Mary eventually broke the stalemate by moving to Owensboro, taking Beulah with her. In later years, Beulah's cousins would report what they had heard from their parents. "She just up and left one day," Bevie Marksberry explained. "It wasn't that she had anything against John," just that she "didn't like farm life." Anna Price heard the same.[3]

Once in Owensboro, Mary filed for divorce. Papers were served on John, and he began paying temporary alimony; but Mary never went any further with her divorce action. If she hoped that John would join her in Owensboro, she was mistaken. He stayed where he was, paid Mary monthly support, and waited for her to return.[4]

As Beulah's father, John had a legal right to take Beulah from Mary, and he could have arranged for her to live at one of his brothers' or sisters' nearby farms. But he did not want to hurt Mary by separating her from her only child or hurt eight-year-old Beulah by separating her from her mother.[5]

By May of 1910, Mary and Beulah were boarding in Owensboro with a widow named Hettie Hardwick. Hettie owned a house at Fourth and Mulberry, not far from the Ohio River and just two blocks south of the city's bawdy-house district in a neighborhood of tinners, coopers, clerks, stenographers, and telephone operators. Twelve people were crowded into this modest home, ten women and girls, ranging in age from seven to seventy-seven, along with Hettie Hardwick's male servant and a female boarder's husband, who traveled with a horse show. Ten-year-old Beulah attended Walnut Street School several blocks away, and Mary worked in a downtown millinery, trimming and refurbishing women's hats. For this work she was paid the barest wages, and there was no permanency to the job. After the spring rush, the owner of the store probably let Mary go, for she would have counted as a temporary employee.[6]

Mary and Beulah Sheriff, circa 1907, shortly after Mary left Beulah's father and moved with Beulah to Owensboro. Courtesy of Betty Sherriff.

Over the next several years, Mary shifted from one low-paying job to another, including, it appears, selling door to door. And Mary and Beulah moved from one cheap residence to another. Although the support Mary received from John ensured that she and Beulah always had money for food, clothing, and rent, her marital situation put her in a socially vulnerable position. In the early twentieth century, a woman who left her husband, even if the two of them were only separated, was considered no better than a divorcée, one step above a "fallen" woman and liable to be "cut," that is, snubbed. As a minister of the era explained, without sympathy, "society shows its disapproval in these cases, because this is the only antidote to divorce we have in this country—'society's snub.' The pulpit or the press does not worry the transgressors much. . . . But society's 'deadly cut' or its 'frigid brow' seems to be more than even the most brazen of them can stand up against." Therefore, Mary had been telling people that she was a widow. She was not the only woman in her circumstance to do so. As one man who grew up in the 1920s recalled, his mother had been so ashamed of having been deserted by his father that she told people she was a widow and instructed her son to say that his father was dead, if anyone asked.[7]

There must have been a friend or two in whom Mary confided the truth of her marital condition, and there were probably people who suspected or found out, despite the lie. But her feeling that she had to keep up the veneer of widowhood meant that Beulah had to tell the lie, too. It is likely that when anyone outside the circle of the knowing asked about her father, she was to say that her father was dead and to volunteer no further information. Mary would have explained that the fib was necessary because people would otherwise think poorly of them, perhaps even snub them.

Circumstances intensified the intimacy between Mary and Beulah in these years of Beulah's childhood, the moving from one place to the next, always living in a single room and sharing a bed. In the warm cocoon of this private world, Beulah's little successes and failures, joys and hurts, were the engrossing drama of Mary's existence. She doted on Beulah and was also controlling. Beulah was likewise bound to her mother with a degree of loyalty and love she would never bestow on any other person. In later years, friends remarked this about her—that the person she cared for most was her mother.[8]

John Sheriff eventually divorced Mary on grounds of abandonment, and in 1912 he married a woman named Martha Howard. Two years later, Mary also remarried, uniting with a widower named Elvin "Eb" Neel, who had two children, Gilbert and Anice. The Neel family lived in Owensboro in a small house at Second and Pearl. By May of 1913, however, when Beulah was thirteen and a half, she was living with her father and stepmother, Martha. This arrangement was probably not her choice, since she was emotionally closer to her mother than to her father and preferred town life. But by law, as well as custom, Beulah had to do what her father decreed, no matter what her mother said, at least until she turned twenty-one or got married.[9]

She was not happy on her father's farm and pined for her mother and friends in Owensboro. Her father let her visit, of course, and during an extended stay in the fall of 1914, she met Perry Stephens, a young linotype operator who worked for the *Owensboro Inquirer*. Perry lived with his parents and siblings in a small house on Second Street, just down the street from the Neel residence. He was twenty-one; she was fifteen. He was shy; she was outgoing. It may be that she initiated their friendship. In any case, the attraction on his side is not difficult to explain. Beulah was tall, slender, and very pretty, with glowing skin, bright blue eyes, and dark red hair. She also had a warm, fun-loving personality. Perry fell madly in love with her.[10]

Beulah became fond of Perry, and when he proposed marriage several months later, she saw it as a way to escape the farm and her father's control and to live in Owensboro near her mother. But she was legally too young to get married, whether in Kentucky or across the Ohio River in Indiana, without her parents' consent. Neither would give it, she knew, but there was another possibility.

It was widely known that the county clerks in Rockport, Indiana, just up the river, were willing to accept flimsy evidence of a person's age, including the word of a friend. Beulah's own parents had eloped to Rockport without so much as a friend to vouch that sixteen-year-old Mary was eighteen. John and Mary had appeared before a clerk named John Baumgaertner, who had filled out the required affidavit of age to make it show that a Mary Stone had appeared before him on March 31 and that she, under oath, had declared that she was a "disinterested person" who knew this Mary Stone and could attest that said Mary Stone was of lawful age to be married without parental consent. Having thus represented Mary as vouching for herself, the accommodating Baumgaertner placed an X on the signature line as her "mark."[11]

Beulah's elopement was more dramatic. In the dim hours of February 11, 1915, she sneaked away from her father's farmhouse and headed off to marry Perry at that same courthouse in Rockport where her parents had wed. This courthouse lay eight miles upriver from Owensboro. But the Ohio River was in a state of massive flooding.[12]

Twelve days earlier, a winter rain had begun falling in Owensboro and its country environs, pooling in the low-lying fields and eddying in the wagon-

Above left, Beulah's first husband, Perry Stephens, around the time of their elopement, when he was about twenty-two years old. [Detail of figure on page 12.] *Above right,* Beulah Sheriff at age fifteen or so. This photo was taken close to the time when she eloped with Perry Stephens. Courtesy of Sharon Watts.

rutted country roads. This gentle rain was the first sign of more threatening weather to come. The Owensboro papers had already begun reporting about conditions near Pittsburgh, where warm rain was melting the snow in the watersheds of the Allegheny and Monongahela Rivers, causing the Ohio River to rise precipitously.[13]

On Monday, February 1st, the front page of Owensboro's morning *Messenger* telegraphed a sobering fact: "Great Volumes of Water Are Coming Down the Ohio River." By Wednesday morning, it was plain to the eye that the river was rising; and over the next two days the Ohio swelled into a roiling mass of dark water that invaded the lowlands on its Indiana side and inched its way up the high banks on its Kentucky side, where Owensboro stood.

On Sunday, the papers reported that the Ohio would probably crest on Tuesday night or Wednesday morning. Nevertheless, the Louisville and Evansville packet service, which made stops at Rockport, would be out of operation for perhaps another week; and the Rounds brothers, who ran a local packet service, were using all their boats to help farmers remove corn to dry ground.

On Thursday, the Sheriff household probably learned the following, thanks to a restoration of mail and newspaper service to their neighborhood. The river had crested in the wee hours of Wednesday morning and was expected to fall rapidly on Thursday. Yet certain boats that regularly ran between Louisville and Evansville were not yet back in service and would not resume their schedules until the river assumed normal conditions. Most of the landings were completely under water. Not only that, the steamers *Golden Girl* and *Jumbo* had been torn from their moorings and were still marooned in a flooded cornfield.[14]

It was about eleven miles from John Sheriff's farm to downtown Owensboro. Beulah would have known that the roads were passable, since the mail had been delivered the day before. After breakfast and before the newspaper arrived, she slipped away in a horse and buggy. If all went well, she would be married before anyone figured out where she was.

Her mother would later describe how Beulah rode into Owensboro "in madcap fashion" and married Perry Stephens. One can picture the fifteen-year-old hurtling through the soggy countryside in her light buggy. The roads were a mess. At Smith Road, she turned east to the Livermore-and-Owensboro Road, then headed north, clattering over the wrought-iron Panther Creek

Owensboro Inquirer composing room crew, circa 1915 (not early 1920s); Perry Stephens (*far left*). Lawrence W. Hagar papers, box 24, item 80, University of Kentucky Libraries.

bridge toward the outskirts of Owensboro, and soon she was clopping past stately homes on well-paved South Frederica Street. Ten minutes later she was rendezvousing with Perry in downtown Owensboro.[15]

The couple enlisted Lucy Hicks, the wife of one of Perry's fellow printers, to go with them to Rockport so that Lucy could vouch—fib—that Beulah was eighteen. When the wedding party reached the Owensboro wharf, they found that the wharf landing was still submerged and that much of the river traffic was still suspended. But packet service had resumed. The Rounds Bros.' ninety-foot shallow-draft vessels needed no landing or wharf boat to take on passengers, since each boat was equipped with a gangway. This happy fact meant that shortly after 10:00 A.M. the wedding party was able to board one of the Rounds Bros.' boats and settle inside its long, covered cabin, a close space smelling of river water and fumes from the gas-powered engine. The captain eased the boat away from shore and maneuvered into the heart of the log-littered, muddy river. The Kentucky shoreline was clearly marked by high banks at Owensboro, but the only signs of the Indiana shoreline were the upper parts of a few farm buildings and partly submerged trees. The river stretched five miles inland on the Indiana side.[16]

Forty minutes later the Rockport bluff came into view, a little mountain in the midst of what must have looked like a large swamp. The Ohio had filled the bottomlands for miles in all directions, but the town, built into the slope of the bluff on the other side of the escarpment, well above the lowlands, was high and dry.[17]

The packet stopped at a muddy strip of land at the foot of the cliff, and the wedding party now followed the steep, winding plank sidewalk up to the town square, where a stained and weather-beaten courthouse stood between a jail and a wood-frame church. There, Beulah and Perry presented themselves to a courthouse clerk and requested a marriage license. Lucy Hicks served as a witness, adding three years to Beulah's age by declaring that Beulah had been born in November of 1896 and was therefore now eighteen. The clerk wrote the necessary particulars into the blanks on the license and turned the document around for the couple's signatures. Perry added his name in a neat scrawl; Beulah signed with a curious mixture of forward and backward slants.[18]

Their marriage might have been solemnized immediately by a justice of the peace, but Perry insisted on being married by the minister of his denomination, the Christian Church of the Disciples of Christ. Elder Leonard Varble was called to the courthouse, or perhaps they found him at his home on Seminary Street and exchanged vows in the tidy Varble parlor with Mrs. Varble looking on.[19]

It was now midday. The wedding trio may have celebrated with lunch in a Rockport restaurant. They certainly would have walked to the nearby river bluff to look out, from the crest of the cliff, at the broad vista of debris-strewn water and drowned fields. Rows of black leafless trees stuck up from the vast waters, marking the flooded shoreline, tracing outlines of submerged islands and invisible roads. In the flinty afternoon sunlight, Beulah was radiant.

One can imagine Perry's exuberance. There must have been something dreamlike about the courtship, an effect of Perry's infatuation, the elopement in the midst of a flood, and the fact he had kept his marital plans a secret from his own family and most of his friends. As for Beulah, she would have felt exhilarated by the knowledge that she was now free from farm life. But perhaps she was also unsettled by the thought that she may have done a reckless thing.[20]

Beulah's mother opposed the marriage from the start. According to family members, Mary always wanted Beulah to become an actress. She spoiled her daughter, told her she was the prettiest girl in school, demanded money from Beulah's father to buy her dresses from fine shops in Owensboro, and nurtured the idea of an acting career that would get them both out of Owensboro and on to "brighter lights." Mary may have thought that all an aspiring young woman needed to break into the movies was prettiness, not thespian training—or perhaps that any necessary training would be provided if only Beulah were discovered. Beulah herself probably enjoyed this fantasy, but she was not committed to it. Her elopement to Perry was a no, not only to her father's plans for her but to her mother's as well.[21]

The marriage was not happy. Perry was devoted to Beulah but controlling, partly because he was older, partly as a matter of temperament. He was also a homebody with little interest in socializing. Beulah felt trapped. At fifteen, she wanted to go out and enjoy the usual amusements or gather with friends at someone's house to pull back the rugs and dance to a victrola. Meanwhile, her mother tried to convince her that she had made a mistake and should leave Perry. Despite social attitudes at the time, this idea did not seem shocking to Beulah. After all, her mother had left her father after eloping at sixteen and then regretting it.[22]

A year into the marriage, Beulah gave birth to a baby boy. She had not felt ready to start a family, but there had been no effective way to prevent a pregnancy without Perry's agreement and cooperation. If he wanted children, her duty was to accept his wishes. They named their son Perry Waller Stephens, after his father, and called him P. W.

Beulah's husband seems to have been an extreme version of the early-twentieth-century father who left the nurture of infants and even toddlers to his wife and other female members of his family. Perry took no interest in P. W. and assigned all the care for him to Beulah. She received help from Mrs. Stephens, but her own mother worked at a local factory and could not assist with P. W. during the day. Beulah felt overwhelmed by motherhood, and Mary kept pressuring her to leave Perry and put the infant in the care of Mrs. Stephens. It was a strange demand from a mother whose life was absorbed by devotion to her own child. But perhaps there was an element of realism and wisdom in the proposal, at least as Mary assessed her daughter's situation. In any case, Beulah did what her mother told her to do. On November 8, 1916, when P. W. was three months old, Beulah told Perry's parents that she was "too young to be a wife and mother" and "wanted to join a moving picture company." (Her mother had probably given her this script.) Then she walked out.[23]

She almost immediately regretted it. For a time, it seemed that a reconciliation was in the offing. Beulah asked Perry to take her back, but she did not want things to be the way they had been before. There were emotional meetings and letters exchanged. In one of these letters, composed in the spring of 1917, Perry declared his undying love for Beulah but gave her an ultimatum. Before he would take her back, she had to stop living a "crooked life" and demonstrate that she could live properly over the course of three months. The expression *crooked life* was a Christian one, the opposite of the "straight and narrow path," which, in the church culture of Perry's upbringing, had to do especially with avoidance of alcohol and tobacco. Perry had undoubtably heard that Beulah was going to parties where she drank.[24]

Perry also knew that Beulah's friends included young men. One was Morton Atchison, the son of an Owensboro attorney, whose family lived in a fine house on fashionable South Frederica Street. In the summer of 1916, Atchison had just completed an illustrious high school career as a top member of the debate team, manager of the high school lyceum, and a regular actor in school plays, which won him a minor part in a local motion picture (a farce called *Owensboro Adopts a Baby*). He was a member of the Owensboro choral society, too, as well as the Elks Lodge's musical troupe, and he had recently been elected president of the Junior Chamber of Commerce. He was also making college plans. Meanwhile, he had a job in the editorial department of the *Owensboro Inquirer*, the newspaper where Perry was employed as a printer. Perhaps Atchison met Beulah at an *Inquirer* social event, such as a company picnic. In any case, he eventually left the *Inquirer*, abandoned his college plans as well, and took a job as a salesman for the Standard Oil Company in Chattanooga, Tennessee. After Beulah left Perry in the fall of 1916, she socialized with Atchison when he made occasional weekend visits to Owensboro.[25]

As Beulah saw it, she was free to do as she wished, since she was no longer with Perry. But her behavior made it difficult for her to negotiate a reconciliation with him. It was probably during these months that she started drinking. Diary entries she wrote in her twenties suggest that she tended to overdrink, sometimes as a way of coping with unhappiness. Getting drunk as a mode of escape likely had its beginnings in the period when her marriage to Perry was heading to a divorce.[26]

Beulah and Perry had been exchanging letters, and in the spring of 1917 he wrote, "I would advise you to go to your father as I think you could be left alone long enough to know just exactly what you want to do." But she did not go live with her father. Nor did she and Perry come to any agreement. He finally filed for divorce. Beulah did not resist.[27]

Just as the divorce proceedings were nearing their conclusion, Beulah was involved in an automobile accident. Morton Atchison had returned to Owensboro for a weekend visit, and he, Beulah, and a few friends had been traveling on a city thoroughfare in a car belonging to Atchison's mother. At some point, Atchison lost control of the vehicle and drove into a telephone pole. Beulah suffered a broken left thigh and lacerations to her right thigh. The time of the accident—after midnight on a Saturday night—suggests that the group had been to a party or maybe to a roadhouse.[28]

Beulah spent the next two months in the city hospital. When she was released, her father insisted that she come live with him. Although she was now eighteen, she was still considered a minor, and custody had reverted to her father when her divorce became final. Beulah responded by petitioning the county court to appoint her mother as her legal guardian. The court made the appointment in February of 1918.[29]

Beulah may have rationalized that leaving her baby in the care of the Stephenses was for the best. P. W. would have a good home, and she herself would be better off unmarried and without the responsibilities of parenthood, which was her mother's view. Yet Beulah never escaped the feeling that she had done something ruinous. Years later, she told a reporter that a divorce causes "a done-for feeling that makes you sure you've already pretty much made a mess of life." Although Mary claimed that Perry had been a cruel husband, Beulah said the fault was not all his. Her friends took her side, she told the reporter, and Perry's friends took his.[30]

If Beulah imagined that tensions would ease after the divorce and that she would be able to visit her son and spend time with him, she was mistaken. Perry turned over all decision-making about P. W. to his parents. It was understood that William and Margaret Stephens would raise the boy, and they told a judge as much during the divorce proceedings. Eventually, Perry took the further step of signing over legal custody of P. W. to them, an act that suggests that he, too, like Beulah, did not want the responsibilities of parenthood. His relationship with his son remained distant. Although they lived in the same house during P. W.'s earliest years—Perry having moved back into his parents' home—Perry took on no parental role. And when P. W. was just four years old, Perry left Owensboro for a job in Evansville, Indiana. Not long after that, he moved to Chicago. In other words, both parents gave up their parenting roles, something for which people in that time generally forgave fathers, in a case of divorce, but not mothers.[31]

According to a family member, when Perry signed over his custodial rights to his parents, the Stephenses asked Beulah to sign a companion document. Her mother told her to comply, and she did. Since Beulah never sued for visitation rights, the document probably formalized a renunciation of those rights. Beulah was not prepared to fight her mother and the Stephenses. The Stephenses were adamant that Beulah should have no more contact with P. W., and this state of affairs proved permanent. Beulah was barred from seeing her son. The Stephenses erected a wall of family silence about Beulah. According to P. W., "she was never mentioned in my presence."[32]

Beulah did, however, make efforts to see P. W. by asking Perry to arrange secret meetings. But it was a hopeless situation. Perry, who showed no interest in helping to raise his son, must have found it almost impossible to take the boy out of the house for a surreptitious meeting with Beulah, without arousing his mother's suspicions. The meetings were doomed to become untenable, in any case, as soon as P. W. was old enough to talk.

The last time Beulah saw P. W. was in the summer or fall of 1918, just before Beulah and the Neel family moved to Louisville. The recollection of this meeting was passed down from Perry to P. W. and from P. W. to his wife, Ruth. P. W. was a toddler by this time. Perry did not tell his parents about the rendezvous, which occurred in Owensboro's Hickman Park at the end of the streetcar line. Beulah took P. W. in her arms and walked around the park with him, saying goodbye.[33]

The Neel family, Beulah included, moved to Louisville in the latter part of 1918. Eb Neel was not with them. In the spring of that year, Eb had landed a better-paying job at Owensboro's Green Mill Distillery. Just days into his new employment and being unaccustomed to its ways and risks, he lost his footing on one of the high walkways of the warehouse and fell, fatally, to the concrete floor.[34]

Eb's death made Mary the head of the family, and it must have been Mary who decided that they should all move to Louisville. According to what one of Beulah's cousins heard, Mary had always wanted Beulah to "be an actress or go into vaudeville," so she took the family to "the bright lights of Louisville" to make that happen. But the family struggled in Louisville, and Mary, who had been employed in factory work in Owensboro, ended up taking in sewing while she waited for a workman's compensation insurance settlement, which was not awarded until November of 1919. Beulah may have worked, too. Whether she made any effort to get into acting is unknown. It is possible that her mother thought that an agent or producer would simply discover her, based on her good looks. It was all a pipe dream.[35]

In the spring of 1919, Beulah took up with a young taxicab driver. The Neels were then living at 815 South Second Street on the edge of downtown in what appears to have been a boardinghouse. Mary may have managed the place. The taxi driver, a shifty fellow named Jack Thorpe, was nothing like the diffident, honest, hardworking Perry. It seems that Jack had been recruited by an auto theft ring. Taxi drivers like Jack did the car stealing, sometimes using their status as chauffeurs to convince a car owner that they would watch the vehicle while the owner was in a restaurant or a shop.[36]

On April 30, 1919, Jack was arrested. The following evening an unhappy Beulah got roaring drunk at a party at the Rossmore Apartments at Fourth and Broadway, then staggered home with the help of two female friends. When she got to the front yard of the house on South Second Street, she began screaming for "her Jack." A small crowd gathered, and police were called. When they arrived, Beulah ran into the house. A police officer followed and found her dancing in the front room. Wittingly or accidentally, the twirling Beulah, who was still quite intoxicated, kicked him in the stomach as he approached her. Then she threw a lamp at him. In the patrol wagon on the way to the police station, she admitted to knowing about her boyfriend's auto heists and declared that she wanted to go to jail to be with him. A week later she appeared in police court on charges of drunkenness and disorderly conduct and was fined $15. It was the second time in a month.[37]

By 1920, most of the Neel family was ready to leave Louisville. Anice wanted to return to Owensboro to marry Lee Bartlett, her childhood sweetheart. Beulah and Mary wanted to go to Chicago. Only Gilbert wished to remain in Louisville.[38]

While the plans to move were under way, Beulah met a man named Albert Annan at a house party. Her Louisville friends described him as a "woman-hater," but he was merely shy around women and lacked the confidence to date them. Beulah's friends dared her to flirt with him. She must have flirted kindly, putting Al at ease. "She was all I thought a woman could be," he later said. Two weeks after Mary and Beulah moved to Chicago, a smitten Al followed. A few weeks later, Beulah married him.[39]

Albert Annan was nothing like Jack Thorpe. Once again, Beulah had married her opposite, another homebody who did not like to go dancing or negotiate a crowded room. But Al's maturity and steadiness were attractive to her. He was eight years older than Beulah, tall, strong, reliable, and hardworking. Despite their differences in personality, the two made a go of it. Information about their life together from 1920 through 1923 suggests that Beulah saw her marriage to Al as a fresh start for her. She felt genuine affection for him, and her social life in these years revolved around him and her mother.[40]

Artist's sketch of Beulah's second husband, Albert Annan. *Owensboro Inquirer,* July 4, 1926, p. 3. Newspapers.com.

Chicago, along with most of the rest of the country, suffered an initial postwar economic depression in the early 1920s, and the Annans struggled to maintain steady employment, even when the downturn eased in 1923. In Louisville, Al had worked as a delivery truck driver and had developed skills as an auto mechanic. In Chicago, he was able to get work as a mechanic in various garages but was unable to find anything permanent. Beulah also worked, for less money, and she, too, had trouble finding a lasting position. At the beginning of 1923, after three years of marriage, the Annans owned no furniture and struggled to save money. In their most desperate times, they may have veered toward the brink of homelessness, a frightening prospect, since there was no family to take them in, not even Beulah's mother, who had no place of her own but lived in boardinghouses. At least once in 1923, they left an apartment and found "a sleeping room."[41]

Frequent job changes caused the Annans to move from neighborhood to neighborhood, making it difficult for them to make and keep friends. This must have bothered Beulah more than Al. He had no interest in going out with friends to the city's cafes and cabarets but preferred a quiet evening at home, occasionally taking his wife to a restaurant or a movie, or enjoying a drive with Beulah, Mary, and Mary's friend John Lydon in John's car. These humdrum details of the Annans' recreations are known only because Beulah recorded them in a diary she kept in 1923 (which one of the Chicago tabloids published after her arrest). This journal was not of the "Dear Diary" variety but rather a line-a-day notebook in which a person jotted down a given day's activities in two or three brief sentences.[42]

Beulah's diary shows her talking to herself about her life, without any calculation or effort to make an impression on others. Since the diary is quite mundane and consists mostly of bare facts about the things she did, one wonders why she bothered to keep it at all, especially since she sometimes went for weeks without making an entry. The most plausible explanation is that she wanted to memorialize her life with Al. Although she was sometimes too busy or tired or forgetful to document an event, the things she recorded were important to her.

One thing of importance to her was the mere fact that she and Al were still together. She calls him "Daddy" and "Sweetie" in the diary and marks six-month anniversaries. "Married three years today," she notes on March 29; and on September 29 she writes, "Today is Daddy's birthday. Married three years, six months today."

The diary begins with a reference to New Year's Eve. Half of Chicago celebrated in the city's restaurants, ballrooms, and cafes, but the Annans stayed home. "We had a pint of Atherton," Beulah wrote. "Saw the New Year in. Went to bed at 2 o'clock. . . . We took a car ride this P.M." Other entries are even more mundane. "Shopped all the afternoon. Sweetie and I went to sixty-third. I bought a new dress and some shoes. Almost broke." "Went up to see Mama. Ate dinner with her and we played poker." "Went over to see mama. Am very sick. Al and I had too much to drink." "Al worked. We ate dinner and went to the show. Saw 'Backbone.' Went over to see Mama. Al and I almost argued." "I went to the country with Al. I drove the car for over two hours. Came home and went to bed very tired." "Rained so hard this afternoon we went to a show." "Had my hair bobbed. Don't know whether I am glad or sorry." "Daddy brought a pint of bottled in bond whisky. I got sick. Had dinner on forty-seventh street." She also noted when she or Al found or lost a job and when they moved out of an apartment or found a new one.

Significantly, no friends are mentioned by name in the diary. Nor does Beulah refer to spending time with *unnamed* friends. In fact, she does not record social activities with any persons other than Al and her mother (and sometimes including her mother's friend John).

She took at least two trips. In the summer of 1922, she and Al went to Michigan together, probably to the twin resort towns of St. Joseph and Benton Harbor, a popular destination just across the lake, served by steamers outfitted for vacationers. The holiday was marred by a theft. One night, while they slept, an intruder entered their room. They never heard the stealthy opening of the door, the light steps to the bedside table. In the morning, Al discovered that his watch and chain were missing; Beulah found that her diamond engagement ring and a cameo ring had been taken.[43]

Beulah took a trip by herself in January of 1923. Her stepmother, Martha, had sent her and Al "a chicken and butter and a big cake." Perhaps the accompanying letter urged her to visit. The couple talked over the possibility, and Beulah recorded the outcome in her diary. "Al and I went downtown. He opened a bank account for himself. Deposited $50. He is going to save while I am in the country." The implication may have been that Al would take a sleeping room while she was away so that he could keep his expenses to a bare minimum.

She left Chicago on a Saturday night in mid-January and made a twelve-hour journey by rail to Owensboro. It was raining when she stepped off the train into the shelter of the canopied platform at Owensboro and saw her father waiting for her, dressed in his floppy hat and overalls. The diary entries for her Kentucky visit seem quite cheery. She was happy to be home and content to spend the days baking, candy-making, helping Martha with familiar farm chores, visiting cousins, and walking through the countryside in weather that warmed to a balmy sixty degrees.[44]

She had intended to make an extended stay in Kentucky, but on Saturday, after just a week, she received a letter from Al telling her that he had lost his job. Sensing he felt demoralized, she decided to return to Chicago. She later noted in her diary that her dad took her to the train depot and stayed until the train departed.

Al eventually found work, and Beulah supplemented the family income by taking short-term employments. By August, she had secured a regular position at Tennent's Model Laundry as an assistant bookkeeper.[15]

On September 30, 1923, Beulah prepared a birthday dinner for Al and invited her mother and John Lydon over for supper. She gave Al a watch to replace the one that had been stolen in Michigan. A week later, Al brought home a pint of bottled-in-bond whisky, and the two of them had dinner at a restaurant on Forty-Seventh Street. Beulah drank too much whisky, and the next day she was sick, which led to an argument with Al, apparently about her drinking. Al told her to "go to hell." She "went out and didn't come home." Al called her at work and told her they would be "friends" next Saturday, which meant they would separate amicably. Beulah's reaction was to get drunk again. The following morning, she was too sick to go to work. The next day she was still sick and called a doctor, who came to the flat and gave her morphine. In her diary, she swore off "moonshine."[46]

On Saturday, October 13, a week after the quarrel, Al packed up his things and left, just as he had said he would. "We quit the best of friends," Beulah wrote. "It is over for good now."

But it was not over. Within weeks, Beulah and Al were back together and looking for a new apartment. They eventually found one on Forty-Sixth Street, just a block east of Cottage Grove Avenue. It was during this period of marital difficulty that Beulah met Harry Kalsted.[47]

In November of 1923, Kalsted began working as a shipping clerk for Tennent's Model Laundry. Unfortunately, Beulah's diary falls silent after her October 13 entry; and she did not start a new diary in 1924. Hence, there are no direct clues to how things were between her and Al during the months after they reconciled, which was also the period when her relationship with Harry evolved from a friendship into an amorous affair. It is likely, however, that Beulah and Al fell back into their old patterns, including their usual quarrels. It is also likely that since Al had walked out on her (even though he had come back), Beulah thought their marriage would not last. In one of her explanations of her affair, she spoke somewhat obliquely about how women in unhappy marriages end up cheating because it is difficult for them to leave a husband if they do not have someone else to go to. She also said that she had hoped her "triangle romance" would not end up the way extramarital affairs usually do and that her relationship with Harry would turn out "like in the story books."[48]

It did not.

2. A SHOOTING

Thursday morning, April 3, 1924. The Annans' windup alarm rang around 6:00 A.M. Al got up and dressed for work, then went out the back door of their first-floor apartment into the alley, where he crossed a wide vacant lot that stretched west from the alley to Cottage Grove Avenue. Moments later, he was waiting in the near-freezing cold for the poorly heated "So. Chicago–92" streetcar that would take him to a mechanics' garage at the Cudahy meat-packing plant in South Chicago, fifty blocks away.[1]

Al was grateful to have a steady job. He made $65 a week, and Beulah brought in $20 or so at Tennent's Model Laundry. They paid $75 a month for their apartment, a single-bedroom, working-class flat in the relatively new Drexel Manor apartments, a U-shaped complex in Kenwood on the south side of Chicago, just north of Hyde Park. This apartment was the nicest place they had yet been able to afford during four years of marriage. They had moved into the unfurnished flat on December 1st and were still paying off the furniture they had purchased for it. They were also saving for a car.[2]

Al's boss and fellow mechanics at the Cudahy garage had the impression that Beulah was the love and light of Al's life, which was certainly how Al liked to think of Beulah. But there were tensions in the marriage, especially over Beulah's tendency to drink too much and too recklessly—she was a risk-taker when it came to testing her luck with liquor of dubious distillation—and, more recently, over her insistence that she had a right to spend time with "her own set of friends."[3]

Yet for most of their four years of marriage, there had been no friends. Beulah and Al had moved from one apartment to the next every several months and had taken various low-paying jobs in different parts of the south side. These circumstances had made it difficult for Beulah to make and keep friends her own age. Now, however, her regular employment at Tennent's Laundry had given her a set of pals. They included Betty, the head book-keeper; Harry, who worked as a shipping clerk; and other young men and women—machine operators and delivery drivers, some married, some not. Coworkers called the boss, William Wilcox, "Billy." They called Harry "Moo." They called Beulah "Red." But when Beulah and Harry became close, she stopped calling him Moo, and he stopped calling her Red. Instead, he called her "Anna." Why is not certain. Perhaps her last name inspired it.[4]

Their trysts did not take place in cabarets or dance halls. In the beginning, Harry simply walked her home. Then they began taking longer walks, and for a while their friendship was merely flirtatious. Eventually, there were kisses. In March, they had sex, twice, but not at her apartment. Although her flat would have been the most securely clandestine place, since Harry had no flat but lived with his sister and her family, it seems that Beulah did not feel comfortable entertaining Harry at home. Perhaps she felt guilty.[5]

But she was in love with Harry. They had either talked about a future together, or she had been thinking about it. From what he had told her, he was due to receive a large sum of money from his family in Minnesota. He may have bragged that he planned to go into his own business when he got this stake.[6]

Meanwhile, Al knew nothing about Beulah's affair. He had never laid eyes on Harry. Nor did Beulah's friends at work know that Beulah's friendship with Harry had gone beyond flirting. Nor did her boss, William Wilcox, who happened to be married to Harry's sister and had given Harry a place to stay.[7]

By 7:30 A.M. on that morning of April 3rd, Beulah was in a chemise, brushing her hair. She had not yet dared to try the boyish, short "shingle bob" that was now in vogue among the chicest of the chic, but six months ago she had let a hairdresser cut her dark-red hair to just below her ears and give it a marcel. Now her hair had grown down to her collar in thick unruly waves, crossing her forehead in a sweep that sometimes dropped over her eyes. She fixed this drooping wave with a bobby pin.[8]

She had to be at the laundry by eight and was feeling the press of time when the telephone rang. It was Harry. He was going to get some wine and wanted to know whether she wanted any. She promised him a dollar for a quart but told him to come quickly since she had to leave for work.[9]

In her closet were several outfits, including a checkered flannel dress, a black crepe dress, and a fawn-colored suit. She selected the suit, her regular work outfit, donned a string of faux pearls, and slipped on an orange-blossom ring. There was a light knocking at the back door. She went through the kitchen, opened the door, and there, in the shadows beneath the wooden staircase, was Harry. She told him to wait while she retrieved a dollar from her pocketbook. Moments later she was pressing the money into his hand.

They agreed that he would bring the wine to her apartment at half past twelve after she got off work; she had Thursday afternoons off.[10]

She closed the back door and went to the front hall closet. She had about ten minutes to get to Tennent's, which was four blocks from her apartment. Not wanting to be late, she pulled on her lamb's-wool coat and "georgette" hat and hurried out of her flat without tidying up or making the bed. It is very likely that on the bed, near Al's pillow, was a gun.[11]

Al had purchased this gun two months earlier. He had first talked about getting a firearm after he and Beulah were robbed during their vacation in Michigan. It was not only the loss of their personal articles that had bothered Al but the fact that a stranger had entered their room while they were sleeping. After this disturbing experience, he had considered purchasing a gun for protection but had put it off. A little over a year later, however, when he and Beulah took a first-floor apartment with a low balcony and a vulnerable back door that opened onto an alley next to a vacant lot, his anxiety about intruders reawakened. Perhaps reports of burglaries in his neighborhood intensified his concern. He would have read newspaper reports about state's attorney Robert Crowe's ongoing efforts to restrict the licensing of handguns in Chicago. And he had probably read or heard that the *Chicago Tribune* was calling for a general prohibition "of the private manufacture or sale to private persons or dealers of any pistol or revolver, or other firearm easily concealed on the person." Hence, he had cause to act before it was too late for him to own a revolver legally. So, three months after moving into the Drexel Manor apartments, Al purchased a used Smith & Wesson revolver, found a place to test it, and fired off a single shot.[12]

According to Beulah, Al kept the gun under his pillow. He wanted to have it close at hand, and he did not have a bedside table. Sleeping with a firearm under one's pillow was an imprudent thing to do, but it was not uncommon. The author of a 1919 article about a child getting hold of a gun kept under a pillow advised that an electric light and a loud shout were better deterrents against a burglar than a gun and that "the most dangerous place to keep a gun is under a pillow." It must have been an all-too-common practice. Every year, in towns and cities across the country, incidents were reported that involved a gun kept under a pillow.[13]

Tennent's Laundry at 4228–30 Cottage Grove Avenue was a three-story edifice, most of it consisting of a large room with a high ceiling and a gallery. On the open floor were large washing machines, mangles, and extractors. Beulah entered the laundry office and found the head bookkeeper, Betty Bergman, going over statements. From hints of impatience in Betty's voice, she could tell that her colleague was still annoyed that Beulah had refused to give her a key to her apartment.[14]

Beulah had no intention of letting Betty entertain a man in her flat, if that is what the request for the key was all about. Beulah had not even let Harry visit her in her apartment, except once, just briefly. But today she was thinking about inviting him in when he brought her the quart of wine.[15]

Phone calls came in to the laundry office all morning, mostly from customers, but one was for Beulah—from a fellow named Billy (not her boss, Billy Wilcox) who owned a car and offered to take her for a drive to Hammond that afternoon. She declined. After she hung up, Betty asked her about the call. Beulah told her it was nothing.[16]

Beulah returned to her apartment shortly after noon and changed from her work outfit into her house dress. The phone rang. It was Harry telling her that he had the wine and wanted to come over. She told him a boy named Billy had offered to take her for a drive. Then she laughed and said she was only joking. She would be waiting for Harry at her flat.[17]

She may have teased him about Billy's offer because something was bothering her. At work that morning, someone had told her some gossip about Harry having been in jail in Minnesota. The rumor, if true, implied that he had not been honest about his past. Beulah wondered what else might be false about him.[18]

The facts were these. Harry had fathered a child by a young woman named Lydia Lindgren. He had been living with his mother and stepfather at the time on a farm in Cambridge, Minnesota. Lydia's father, who had a nearby farm, was the brother of Harry's stepfather. When Harry refused to take responsibility for Lydia and baby Harriet—the name "Harriet" being a declaration of the child's paternity—Lydia swore out a criminal complaint for bastardy. Wanting to avoid a prison sentence but being too lazy to secure steady employment and support Lydia and the baby, Harry married Lydia and moved in with her family. Lydia was soon pregnant again. Harry, unhappy as a married man with a growing family, grew morose; and on April 17, 1918, the day that Lydia went into labor with their second child, Harry left the house for good.[19]

Over the next couple of years, Harry avoided registering for the draft, sponged off the family of a boyhood friend in Chicago, and, when they threw him out, finagled hospitality from other newfound friends, applying his charm. In August of 1920—broke, with no place to stay, and having worn out all his welcomes in Chicago—he returned to Cambridge and moved in with his mother and stepfather. Whether Lydia and his children immediately joined him is unknown. He received no wages from his father-in-law, only

Harry Kalsted, shot to death by Beulah Annan on April 3, 1924, shown as he appeared circa 1918. *Chicago Tribune*, April 4, 1924, p. 40. Newspapers.com.

room and board, perhaps because the work he did was minimal. In any case, he did not support Lydia and the children. She lost patience and swore out a complaint for child desertion. Harry called her bluff and was unable to reverse course in time to avoid a legal judgment against himself. A court sentenced him to prison, and Lydia divorced him.[20]

Harry was an inmate at St. Cloud Reformatory from July 1921 until his parole in August of 1923. Three months later, in October of 1923, having been discharged from parole, he took a train to Chicago and persuaded his sister Ella to take him in. Ella's husband, William Wilcox, gave him a job at Tennent's. Over the next several months, Harry lived at the Wilcoxes, worked at Tennent's, and made friends there. But he did not tell anyone at Tennent's the truth about his Minnesota past. Instead, he claimed that he had been a successful farmer and had a sizable sum of money coming to him from his family. In the idiom of the times, he was a ne'er-do-well—not that this justified what was about to happen to him.[21]

Harry arrived at Beulah's apartment around 12:40 in the afternoon with two quarts of wine. She let him in the back door and suggested they have some. Six hours later, when police searched the Annan apartment, they found Harry's hat, overcoat, and suit coat in the bedroom on the bed. Either Beulah had invited Harry to put them there or she had put them there. When she was questioned, Beulah could not recall where exactly in the bedroom Harry's things had been—whether on the bed or on a chair. Hence, it is perhaps more likely that she had simply invited Harry to put his things in the bedroom. In that case, and if Al's gun was on the bed, Harry may have seen the revolver and asked Beulah about it.[22]

A news photographer's photo of a corner of the Annans' living room as it looked on the day of the shooting, showing the victrola and liquor bottles. *Chicago American*, April 4, 1924, p. 1.

Shortly after Harry entered the apartment, he and Beulah sat down on the living-room sofa and began drinking wine, smoking, and talking. They had finished off one of the quarts and were into the second when they began kissing. She knew he wanted to "have a jazz," a euphemism for sex, and she gave in to him. Then they drank the rest of the wine and smoked a few more cigarettes.[23]

They were now completely drunk, and at this point Harry brought up Billy, the fellow with the automobile who had offered to take her for a drive. Beulah laughed and said she had only been kidding. Harry seemed doubtful and told her that she would be a whore if she had gone with Billy. He was furious with jealousy. Beulah, stung by the foul name, brought up the rumor she had heard from Betty and asked Harry whether he had ever been in jail. He admitted that he had, and they started quarreling about whether he had been honest about his past and his claims that "he had a lot of money and [that] his people were sending him money." She said he was "nothing" and called him a "jail-bird."[24]

The argument continued, growing more heated. Then Harry said, "To hell with you!" He "jumped up" and began to stagger past her, stepping between the edge of the coffee table and Beulah, who was sitting at the end of the couch, beyond which was the short hallway to the bedroom. Realizing that Harry meant to go there, she got up, too, and they both "beat it for the bedroom," as she later described it, although they probably moved fumblingly, given how intoxicated they both were.

What happened next eludes exact reconstruction, and it is possible that Beulah, even in her most honest account, had trouble remembering every detail and the precise sequence of events, due to her drunken state. All that is certain is that within a minute of their entering the bedroom, Harry was dead from a gunshot wound.

That minute in the bedroom became the crucial focus of Beulah's trial for murder. The following facts are indisputable. Harry was more or less sideways to Beulah when she pulled the trigger, whether because he was turning to go or because he was reaching toward her. The bullet entered his back obliquely, very close to his right side and not far below the armpit, and it moved laterally through his heart and lungs before coming to rest near a rib on his left side. He died almost instantly. Beulah dropped the gun on the bed. Harry's overcoat, suit coat, and hat were also on the bed. Police noted that the bed was unmade and that Harry's body was on the floor between the bed and the wall, with his head near the head of the bed and his feet in the bedroom doorway. Beulah's house dress and stockings were stained with blood.[25]

According to what prosecutors claimed, the shooting happened as follows. Harry, intending to leave the apartment, went to the bedroom to get his hat and coat. Beulah followed, went to the bedroom dresser, took Al's gun from a drawer in the dresser, and shot Harry as he turned to leave. Her motive: she was angry because Harry had said he was "through" with her.

Beulah told more than one story, but her most honest version, according to the prosecutors themselves, was a statement she gave at the Hyde Park police station at 12:30 A.M. The prosecutors referred to this after-midnight statement as her confession, and they introduced it as the centerpiece of their evidence at her trial. In this account, Beulah said that when she and Harry entered the bedroom, she "grabbed" for the gun and Harry "grabbed for what was left, there wasn't anything there." This implied that the gun was within Harry's reach when he stood by the bed and that he tried to get hold of it. The prosecutor who led Beulah through the questions that produced the after-midnight statement never asked her why she went into the bedroom or why she reached for the gun or what she thought Harry meant to do when he reached for it. The prosecutor did ask her what she did after she shot Harry, and she said that "he was falling and I grabbed him and held him up." This implied that the shooting occurred as the two of them stood side by side next to the bed, between the bed and the wall (not with Beulah across the room at the dresser). It also explained how she got blood on her dress.[26]

Whether the gun was already on the bed or in the dresser drawer when Beulah and Harry entered the bedroom was never clarified. Ten days after the incident, two police officers named Michael Collins and James Mc-Laughlin filed a report in which they stated, among other things, that when they joined officer Thomas Torpy and his partner at the scene, they asked Al where the gun was kept and he answered, "in the dresser drawer." At Beulah's trial, sergeant Malachi Murphy, who had taken a statement from Al at the Hyde Park police station, testified that Al told him the same thing. But Beulah claimed that the gun was always under Al's pillow at night and that on the day in question it was uncovered on the unmade bed. She said this to William Wilcox just an hour before she made her after-midnight statement, and it fit her subsequent description of how she and Harry had both reached for the revolver.[27]

Were the prosecutors' assertions regarding the location of the gun a true and complete statement of the matter? One would have no reason to doubt their claim were it not for the fact that they did not introduce the testimony about the gun at the inquest held on April 4. Nor did Al say anything about where the gun was kept in his typed statement, which Sergeant Murphy took from him at the time of Beulah's arrest. Furthermore, at the inquest, when Beulah's attorney made a great deal of Beulah's claim that the gun was always on the bed, over protests from the prosecutor, and when that same prosecutor put on his own witness, Officer Torpy, to testify about the gun, he did not ask Torpy to tell whether Al had said anything about where the gun was kept. Nor did the prosecutor call officers Murphy, Collins, or McLaughlin to testify at the inquest, even though all three were stationed at the Hyde Park police station, in whose wardroom the inquest was held. And when the coroner invited Al to testify at the inquest, the prosecutors did not ask him where he kept his revolver.[28]

Was it only incompetence that caused the prosecutors not to provide the coroner's jury with testimony about where the gun was when Harry and Beulah entered the bedroom? Or did they not want Al to testify that he kept the gun under his pillow? The Chicago police were not beyond lying to help out a case, and they would have known that they could not be contradicted by Al at the *trial* because he would not be permitted to testify against his wife. The fact that the earliest police claim that Al said the gun was kept in the dresser drawer did not appear in the record until after the inquest, where Al had been allowed to testify, raises suspicions. In any event, in the crucial passage in her after-midnight statement, Beulah implied that the gun had been in plain sight on the bed. Moreover, she had already said the same thing an hour or two earlier, at her flat, when she was still claiming that Harry was an intruder who tried to rape her. Significantly, in that version of the shooting, the location of the gun did not matter. Arguably, she had referred to it as being on the bed because that is where it had been.

One more clue about this subject appeared in something Beulah told reporters on the day after the inquest. She had never fired a gun before in her life, she said, except once on New Year's Eve. "Every day" she would pick up Al's gun "so carefully" because she was "afraid of it." She did not explain why she would pick up the gun every day; that detail was incidental to her point about how averse she was to guns. Yet the remark seemed to imply that there had been a routine. Did she return the revolver each morning from the bed to the dresser drawer or to its precise place under the pillow if it had shifted, when she made the bed—if she made the bed?[29]

───────────

It was around three o'clock in the afternoon when Beulah shot Harry. When she squeezed the trigger, she felt as if she "jerked the gun from the front." It must have been the recoil, but it made her think she had missed.

When Harry said, "My God Anna, you've killed me," she told him, "No, Harry, you're all right, you're not shot," and she put her arms around him to keep him from falling. Then blood started coming from his mouth, and he fell back against the wall and slumped to the floor between the bed and the wall.[30]

She knelt beside him and began rubbing his face and his hands to revive him. His hands felt warm and his face was warm, but he wasn't talking or moving, and his eyes were closed. She pushed his eyelids up to see if he might still be alive.[31]

He appeared to be dead. His eyes did not move. He was absolutely still, and his shirt was red with the blood that had poured from his mouth and nose but no longer flowed. She could not think of what to do for him. Because she was drunk and believed he was dead (which he was), she did not think to call a doctor. Instead, she fetched a washcloth from the bathroom and tried to wipe away the blood on his mouth and chin.[32]

Then she heard voices in the courtyard, children playing and calling to each other. She realized that the neighbors could have heard the quarrel and the gunshot. She was terrified that someone might investigate and find Harry dead on her bedroom floor, so she went to the living room to put a record on the victrola to give the impression that everything was all right in her flat.[33]

The record was a thick black shellac disc, a recording of the faux Hawaiian song "Hula Lou" sung by a white stage singer to the jaunty strains of a jazz band. When Beulah wound up the victrola and went to lower the head of the tonearm onto the disc, she realized it had no needle. So she located the needle box, extracted a needle, fixed it in the armature, and lowered the tonearm again. The needle scratched in the groove, and sounds of a jazz band came through the horn, followed by the singer's words, "Well you can talk all you want about women. . . ." Beulah's hands were still sticky with blood, and she probably did not notice that they had left smears on the record, the crank, the needle box, and the variable speed dial.[34]

The circumstances looked bad for her. She had shot a man, a coworker, in her apartment while her husband was at work. Delay in reporting the incident to the police would only make things worse by suggesting "consciousness of guilt." Moreover, anything else she might do to hide what had happened would only reinforce that impression. But these risks did not occur to her. She could not think clearly. She began pacing. She walked the apartment, then sat in the kitchen, then paced again. Just as often she went to the bedroom to see whether the thing was real. She was still very drunk, and everything seemed dreamlike. But when she went to the bedroom, Harry's body was always there, collapsed awkwardly on the floor between the bed and the wall, his white silk shirt red with blood, his face white.[35]

By four o'clock, cried out but still intoxicated, Beulah started thinking seriously about how to avoid being implicated in Harry's death. She considered that if she could get rid of Harry's body, maybe get it into the back alley without anyone seeing, the police would conclude that he had been shot by someone trying to rob him.[36]

Now that she had a plan, she went to work. First, she put away the drinking glasses they had used and placed the empty quart wine bottles next to the stove. Then she called the laundry, intending to speak to her boss, Billy Wilcox, and to ask him whether he knew where Harry was. Betty Bergman answered the phone. Beulah was not sure what to say, so she asked her what she was doing.

> "I'm awfully busy," Betty said.
> "Is Billy there?"
> "You know he has been in and out already."
> "Is Moo there?"
> "You know he hasn't been here all day long."
> "That's funny, I had an appointment with him for a quarter after twelve and he hasn't shown up."
> "What's the matter, Red, you sound kinda stewed."
> "No, I haven't had a drink all day. I talk queerly because I'm trying to talk to you and read the telephone directory at the same time."[37]

She hung up the phone and went to the bedroom. She knew she could not pick up Harry's body and carry it. It is possible that she tried to drag him, moving him a foot or two before giving up because it was too ghastly.[38]

She now realized that if she did nothing, Al would be the first one to know what had happened. He would find out when he arrived home from work around nine o'clock. She could wait until then, or she could call him now. She could not bear the thought of waiting for hours in the apartment with Harry dead in her bedroom. So she called Al.

She was still drunk and had difficulty remembering the number for the Cudahy garage. After a series of misdials, some to the same party, she heard an annoyed voice say, "Refer to your directory." She went to the desk and found a piece of paper with Al's work number on it. This time she dialed successfully, got the garage, and asked for Al. When she heard his voice on the line, she cried, "My God, I've killed a man."[39]

Drexel Manor, number 817, on East Forty-Sixth Street as the building looks today (lacking its original balconies). The Annan apartment was on the first floor (*left*). Photo by Charles Cosgrove.

Beulah's telephone call came in to the Cudahy garage around 4:45. It took Al an hour to get home because the Yellow Cab he hired was delayed by a flat tire. When Beulah saw him, she sobbed, "Daddy, I killed a man." Al asked where the man was. When she told him, he went to the bedroom and saw the body on the floor and the gun lying on the bed. He picked up the gun and put it in his pocket, then went back to Beulah and said, "Tell me just how it was." She kept saying, "Harry, Harry, I killed him." At some point she told Al that she shot Harry because he made "unwelcome advances."[40]

It is possible that during the fifteen or twenty minutes between Al's arrival home and his eventual phone call to the police, Beulah tried to persuade him to help her get rid of the body, or perhaps she hoped that he would do that on his own initiative. Instead, he told her, "You've got to give yourself up." She refused. Finally, he went to the telephone; when the call went through to the police, Beulah grabbed the receiver and shrieked, "I've just killed my husband!"[41]

Fifteen minutes later the police arrived.

3. AN ALLEGED CONFESSION

Officers Thomas Torpy and Joseph Kelly were first on the scene. After learning almost nothing from Al, except that Beulah had shot a man whose dead body lay in their bedroom, Torpy asked Beulah why she had shot him. She said, "I don't know," and otherwise refused to answer.[1]

More police arrived. Officers Michael Collins and James McLaughlin asked Beulah, in front of Al, whether Kalsted had been in her apartment on any other occasion. According to their report, her response was "O God, do I have to answer that?" Al told her to answer. She refused.[2]

The police could see that Beulah was drunk, and certain details about the physical scene led them to conclude that she and Kalsted had spent time drinking together on the couch. So, at 7:15 P.M., after an hour of unsuccessful questioning at the flat, they took both Beulah and Al to the Hyde Park police station. Once there, however, they realized that they needed to collect Beulah's blood-stained clothing as evidence. So they took her back to her flat and asked her to change clothes. Beulah put on her suit dress and a white blouse.[3]

Assistant state's attorneys Bert Cronson, William McLaughlin, and Roy Woods also came to the apartment. They questioned Beulah off and on without getting any satisfactory account of the shooting. Around 11:30 P.M. Woods asked William Wilcox to come to the apartment to see whether he could get Beulah to open up. At Woods's urging, Wilcox explained to Beulah that Mr. Woods was a friend of his and that she should talk to him; Woods himself told her more than once that it would be "better" for her if she talked. Beulah agreed to talk with Cronson, Woods, and McLaughlin, so long as no police were present. The prosecutors took her into the kitchen and closed the door. Wilcox went with them.[4]

Some minutes later, a shorthand reporter named Elbert Allen arrived. Allen was one of many stenographers who worked for the court system. Court reporters took down testimony at hearings, inquests, and trials and were sometimes asked to record questioning. Earlier in the evening, Allen had been summoned to the Hyde Park police station to record the questioning of Beulah there; but since the prosecutors were now interviewing her at her apartment, Allen was called there. He later testified that when he arrived at the flat, Beulah was in the kitchen talking to Assistant State's Attorney McLaughlin. When Beulah was asked why she shot Kalsted, "she said she didn't know." She appeared "greatly agitated and worried," Allen said, "almost hysterical, mingling smiles with tears."[5]

What happened next became a subject of dispute at the trial. Beulah had been encouraged by Wilcox to believe that Woods, who was Wilcox's "friend," wanted to help her. This is why she had agreed to talk to him. "We went into the kitchen," she explained, "and he said, 'Don't you know me?' and I said 'No.' And he said, 'I am Roy C. Woods, and I am a customer of Mr. Wilcox and a personal friend of his.' Then he told me not to be afraid, that I had shot the man in my own house, and that it was no crime." Wilcox later testified that he heard Woods say, repeatedly, that it would "be better for her if she would tell everything."[6]

What would make it "better"? According to the prosecutors, Beulah asked Woods if he could "frame it to look like an accident," and Woods told her, "You don't frame anything with me." It is possible that this interchange was the result of a misunderstanding. The Chicago police referred to incidents of all kinds, including murders, as *accidents*. The police report on the shooting carried the heading "accident," and at the inquest the next day, where Woods presented his case against Beulah, he referred to the shooting as an "accident," meaning an incident. If Woods used that term with Beulah, she might well have misunderstood his meaning, thinking that they were inclined to treat what had happened as an accident.[7]

After Woods made it clear that he was not going to frame anything, Beulah gave an account of the shooting. Court reporter Allen took down what she said. This kitchen statement was the first of two statements later submitted at Beulah's trial. Unfortunately, it is known only in bits and pieces reported in the newspapers. According to these reports, Beulah claimed that she knew Harry Kalsted only casually. He came to her apartment unannounced and told her he was "crazy" about her. Then he tried to "make love" to her. When she retreated to the bedroom, he followed with a "look in his eye." Afraid he was going to rape her, she grabbed the revolver, which was on the bed, under a pillow. She warned him not to come any closer. When he moved toward her, she closed her eyes and shot him.[8]

Woods and his fellow prosecutors did not believe Beulah's story, at least not the claim that Kalsted tried to rape her. They also confronted her with the fact that Kalsted was shot in the back, which was technically true, although misleading, since the shot entered the far-right side of his back, laterally, and passed through his torso to his left side. Kalsted must have been sideways to Beulah when she shot him.[9]

Unsatisfied with what they had heard, the prosecutors took Beulah back to the Hyde Park police station. Court reporter Allen went with them and so did William Wilcox. Again the prosecutors confronted Beulah with the evidence they had about the location of the bullet wound and the signs that there had been a party in the flat. By this time it was after midnight, and Beulah, who had sobered up and was feeling exhausted and helpless, finally did what Wilcox had been urging her to do—"to tell all about it" because "it would relieve her." She gave what the prosecutors later touted as "a true account" in answers to a series of questions by assistant state's attorney Roy Woods. This after-midnight interview became the foundation of the state's case against Beulah, and it has survived intact.[10]

Roy Charles Woods was born in Osage, Iowa, in 1880. The Woods family moved to St. Louis when Roy was in his teens, and he attended college there, entering the workforce on the cusp of the new century. Eventually, Woods wound up in Chicago, where he tried his hand at various employments, including real estate, before turning to law. By the time he was thirty, he was an investigator for the state's attorney general; and in 1922, Cook County state's attorney Robert Crowe hired him as a prosecutor.[11]

Regarded as a "tough egg" who could get things done, Woods was soon drawn into the great intrigue of his life, during which aspects of his personality were revealed that shed light on the way he handled his interrogation of Beulah. According to accounts that Woods gave to a handful of people over the years, he was recruited in 1923 by persons in the State Department (and by a New Yorker who supposedly represented the Russian royal family) to travel to Poland to rescue twenty-five-year-old Tatiana Nikolaevna, a daughter of deposed Russian tsar Nicholas II and the only member of the royal family, Woods was told, who had escaped execution. The plan was to extract Tatiana from a village in Poland where she was living with a peasant family under an assumed name. The operation also involved transfer of the Russian royal jewels to the United States.[12]

In May of 1923, Woods secured a "Special Series" emergency passport, and in June journeyed to Warsaw, where he took up residence in the once luxurious but by then somewhat war-beaten Bristol Hotel. On July 16, he

Assistant state's attorney Roy C. Woods, who led the interrogation of Beulah Annan, as he appeared in his 1923 passport photo at the time of his secret mission to Poland. Ancestry.com.

happened to meet an American journalist named Kenneth Roberts, who was also in residence at the Bristol. The two men talked on several occasions, and Roberts noted the substance of these conversations in his diary and subsequently recounted them in his autobiography. Others who spoke to Woods in later years gathered further particulars.[13]

Roberts found Woods's claims and plan so implausible that he suspected Woods might be involved in a hoax. On more than one occasion, he pointed out the many reasons for doubting that the woman Woods had visited in the Polish village was Tatiana or that the Russian crown jewels were packed in crates somewhere in Poland, ready to be shipped to America. Woods was stubborn, however, and brushed all contrary evidence aside.[14]

Despite what appear to have been unshakable beliefs on Woods's part, the packed crates he had been shown contained no royal jewels, and the woman he had met was not Tatiana. Tatiana Romanov had been executed with the rest of her family in Ekaterinburg, Siberia, two years before, in a massacre that was widely reported in the newspapers. Yet rumors had continued to circulate about this or that supposed survivor. Imposters kept appearing in various parts of Europe, and the gullible were taken in. Roy Woods and certain officials at the State Department appear to have been among the credulous.[15]

The outcome of Woods's mission was as follows. In November, after four months' effort, including numerous hopeful visits to the peasant woman who claimed to be Tatiana (to whose family he brought gifts of food and small amounts of cash), Woods left Poland empty-handed yet determined to return and complete his assignment. In later years, he spoke only rarely and rather obliquely about his secret assignment.[16]

In April of 1924, six months after his failed effort in Poland, Woods was the lead interrogator when Beulah Annan made her statement at 12:30 A.M. in the Hyde Park police station. His questioning of her evinced the same tendency to resist countervailing evidence, once he had made up his mind about a thing, which Roberts had observed about him in Warsaw. The interview was a study in selective focus, designed to elicit only the answers the prosecutor wanted and to avoid giving Beulah a chance to divulge exculpatory information. It was not only Woods's personality that dictated his one-sided approach. In 1920s Chicago, police and prosecutors tended to assume the guilt of suspects and to interrogate them accordingly. The transcript of Beulah's after-midnight "confession" reveals an assistant state's attorney seeking a confirmation of his theory. As for Beulah, her responses to Woods sound perfectly frank, not evasive or contrived. For example, she divulged details about her affair with Kalsted, including how many times they had been intimate. She could have kept these incriminating details a secret, but instead she spoke frankly and unguardedly about them. Yet when she told Woods things that did not fit his theory, he did not follow up but instead tried to get answers that suited his hypothesis.[17]

Had Woods's sole aim been to establish all the relevant facts, he would have focused on the four main issues on which everything hinged. First, exactly where was the gun when Beulah got hold of it—on the bed or in a bureau drawer? Second, what did Kalsted do in the moments just before Beulah shot him—reach for the gun or turn to leave? Third, what was their proximity to each other when Beulah pulled the trigger? Were they separated by several feet or more, with Kalsted in the doorway and Beulah near the bureau, or close to each other between the bed and the wall, perhaps engaged in a physical struggle? Finally, why did Beulah shoot Kalsted?

Woods asked Beulah none of these questions. He was convinced that the couple had gotten into an argument over a certain "Billy the boy with the automobile" and that this argument escalated to a point where a disgusted Kalsted declared that he was "through" and went to the bedroom to fetch his hat and coat; Beulah followed, took the gun from the dresser drawer, and shot him as he turned to leave.

In pursuit of this theory, Woods asked Beulah, "What did you argue about?" She said, "I had heard he had been in jail and I asked him about

Beulah Annan in police custody. DN-0076797, *Chicago Daily News* collection, Chicago History Museum.

it, and he said he had." Woods asked, "Did he say anything about Billy the boy with the automobile?" Beulah said, "Oh yes, but that wasn't much; the argument was mostly because he had been in jail, and he had always told me he had a lot of money and his people were sending him money." Woods repeated the question about Billy. "When did you tell him that Billy had called you up and you said you couldn't meet him at 12:15?" Beulah explained that she had mentioned Billy to Kalsted not when they were in the flat but earlier in the afternoon, on the phone, before Kalsted came over. "I told him when he called me up and told me he had the wine, and I only laughed and said I was joking, that was all." Woods was still not satisfied. "When you were on the lounge there," he asked, "did he say anything to you about Billy?" Beulah answered, "Oh, he said 'I'm glad you didn't go with him' or 'If you do it you would have been—.'" She did not finish this sentence, and Woods asked, "Now what did he say to you?" Beulah was briefly nonplussed. "Oh, well, just what do you mean?" Woods became more specific. "Did he say anything to you about your having done things you shouldn't do?" Beulah answered, "Oh, yes, and I said to him 'Well, you are nothing' and 'a son of a bitch,' I suppose." Woods asked what Kalsted said to that. Beulah answered, "He jumped up and we both beat it for the bedroom."

"What did he do? Jump up?" Woods asked.

Beulah did not answer this last question with a simple yes but went back to the prior name-calling. "Oh, I don't know. I might have called him something." This did not satisfy Woods. "Did he say anything to you about being through with you?" Woods wanted her to say that Kalsted had declared he was "through" and had then jumped up, but Beulah did not remember it that way. "Oh, he might have said, 'To hell with you' or something like that." Woods repeated the question, since it was the lynchpin of his theory. "Did he say he was through with you?" Beulah answered, "That was after I told him he was a jailbird and he didn't have any money, and he was always blowing around to me that he did have." It appeared, then, that Kalsted had said he was "through" earlier in the argument and not as a final declaration as he was getting up to leave. It was a small point, but Woods's insistence on it showed how doggedly he tried to get Beulah to say that she shot Kalsted because he was through with her.

After Beulah told Woods that Kalsted had jumped up when she called him a name and that "we both beat it to the bedroom," Woods did not ask her why. Instead, he phrased a question that somewhat misrepresented what Beulah had just told him. "Then you say he jumped up and rushed to the bedroom?" Beulah had said "we," and her next answer repeated in substance her statement that they *both* got up at the same time. "I was on the couch nearest the [bedroom] door," she explained, "and I was ahead of him." But again, Woods did not ask her why they both would have beat it to the bedroom after Beulah called Kalsted a name, not even why *she* had rushed to the bedroom.

Instead he asked, "What did you do in the bedroom?" "I grabbed for the gun," Beulah said. The logical follow-up was to ask where the gun was when she grabbed for it. But Woods did not ask that. Instead, he said, "And what did he grab for?" Woods clearly expected Beulah to say that Kalsted had grabbed for *his hat and coat.* Her answer took him by surprise: "He grabbed for what was left. There wasn't anything there." This posed a problem for Woods's theory, since it implied that Kalsted had reached for the gun. That in turn implied that the gun had been on the bed. Did Beulah mean that she and Kalsted had beat it to the bedroom because the gun was there? In that case, since Kalsted had "jumped up" first, was it he who had initiated this rush for the gun? Had there been some reference to the gun during their argument because Kalsted had seen it on the bed when he arrived at the apartment and put his hat and coat in the bedroom?

Woods did not ask Beulah whether Kalsted knew about the gun on the bed. He did not ask her why Kalsted grabbed for the gun when he rushed into the bedroom. And he did not ask her why she reached for the gun. He did not even ask her what she did next or what Kalsted did next, so as to establish the exact sequence of events that led to the moment when she pulled the trigger.

Instead, Woods backtracked, and his next question showed that he was still trying to get Beulah to admit that she shot Kalsted as he was going for his hat and coat. First, he asked whether Kalsted was wearing those things when he went into the bedroom. Beulah said he was not, that his hat and coat were on the bed or on a chair at the end of the bed. Woods did not ask how they got there, whether it was Beulah or Kalsted who had taken them into the bedroom. Perhaps Woods did not want to hear the answer. Instead, Woods asked a loaded question. "Did he get his hat and coat?" Beulah answered, "No, he didn't get that far." Woods prompted, "Why didn't he get that far?" Beulah answered, "Darned good reason." Woods asked her to explain. She answered, "I shot him." The transcript does not disclose whether she said "darned good reason" angrily, defiantly, softly, bitterly, regretfully, or with some other tone. The typed words themselves sound damning, unless she meant that she was defending herself. As for the context, nothing in the transcript suggests that she was angry or defiant when she uttered these words to Woods. And in her next few sentences, she described how she reached out and held Kalsted to keep him from falling, telling him that he was "not shot."

Woods himself may have been tired. By this point, it must have been around 1:00 A.M. In any case, at the most crucial point in the interrogation, he failed to ask Beulah the most obvious question: *Why did you shoot him?* Instead, he moved on, and the interview ended without that question being asked.

Woods's careful avoidance of any line of questioning that might have led to Beulah saying that Kalsted had seen the gun in the bedroom earlier in the afternoon was crucial to his pursuit of his theory of the shooting. For if Kalsted had seen the gun or had even referenced it at some point during the argument, the facts on which Woods based his theory admitted an opposite interpretation. Beulah and Kalsted were both very angry at each other. Hence, if anger was a motive to kill, Kalsted had the same motive that Beulah did. Moreover, it was also possible that drunkenness caused them to misinterpret each other's intentions and gestures in the bedroom, each thinking the other meant to do harm with the gun. Woods seems not to have realized that if he had asked Beulah directly why she shot Kalsted, she might have admitted to having killed him in anger; that if, alternatively, she had provided an exculpatory explanation instead, then the prosecutors could have spared themselves a defeat at trial by dropping the case for lack of sufficient evidence. After all, there was no living witness except Beulah, and her most honest account of the shooting described how she shot Harry after he reached for the gun.

In an interview with one or more reporters on Friday morning, some eight hours after the interrogation in the Hyde Park police station, Beulah repeated the account she had given to Woods. She admitted to the affair, the drinking and sexual intercourse in the apartment on the afternoon in question, the argument, the rush to the bedroom, and the grab for the gun, which she described by telling how, when Harry "reached out to pick the gun off the bed, I reached around him and grabbed it." Then she added, "They say I shot him in the back, but it must have been sort of under the arm."[18]

"They" may have been the morning papers, quoting Roy Woods, for the *Daily News* told its readers that day, "according to the story she told Mr. Woods, Mrs. Annan tantalized her admirer with tales of another man, 'a handsome southerner,' until he started to leave her. When she saw in his eyes that he would never return, she shot him."[19]

Beulah must have been surprised to discover that Woods and his fellow prosecutors were claiming that she had confessed to murdering Harry. She did not think that she had confessed to murder. She had confessed to the affair, and she had explained how the shooting took place. She and Harry had both grabbed for the gun, and she had gotten hold of it before he did. She believed this exonerated her. In fact, it did, but only if she had been in genuine fear of serious bodily harm when she pulled the trigger.

4. POLICE AND PROSECUTORS SHAPE THE NARRATIVE

A number of Chicago newspapers relied on the City News Bureau for a good deal of their initial reporting on newsworthy events. City News posted reporters in shifts around the clock at the city's police stations, and in the 1920s the Chicago evening papers also assigned their own reporters to the police beat. Hence, when Beulah was brought to the Hyde Park station just after midnight, the posted reporters were present to pump police officers for information and to receive any statements that Roy Woods or one of the other prosecutors wished to make to the press. This explains why all the initial newspaper accounts of the shooting reported the same basic information about Beulah's "confession." The only information initially available to the papers derived from the police and prosecutors.[1]

This information about the shooting was calculated to make a first, indelible impression on the public mind. Unfortunately, it contained crucially misleading and downright false claims. Joseph Springer, the coroner's physician, had performed an autopsy in the apartment and had also written his report there—a handwritten note that he provided to the police or prosecutors before leaving the scene. This report stated that the bullet passed directly through Kalsted's heart, which implied that Kalsted died almost instantly, which is exactly what Springer later testified at the trial. Springer's finding supported what Beulah told Woods: that she knew, just minutes after the shooting, that Harry was dead. But the prosecutors preferred a faulty guess about time of death that Dr. Clifford Oliver, the first physician on the scene, had offered. When Oliver arrived at 6:25 P.M., he opined that Kalsted had been dead for only twenty or thirty minutes. Relying on Oliver, who had made no attempt to determine the exact cause of death, the police told reporters that Beulah had played a jazz record while Kalsted lay dying, implying that hours had passed while she amused herself and he slowly slipped away. They even claimed that she had danced around the body like a "modern Salome," a reference to a Gospel story about the stepdaughter of Herod Antipas, who danced at Herod's birthday party and then demanded the head of John the Baptist on a platter as her reward. The prosecutors' comparison inspired headlines such as "Woman Plays Jazz Air as Victim Dies" and "Woman in Salome Dance after Killing Tells Prosecutor She Played Jazz Record and Kissed Fallen Victim."[2]

Dr. Clifford Oliver's inaccurate handwritten note, which he composed at the scene of the shooting on April 3, 1924. MHK.

Prosecutors also told reporters that Beulah had confessed to *murdering* Kalsted, that she had shot him because he said he was "through" with her. This was Woods's theory, not something Beulah had said in her after-midnight statement. Moreover, the prosecutors omitted mention of something that Beulah had told them—that Kalsted had reached for the gun.

Meanwhile, Beulah was at the South Clark Street jail. She had been transferred there around two in the morning and had been placed in the women's cellblock of the jail's Harrison Street annex. There she had spent the next several hours unsuccessfully trying to fall asleep. In the morning, she was conducted to the matron's room at the front of the women's cellblock to await transport to the coroner's inquest. At least two reporters found her there, one from the *Daily News* and another from the *Herald and Examiner.* Reporters from the *Daily Journal, Evening Post,* and *American* also filed stories based on news gathered that morning, and they quoted statements that Beulah had supposedly made during her detention at the Clark Street station. These accounts contradicted what the *Daily News* and *Herald and Examiner* reported.[3]

It is doubtful that the *Daily Journal, Evening Post,* and *American* got their quotations directly from Beulah. Although 1920s newspaper quotations of what subjects reportedly said gave impressions of immediacy and precision, they were often mere paraphrases or secondhand accounts. It would have required careful comparative detective work by newspaper readers to have discovered the chain of mediations that led to words placed between quotation marks.

The *Daily Journal, Evening Post,* and *American* all claimed that Beulah said, "He was my greatest love. Rather than see him leave me, I killed him," and "I'm glad I did it. It ended an affair that was wrecking my life." This was the *Post's* version. The other two papers used almost the same wording. Moreover, according to the *Daily Journal,* Beulah said these things to "a Journal reporter, who interviewed her before the inquest, while she still occupied a cell in the women's quarters of the South Clark station." But the *American* attributed these same statements to the confession she made to Roy Woods just after midnight, which did not in fact contain them. And the *Post,* which placed her in her cell, claimed that she made the statements to one of the matrons, which implies that a matron quoted to the reporters what Beulah had supposedly said privately. Since reporters routinely phoned in their notes to "rewrite men," who worked up the notes into a story, the differences in location were probably due to different inferences drawn by rewrite staff from phoned-in reports that referred to Woods or to the station or to a police matron.[4]

The *Daily News* gave a different account, one that did not include any of the statements attributed to Beulah by the *Journal*, the *Post*, and the *American*. In fact, what it quoted from Beulah was quite the opposite. Moreover, the *Daily News* included a detail that implied the reporter had interviewed Beulah directly. At the close of Beulah's remarks, the paper noted, she "leaned forward in her chair" in a gesture that signaled she was done talking. Since the women's cells at the South Clark station did not have chairs, the implication is that Beulah was in the matron's room.[5]

An account in the *Herald and Examiner* also differed from those of the *Journal*, the *Post*, and the *American*; and it not only placed the interview in the matron's room but overlapped in content with the *Daily News* and also mentioned a gesture—Beulah looking over at the matron at one point.[6]

Significantly, the *Daily News* version was very similar to what Beulah had stated just hours earlier in her after-midnight statement:

> I taunted Harry with the fact that he had been in jail once and he said something nasty back to me. Seems like we just wanted to make each other mad—and to hurt each other. I finally called him a name. Harry said, "You won't call me a name like that," and he started toward the bedroom. There was only one thing he could have been going into the bedroom for. The gun was there—in plain sight. It had been under the pillow where it was always kept, but the pillow was turned back and it showed. I ran, and as he reached out to pick the gun off the bed, I reached around him and grabbed it. Then I shot.

The similarity of this report to Beulah's account in her after-midnight statement suggests that it is a good paraphrase of what Beulah related. That said—and despite the quotation marks—these words are not a stenographer's verbatim transcription. At least they cannot be assumed to be that exact. Newspapers of the era routinely put paraphrase between quotation marks. Hence, even if this quotation conveys the drift of what Beulah said and some of her words, it is impossible to know just which words are hers and which are the reporter's or rewrite man's; nor can one even be sure whether all the statements are in their original order, much less what may have been left out.[7]

The *Herald and Examiner* reported little of Beulah's interview in the matron's room but agreed in substance with the *Daily News* report. While she awaited transport to the inquest, the paper said, Beulah mused to the police matron, saying, "I don't believe I ever loved anybody very much. You know how it is, you keep looking and looking for the great, mad, unreasonable passion. But it never, never comes." The *Daily News* phrased this comment as follows: "I didn't love Harry so much—but he brought me wine and made a fuss over me and thought I was pretty. I don't think I ever loved anybody very much. You know how it is—you keep looking and looking all the time for someone you can really love." By contrast, the *Journal*, the *Post*, and the *American* quoted her as saying that Harry was her "greatest love" and that she was "glad" she killed him because the affair was "wrecking" her life.[8]

It turns out that Beulah was not the only accused killer whom the press quoted as saying, "I'm glad I did it." This declaration was attributed to others as well. Some of them may well have been glad, but did they all *say so* as part of an admission to the police or reporters? When a woman named Frances Kowalkowski was arrested for allegedly killing her husband because he never spoke a pleasant word to her, a police officer claimed that she had declared to him in Polish, "I poisoned my husband, and I'm glad I did." Despite this supposed confession, prosecutors found insufficient evidence to bring her to trial. They must have concluded that the officer's testimony was not credible. Or else the paper who quoted him erred. This example, together with a recurrence of instances where an accused person was reported to have made the same declaration, raises the suspicion that "I'm glad I did it" was a trope, a cliché and ready-made interpretation of a homicide that police sometimes fed to reporters and that papers sometimes used on their own initiative. One or the other origin probably explains the attribution of these words to Beulah, especially given the contradictions and confused sourcing in the newspaper accounts of her Friday-morning statements. In fact, the following day, when she sat in the county jail and read what the papers were saying about her, she protested, "I never said I was glad!"[9]

"Glad I Killed Him." *Chicago Tribune*, September 24, 1926, p. 3. Newspapers.com.

> ## "GLAD I KILLED HIM," SAYS WIFE OF MATE'S DEATH
>
> Mrs. Marguerithe Delveaux, 50 year old mother of three sons, went to sleep last night in her cell at the South Chicago police station still smiling and declaring yesterday had been the happiest day of her life. Yesterday morning she had shot and killed her husband, John, ending a quarrel that had lasted most of their 28 years of married life, she said.

Another common expression attributed to women accused of murdering lovers was that they killed the man "rather than lose him." The appearance of this phrase in the plot summary of a 1907 novel suggests its cultural currency: "At the first suggestion of cooling ardour she prefers to slay him rather than to lose him." The author did not need to explain the phrase, since everyone knew what it meant, just as everyone knew the import when a 1924 newspaper article about three women held in Cook County Jail on murder charges—Elizabeth Uncapher, Belva Gaertner, and Beulah Annan—declared that each of them was "a 'woman scorned' who shot the man 'rather than lose him.'" The author of that statement was Maurine Watkins. Her quotation marks tagged the phrases as conventional. Moreover, when Watkins wrote *Chicago*, she had fictional reporter Jake apply the formula to Roxie Hart as a shorthand for explaining to a newspaper photographer what Roxie's case was all about—"Hot stuff: she kills him rather than lose him."[10]

> Of the four awaiting trial, the cases of Mrs. Annan and Mrs. Belva Gaertner would seem most similar to Elizabeth Unkafer's; each is accused of shooting a man, not her husband, with whom her relations were at least questioned; each is supposed to be "a woman scorned" who shot the man "rather than lose him." But neither was at all disconcerted by Mrs. Unkafer's sentence

A 'woman scorned' who shot the man 'rather than lose him.'" Article by Maurine Watkins, *Chicago Daily Tribune*, May 9, 1924, p. 6. Newspapers.com.

To summarize, the stories in the *Journal,* the *Post,* and the *American* about Beulah's Friday-morning remarks in the Clark Street jail were completely at odds with what the *Daily News* reported. They also showed confusion about whether Beulah was in her cell or in the matron's room when she made the supposed remarks, and they disagreed about whether the reporters acquired the remarks directly from Beulah or indirectly from police and prosecutors or a matron. Finally, they featured two clichés that suited the prosecutors' view of Beulah's case but were not in Beulah's after-midnight statement and in fact contradicted it. Hence, it is doubtful that Beulah ever said that she killed Kalsted "rather than lose him" and was "glad" she did it. In fact, just hours later, while waiting for the inquest to begin, she was asking police to let her see Harry, even though "it would only make me feel worse."[11]

5. INQUEST INTO THE DEATH OF HARRY KALSTED

The inquest was held at 2:00 P.M. on Friday afternoon, a mere twelve hours after Beulah gave her after-midnight statement to Roy Woods. When that statement was read aloud at the proceeding, any reporters who paid close attention would have realized how misleading the morning's communications from the prosecutors had been. They had claimed that Beulah had confessed to murdering Kalsted. But in her after-midnight statement, Beulah had said that she shot Kalsted after both of them reached for the gun. At the very least, this muddied the waters and raised a host of unanswered questions.

The inquest began at Boydston Brothers undertaking parlors and concluded at the Hyde Park police station. Boydston's was at 4227–29 South Cottage Grove Avenue. Kalsted's body had been brought there the night before, at the request of William Wilcox, and it was now on a table in a back room, where the coroner's jurors were to view it as part of the proceedings. Wilcox knew Frank and Charles Boydston because their business shared a building with Tennent's Model Laundry.[1]

One of the reporters covering the inquest was Maurine Watkins. In an account composed later that day, Watkins noted that Beulah had seemed reflective, not nervous, and had "talked of her early life in Kentucky and her little 7 year old son of a former marriage." Watkins added that, according to the general consensus, Beulah was "the prettiest woman ever accused of murder in Chicago—young, slender, with bobbed auburn hair, wide set, appealing blue eyes; tip-tilted nose, translucent skin, faintly, very faintly rouged, an ingenuous smile, an intelligent expression—an 'awfully nice girl' and more than usually pretty."[2]

The preliminaries of the inquest commenced at Boydston's, shortly after 2:00 P.M. William McLaughlin and Roy Woods represented the state. Beulah's attorney, William O'Brien, was on his way. When the coroner inquired whether a relative of the deceased was present, Kalsted's brother-in-law

William Wilcox spoke up, and so did Harry's brother Richard, who lived fifty miles west of Chicago in the town of Aurora and had traveled in by train that morning. When the coroner asked Richard to provide particulars about Harry, Richard could not recall Harry's middle name or whether he even had one. It had been some time since he had seen his brother, and they were not close. During these preliminaries, Beulah's attorney arrived and identified himself. O'Brien knew little about the case and had almost certainly not yet spoken to Beulah.

Beulah Annan's defense attorney, William W. O'Brien. DN-0081117, *Chicago Daily News* collection, Chicago History Museum.

Six prospective jurors were questioned briefly. All were white men from the south side—an electrician, a mechanic, two merchants, a sign painter, and a retiree. Assistant State's Attorney McLaughlin had a single question for them: "Would the fact that the lady who might be charged with the killing in this case should be a good-looking woman, would that make any difference with any of you gentlemen? You would have no more hesitancy in bringing in a verdict against a woman than a man?"

There was a pause. Then one of the jurors said, "Absolute justice."

It was now nearly three o'clock. The coroner directed the jurors to the morgue to view the body and be sworn in. After the viewing, the coroner, court reporter, lawyers, jurors, and Beulah all piled into cars and headed to the Hyde Park police station for the continuation of the inquest, where the prosecutors put William Wilcox on the stand. Wilcox was an important witness for two reasons. First, Harry Kalsted had been his employee and had been living at his house. Second, Assistant State's Attorney Woods had called him to the Annan apartment around 11:00 P.M. to help Woods and McLaughlin get the truth out of Beulah. Wilcox had also been taken by the prosecutors to the police station, an hour or so later, so that he could sit in on the questioning that produced Beulah's after-midnight statement.

From the witness chair, Wilcox rehearsed what Beulah had said at the police station, as best he could recall, and toward the end he summarized the moments of the shooting. "She said last night that he said 'if that is the kind of woman you are, I am through with it'—I didn't—possibly what I think, he attempted to leave, and both made a dive for the bedroom." The sequence of elements in this summary, together with his opinion that "possibly what I think, he attempted to leave," showed the influence of the prosecutor's viewpoint. Woods, no doubt pleased, prompted him. "Didn't she say she was first?" This referred to Beulah's comment that when she and Kalsted "jumped up," she was on the end of the sofa nearest the bedroom door. Wilcox answered, "Yes, and they both grabbed—." At this point the coroner interrupted with a "What?" And Beulah's attorney, O'Brien, asked, "Grabbed what?" Wilcox answered, "The gun, it was in the middle of the bed, said it was in the middle of the bed uncovered, and she grabbed and beat him to it—I don't know the exact words, they are there in the statement, but she said there was nothing left for him to grab."

The words about the gun being in the middle of the bed were not expressly in the after-midnight statement. Therefore, Woods asked Wilcox whether he was describing what Beulah had said at the station or what she had said in her first statement, taken down in the kitchen of her apartment. Wilcox said,

"No, I think in the station." Woods asked, "Was there anything said about the deceased grabbing for the gun in the house?" The question was confusing because "in the house" could have referred to where Kalsted was when he grabbed for the gun or where Beulah was when she made the remark. Woods had meant the latter, and Wilcox seems to have understood that. "Why, not for the gun," Wilcox answered. O'Brien interjected, "What is that?" Wilcox said, "Not for the gun that I know of." O'Brien interrupted, not understanding that Woods's question had been about the kitchen statement. "Didn't both go there and dive for the gun?" O'Brien asked. Wilcox answered, based on what he had heard Beulah say at the police station, "I don't know whether for the gun or not, both made a grab; I suppose it was for the gun, because she beat him to it." O'Brien asked, "That is, they both dived for it?" "Both dived for it," Wilcox said.

The questioning continued, and at one point Woods, wanting to emphasize to Wilcox that the focus of his questions was what Beulah had said at the station, not in her flat, referred explicitly to the statement taken down in the station by the shorthand reporter. O'Brien's ears perked up. This was the first he had heard about a shorthand reporter. Therefore, he suggested that if they had a statement, it should be read aloud. That was then done.

Wilcox remained in the witness chair during the reading, and afterward O'Brien posed a few more questions to him.

O'BRIEN: Tell us about the revolver. All about the revolver.
WILCOX: I don't know anything about the revolver. I don't even know that it was her revolver.
O'BRIEN: Was it hers or her husband's.
WILCOX: I could not tell you that.
O'BRIEN: Did you ask her?
WILCOX: No.
O'BRIEN: Ask her any questions?
WILCOX: I did ask her where it was and she said on the bed.
O'BRIEN: Do you know who owned the revolver?
WILCOX: No I don't.
O'BRIEN: Did you ask her?
WILCOX: She said it was her husband's.
O'BRIEN: Did you ask her how it came to be on the bed?
WILCOX: Yes sir.
O'BRIEN: What did she say?
WILCOX: Said it was always there.
O'BRIEN: Always on the bed?

WILCOX: Always under the pillow.
O'BRIEN: Always under the pillow.
WILCOX: Yes sir.
O'BRIEN: Did you ask her if she put it there?
WILCOX: No.
O'BRIEN: Did you ask her who put it there?
WILCOX: No, I didn't.

Wilcox's testimony is the best evidence that the gun had in fact been on the bed at the time of the shooting, since the exact location of the revolver in the bedroom was incidental to the version of the shooting Beulah gave when Wilcox and the prosecutors questioned her in her apartment. That version pictured an attempted rape with Beulah retreating to the bedroom, getting the gun, and shooting Kalsted as he attempted to attack her. Had the gun been in the dresser drawer, Beulah would have had no reason to have lied by claiming that the gun was on the bed. Hence, as a merely incidental element of that story, the detail about the gun being on the bed was credible.

According to Wilcox, Beulah told him two things about the gun, which he distinguished. One was that the gun had been on the bed, uncovered, meaning that this had been its position at the time of the shooting. The other was that it was always kept under the pillow. It appears that before Beulah gave her "kitchen statement" to Woods and his colleagues, she had rehearsed it privately to Wilcox—to "Billy" as she knew him—probably when he was trying to persuade her to talk to Woods. This would explain why Woods was unaware that when Beulah was "in the house," she had referred to the location of the gun. In fact, according to Wilcox, the first thing she said to him about the gun was that it was on the bed but not that it was under the pillow. This clarification came up in one of O'Brien's follow-up questions. He wanted to be sure he had correctly understood Wilcox's earlier testimony that the gun was always under the pillow:

O'BRIEN: The revolver was under the pillow?
WILCOX: It was on the bed she told me.
O'BRIEN: Did she say it was under the pillow?
WILCOX: No, she told me this first herself.

"This" referred to the answer he had just given. In other words, when Wilcox first asked Beulah where the gun had been at the time of the shooting, Beulah had said, "on the bed." Moreover, earlier in his testimony, he had recalled her saying that the gun had been "in the middle of the bed uncovered" (when she and Kalsted reached for it). Yet he had also just testified that, according to Beulah, the gun was "always under the pillow." There was no actual contradiction, only a confusion caused by the way O'Brien's questions were phrased to Wilcox and the order in which they were posed. In her private conversation with Wilcox, she had told him that the gun was in the middle of the bed when she retreated to the bedroom to defend herself. And when Wilcox asked her where the gun was kept, she had said, "always kept under the pillow."[3]

Woods objected again and again to O'Brien's line of questioning about the gun because he did not want the coroner's jury to hear testimony that placed the gun in full view on the bed at the time when Beulah and Kalsted entered the bedroom, since that would have lent credence to Beulah's claim that Kalsted had reached for the revolver. And he also did not want them to hear that she had made these statements as part of her first version of the shooting, a version in which it did not matter where in the bedroom the gun had been or whether it had been visible. But the coroner let O'Brien continue.

O'Brien returned to the subject of the "dive" for the gun. Beulah had described it in her after-midnight statement, and that statement had already been read aloud. But O'Brien seems not to have realized that everything Wilcox knew about the dive for the gun was in that statement. Wilcox's answers simply echoed it.

O'BRIEN: She said they were both trying to get the revolver? Both dove for it?

WILCOX: Both dove for the revolver.

O'BRIEN: Did you ask her why she was trying to get it?

WILCOX: No, I didn't.

O'BRIEN: You didn't think they were diving to be in there for any other reason?

WILCOX: No.

O'BRIEN: Did you ask her?

WILCOX: I am not an attorney; am not a diver.

Wilcox had a wry sense of humor. Earlier, when asked whether his brother-in-law Harry was employed, he had answered that the dead man was "unemployed at present." Now, in defending himself for failing to ask Beulah all the pertinent questions, he explained that he was not an attorney and not a "diver." The reporters and jurymen probably chuckled, and Woods called out an objection to what he called "persecution of the state's attorney's witness."

"Of course," O'Brien said, "I have got to be sensible here whether the state's attorney has or not. The idea of my persecuting these witnesses. Mr. Coroner, that would be a perfect question to this inquiry along that direction."

"What is it?" the coroner asked.

"About the revolver."

The coroner decided to ask the question himself. "Mr. Wilcox, did you say also something to the effect—where now did you see the revolver?"

"I see it in the station."

"Ask him to tell all he knows," O'Brien said.

Wilcox had nothing more to tell.

The coroner asked Al to take the stand. Under Illinois law, a husband was not permitted to testify against his wife at a criminal trial, but he could be a witness at a coroner's inquest. Al said he had arrived home just before six. Beulah refused to tell him what had happened. "I could not make her talk," he said. "She was too hysterical to talk." No one asked Al whether he kept his gun under his pillow.

The statement of Dr. Joseph Springer, the coroner's physician, was then read aloud by the clerk. It stated that the bullet passed obliquely through Kalsted's torso from right to left and passed directly through Kalsted's heart. This meant that Kalsted remained conscious for no more than a few seconds. Springer would later opine that death had been "instantaneous." What Beulah recalled, and had told the prosecutors, was that Kalsted gasped out a few words, passed out, and showed no more signs of life.

After Springer's statement had been read, the coroner asked Beulah to take the witness chair. Once he had asked for her name, address, and occupation, the coroner explained that she did not need to testify unless she wanted to. She answered awkwardly, "No, I have not a statement to make."

"You don't want to testify?"

"No sir."

The witness phase of the inquest was now ended. The six jurors retired to an adjacent room and returned shortly with their decision: "We the jury recommend that one said Beulah Annan now under arrest be held to the Grand Jury on a charge of murder until discharged by due process of law."

6. FINDING BEULAH BEHIND THE PRESS'S TROPES AND PARAQUOTATIONS

Following the Friday afternoon inquest at the Hyde Park police station, Beulah was taken to Cook County Jail, a large stone structure at the corner of Dearborn and Illinois Streets in Chicago's north "Loop." There she was searched by a matron, assigned a prison number, and made to bathe. A jail physician listened to her heart and lungs and examined her for venereal disease. All of this was routine.[1]

Next, she was conducted to the regular women's cellblock and brought before a sturdy steel door next to a steel grille. The door opened, and a matron wearing a dark dress with a big white apron ushered her inside and guided her through the somewhat narrow space between a row of white dining tables and a bank of steel-faced cell doors to number 557, the six-by-eight-foot cubicle that would be her home for the next forty-nine days.[2]

The women's cellblocks occupied the fifth, sixth, and seventh floors of the newer part of the jail, with parallel rows of steel cell doors facing narrow, rectangular common areas on the fifth and sixth floors. Wooden dining tables painted in white enamel and banked by low stools filled the common area of the fifth floor. Stairways led up to the sixth and seventh floors, which were constructed so that the seventh-floor corridors formed a balcony, with short steel railings, above the common area of the sixth floor. This sixth-floor commons served as a recreation room and was arranged with narrow tables and benches, a radio, and an upright piano. Here the women talked, played cards, and pored over the newspapers.[3]

On Saturday morning, when the inmates of the women's jail were released from their cells for breakfast and morning "exercise," Beulah probably got a look at what the papers were saying about her. Reading the conflicting Friday stories about what she had allegedly confessed about the shooting,

Fifth-floor dining area of the women's wing of Cook County Jail in 1922. When Beulah was an inmate, she occupied cell number 557. Chicago Community Trust, *Reports Comprising the Survey of the Cook County Jail*, p. 123.

she discovered something that had probably never occurred to her before, namely, that it was common for the papers not only to exaggerate but even to invent and that words between quotation marks were often mere paraphrase or false secondhand reports.

The *Chicago American*'s initial reporting was quite melodramatic, especially in its account of the hours Beulah spent with Harry Kalsted's body before she called Al. Interlacing its description with lines taken from the lyrics of the record that police found on the turntable of the Annans' victrola, the *American* gave a vivid account:

> "Her name was Hula Lou, the kind of gal that never could be true—"
>
> In the apartment at 817 East Forty-Sixth Street, a woman sat on the floor, a pretty young woman with bobbed hair and a man's head in her arms. A group of children passed under the open window—joined hands—dancing to the music.
>
> A dance of death.
>
> The fumes of wine—blood red raw wine—hovered close in the room. A stain that was not wine spread over the woman's garments.

Women's sixth-floor recreation area, Cook County Jail (1922). Chicago Community Trust, *Reports Comprising the Survey of the Cook County Jail*, p. 113.

"Harry! Harry! Speak to me. Speak to me. Do you hear? Say something! Oh . . . God . . . help me. . . ."

"She's got more sweeties than a dog has fleas.
I never knew—
A man who wouldn't shoot a Dan McGrew. . . ."

What had been a man became an empty shell.

The woman rained kisses on still cold lips. Hovering shadows filled the room, gathered in back of the dresser and beneath the bed—ready—waiting to pounce down upon her.

Downstairs, the mailman—with a letter addressed to Mrs. Beulah Annan. The doorbell rang.

Harry Kalstead's requiem.

Panic—terror—stark agony of dark. The woman screamed, stifling the sound with blood-stained hands.

Laughter—a woman's laughter from an apartment across the way—mocked her. The clock—ticking steadily—stolidly, sternly, took on a voice—a voice that said:

"Mur-der, mur-der, mur-der, mur-. . . ."[4]

The *Chicago American* and the *Chicago Herald and Examiner* were owned by newspaper magnate William Randolph Hearst, whose motto was "90% entertainment, 10% information—and the information without boring you." At Hearst tabloids, sensationalism was the order of the day. As one reporter famously put it, a Hearst paper was like "a screaming woman running down the street with her throat cut." To achieve high drama, reporters and rewrite staff were expected to "hype up" stories, stretching facts and sometimes even fabricating details in order to achieve melodramatic effects.[5]

The almost novelistic freedom granted to Hearst reporters was limited by restrictions when it came to two subjects: sex and women. Anything connected with sex had to be couched in decorous language. (Words such as *rape, gonorrhea, syphilis, breast,* and *pregnant* were not permitted.) And all reporting on women was supposed to conform to Hearst's view of them as guardians of the national morality. Hearst believed in "the innocence of women" and "the essential goodness of even the fallen." Reporters who wrote for his papers served this idealistic view of feminine nature by mixing pathos with gentle moral judgment, presenting the "moral lesson" of a wayward woman's life in an emotionally engaging way, "with glowing adjective and picturesque fancy." The *American*'s melodramatic portrayal of Beulah implied that, having killed Kalsted in anger, she was immediately filled with remorse, proof of a reawakening of her innate conscience, which suggested the possibility of rehabilitation.[6]

Reporters, often with photographers in tow, were free to conduct interviews in the cellblocks on any day of the week. Hearst photographers liked to pose female defendants in artificial scenes. Thus, when *Herald and Examiner* reporter Leola Allard showed up at the jail on Saturday morning, she brought along a photographer, who posed Beulah in various repentant attitudes: reading a Bible, gripping her cell bars and gazing heavenward, laying her head on her arm in a sorrowful gesture. The next day, when these photographs appeared in the paper, the caption beneath the Bible-reading image claimed that Beulah had happened "to open her Bible in jail to the twentieth verse of the first chapter of Proverbs," which read, "Wine is a mocker."[7]

"Crime news as entertainment" was nothing new. For decades newspapers had been turning homicides into headline news, and the so-called yellow journalism of the tabloids had been hyping crime stories and scandals with exaggeration, invention, emotional scene-painting, and gratuitous sensationalism

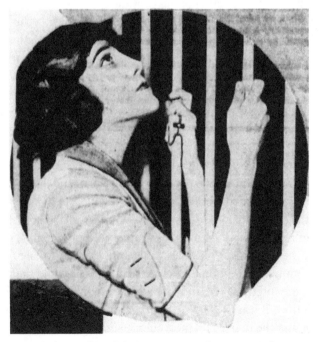

Staged photo of Beulah Annan in Cook County Jail. Originally published in the *Herald and Examiner*, April 7, 1924, p. 3; reprinted in the *Star Tribune* (Minneapolis), August 8, 1926, magazine sec., p. 3. Newspapers.com.

in order to feed—and profit from—the public's appetite for anything seamy, salacious, or grisly. Sensationalism in the news business was so pervasive that the average newspaper reader probably did not think it incongruous that homicides involving ordinary citizens who were otherwise not socially or politically influential were reported in bold front-page headlines alongside news about presidential speeches, congressional legislation, scientific discoveries, world events, and other matters of much greater social and national import.

Criticism had been directed against yellow journalism for several decades. Many instances of the terms *yellow journalism* and *yellow newspapers* and the like can be found in newspaper comments from the 1880s onward. The remarks reflect both the ongoing criticism of the tabloid style and the ongoing currency of public understanding of what *yellow journalism* meant. The tabloids "sensationalize vice and crime, 'play up' trivialities, exploit the private affairs of prominent people, embroider facts, and offend against good taste with screech, blare, and color." So wrote Edward Ross in 1910, summarizing a common view and adding that the tabloids also suppressed and distorted news to their commercial and political advantages. The question was posed to a group of Chicago newspaper editors at a City Club gathering in 1921 of whether their profession did not devote too much ink "to sensationalism and the sordid details of crime." The editors responded that they did not consider themselves censors and were merely giving the public what it wanted. The following year, progressive Chicagoan Victor Yarros lamented that serious denunciation of yellow journalism tended to be heard only "in advanced reform circles or in private homes."[8]

Yarros was no doubt right that people of a certain social class and upbringing were more vexed about yellow journalism than the average citizen was. Most people wanted their newspaper to both inform and entertain, and for that reason most papers included stories that lent themselves to sensationalism. Even the papers that prided themselves on factual accuracy engaged in a bit of dramatic hyping. Not only that, police and prosecutors, wise to the methods of the press, gave out facts in terms meant to titillate or shock or otherwise command attention. It was police officers who told the papers that Beulah was the "prettiest" or "most beautiful" woman ever held for murder in Cook County. It was they who tagged her "a model Salome." The labels stuck. It was also the police and prosecutors who told the papers that Beulah danced to jazz for hours while Kalsted lay dead or dying.[9]

The nature of the record on the phonograph was incidental to the investigation of the shooting, but—prompted by the police and prosecutors—the papers went out of their way to mention that the record was "jazz" music;

and they referred to the jazz record as often as they mentioned how pretty Beulah was. The *American* called Beulah "the jazz slayer."[10]

As a keyword of the 1920s, *jazz* referred to a complicated subject, musically and culturally. At the turn of the century, when early forms of African American music that contributed to the emergence of jazz began appearing in wider American culture, many white Americans regarded those styles as degrading and morally suspect on *racial* grounds. By the late teens, however, many white people had embraced jazz. More precisely, they enjoyed jazzy music performed by white bands and applied the term *jazz* to any new dance music that was upbeat, a bit syncopated, and featured one or more saxophones. In fact, some white musicians claimed to be the real inventors of jazz. Around 1916, for example, a white Chicago band, destined to become immensely popular through its recordings, styled itself "The Original Dixieland Jazz Band." And even if most of the public took for granted that Black musicians had "invented" jazz, a majority of white people knew only the jazz styles created for them by white band leaders. They were also led to believe that white jazz was more cultivated than the Black variety. The promoters for band-leader Paul Whiteman's music, for example, told the public that Whiteman had "tamed" jazz. Meanwhile, some white Chicagoans frequented the southside "black-and-tans," clubs operated by white owners that featured a variety of African American shows; and a small number of young white musicians headed into Black neighborhood clubs after hours to listen to cutting-edge jazz and, if possible, to sit in with Black musicians.[11]

White Chicagoans danced to every variety of white jazz at downtown hotel ballrooms, neighborhood dance halls, and a wide range of cafes and cabarets. Parents and teenagers even enjoyed jazz at local school events. Thus, on the evening of March 14, 1923, the Parent-Teacher Association in a white neighborhood on Chicago's south side hosted a supper in a field house, where one person gave a reading from *Les Misérables*, another sang a solo, two others sang a duet, and some boys from Lindblom High School provided "jazz music" as part of a "delightful program." The report of this event appeared in *Sullivan's Englewood Times*, a neighborhood paper that served the white, working-class, and largely churchgoing community of Englewood on Chicago's south side. Not everyone in urban America approved of jazz, but Mr. Sullivan published no editorial condemnations of jazz, and when forty-three-year-old Hallie Lauritsen wrote a letter to his paper urging parents to teach their children better music than the "jazz" that teenagers liked to play on the "music machine," she felt obliged to assure her neighbors that she had "no quarrel with the young ones' taste."[12]

Scene from an ad for the movie *Nice People*, depicting white people enjoying the music of a white jazz band at a city cabaret. *Ironwood (MI) Daily Globe*, March 19, 1923, p. 2. Newspapers.com.

Jazz also became a metaphor for the new lifestyles of the "Jazz Age." "Our language turned jazzy," one paper commented in 1921, looking back over trends of the last few years. "Our costumes took the last form of jazz, we began to live a jazz life." Other pundits applied the expression *jazz life* to the fast pace of modern existence, the obsession with speed—speedy automobiles, speedy trains, speedy telephone connections. Meanwhile, movies and their advertisements gave the impression that it was ultramodern people—glamorous, trendy men and women—who lived the jazz life.[13]

Not surprisingly, the jazz life was also blamed for cultural decline. It had given birth to an "orgy of spending," declared one pundit. People were cashing in their war bonds and throwing money away on jewelry, fine food, automobiles, and amusements generally. Another article lamented that an "epidemic of jazz" had "spread over the country, evolving from jazz melodies to a form of jazz life characterized by fatalism, indifference, recklessness, and immorality." Marriage was threatened, warned another, claiming that married couples were getting divorced at an alarming rate because "the call of jazz life is stronger with them than the ties of home and family." Jazz *music* was not even necessary to a jazz life: "Were they jaded by the jazz-life of gin and girls?" asked Maurine Watkins, referring to accused "thrill killers" Nathan Leopold and Richard Loeb, whose musical preferences were never disclosed in the press and could well have been classical. In any case, most people did not really think that jazz itself was a cause of moral decline, which is why it was so funny for 1927 theater audiences to hear the *Chicago* character Mary Sunshine ask Kitty "the Tiger Girl" Baxter what had caused her to take up a life of crime— "Was it *jazz*?"[14]

Moviemakers capitalized on the public's interest in the steamier sides of jazz life and depicted not only "flaming youth" engaged in petting parties and other risqué behavior but also reckless, well-heeled married pleasure-seekers living the jazz life as they pursued amorous illicit liaisons in cabarets and other places of amusement. Most moviegoers did not participate in the latter forms of jazz life, but they found it deliciously entertaining to watch jazzy transgressors in action.

Movie ad for *Flaming Youth*. *Zanesville (OH) Times Recorder*, May 2, 1924, p. 18.

They also liked to read about them in the newspaper. Stories about Beulah's tryst with Harry Kalsted, the wine-drinking, and the jazz record on her victrola suggested that Beulah led a jazz life of the scandalous sort. In fact, Beulah was not a regular cabaret-goer, and her relationship with Kalsted had been an old-fashioned extramarital affair. She and Harry had not frequented cabarets; they had gone on walks; and the amorous meeting on the fateful Thursday afternoon had been a singular event. But the newspapers preferred to fit Beulah to a formula. Although the fact that a twenty-three-year-old Chicago woman owned a jazz record was not in itself eyebrow-raising, mentioning "jazz" as the coda to a "wine party," an adulterous affair, and a homicide made the whole set of details sizzle.

1923 ad for a movie purporting to depict "jazz married life." *Fort Worth Star-Telegram*, May 11, 1923, p. 6. Newspapers.com.

According to the transcript of her after-midnight statement, Beulah played the record just once. A United Press story, printed in many out-of-town papers, placed a more melodramatic account into her mouth: "I put on a record and took Harry in my arms, and cried and cried. I kept putting on records and as each one played I took him in my arms and tried to call him back to me."[15]

This was not the only instance of swollen paraphrase masquerading as verbatim quotation in a newspaper story about Beulah. It was customary for reporters and rewrite staff to put their own paraphrase between quotation marks. The Hearst papers used this license to make Beulah sound like a character in a dime novel. Other papers were more restrained, but they, too, put words in Beulah's mouth, polishing her speaking style and rephrasing her comments in ways that sometimes altered the meaning. These practices explain why the Beulah of newspaper interviews says contradictory things from one paper to the next, sometimes reflecting philosophically on life and love, and always speaking in grammatically correct, well-turned phrases. Most newspaper readers probably assumed that when a newspaper they regarded as trustworthy put words between quotation marks, those marks implied verbatim transcription. Moreover, the very style of straight-news reporting gave the impression of unfiltered description and stenographic quotation. Few members of the public realized that reporters often phoned in stories to rewrite staff, who turned rough notes into orderly prose and exercised a good deal of freedom in the use of quotation marks.[16]

This free approach to quotation went back to at least the closing decades of the nineteenth century. In an article published in *Writer* in 1889, a reporter named John Arthur explained that when a subject refused to talk to him, he would invent an interview, "obtaining my information through a third party and 'faking' my interview accordingly." Several years later, in an 1894 handbook on journalism, William Shuman commented on the approach to interviews that had recently come into vogue at Hearst papers. "The best writers of interviews," he explained, "now put their matter in much the same shape as that used by a popular novelist." When they do their job well, "more than half the words credited to the speaker may never have been uttered by him at all, and yet the report as a whole may be fairer to him and please him better than would a verbatim interview written after the old style." Of course, not every interviewee was pleased.[17]

The novelistic approach of the Hearst papers was not universal, but a 1916 handbook shows that even the journalistic standards taught at universities allowed for considerable license. Grant Hyde, a professor at the University of Wisconsin whose book on newspaper writing went through multiple print-ings, gave out a dictum on quotation that started out rigorous and grew progressively more permissive. "Be sure that the quotations are the speaker's exact words or very nearly his exact words," Hyde instructed, "so that he cannot accuse you of misquoting him. The spirit of the words must be in the quotation, anyway." Most reporters of the era had not been to journalism school and did not read handbooks like Hyde's, but even the most scrupulous among them felt free to enclose between quotation marks their own, better formulations of what they took someone's meaning to be. For lack of a better term, I call this *paraquotation*.[18]

The custom of paraquotation explains one of the rules in the style sheet given to reporters at the *Kansas City Star*, a newspaper of high journalistic principle. Quoted words should "preserve the atmosphere" of the subject's speech, the style sheet said. For example, "in quoting a child, do not let him say, 'Inadvertently, I picked up the stone and threw it.'" Revealingly, this example assumes that newspaper staff would not as a rule quote a child verbatim but would paraphrase a child's statement and place the paraphrase between quotation marks. License of this kind was not countenanced in other fields of writing, not even in junior-high essays and reports. Yet the *Star* was not cavalier about factual accuracy. The paper's founder, William Rockhill Nelson, used to stress that the most important person in the news business was "the reporter who can get facts straight and put them into plain concise language."[19]

For reporters and rewrite men, paraquoting was not only a way to make a subject's remarks more interesting; it was a practical necessity. Beat reporters had street smarts but were typically not "writers." They phoned in scraps of information or turned in handwritten jottings to rewrite men, who had to make sense of these notes and convert them into good newspaper prose under the pressure of brutal deadlines in an era when city papers put out multiple editions a day.

Moreover, given the low level of formal schooling among most city reporters, it may have been an understatement when Charles Olin remarked in his 1906 handbook on journalism that "not one reporter in ten is a stenographer." Probably not one in a hundred possessed that skill. And in any case, reporters were instructed that when conducting an interview, they should *not* take notes but should rely on their memories. "In interviewing, as in all reporting, the newspaper man should not take notes in the presence of the person with whom he is talking unless he feels sure it can be done without affecting the freedom and ease with which the man will talk." So wrote Willard Bleyer, advising that it was important to remember and write down verbatim, as best one could, the most important statements but doing so only after the interview, outside the subject's presence. An article on "newspaper accuracy" in *New Outlook* said the same thing. "Newspaper interviews as a rule are not stenographically reported," the author explained. "The correspondent holds his conversation with the person he is interviewing, and after the interview is concluded endeavors as well as he can, to write out a report of the conversation." All of this explains why one of the things that made actor

Charles Bickford most authentic when he played the role of Jake the reporter in Maurine Watkins's *Chicago* was "the absence of notebook and pencil."[20]

The practice of paraquotation ranged from trivial matters to significant ones. According to the *Daily News*, when Beulah was questioned by Roy Woods, she said, "Then I suddenly came to my senses and telephoned my husband where he is employed at 9120 Baltimore avenue." This was not a verbatim quotation from her after-midnight statement. Moreover, had Beulah expressed herself in such a sentence, she would have said something like "I telephoned my husband *at work*." The reporter, quoting Woods quoting Beulah, felt comfortable conveying the gist of her words and specifying the address of Al's workplace, thus making a trivial and expedient change, which he did not hesitate to include between the quotation marks.[21]

More consequential were reporters' paraphrases of police statements of pertinent facts, prosecutors' theories of a case, and defendants' accounts of events and feelings. The first story about Beulah in the *Evening Post* was vague about the source of its quotations. A Friday-morning jailhouse declaration was reported as though a *Post* reporter had been present when Beulah made it. But the account went on to quote something Beulah had said "to a matron," which suggested indirect sourcing. The *Post* then purported to quote directly from the "confession" that Beulah had made several hours before. Since the transcript of the after-midnight statement was still being prepared, the paper must have quoted what police or prosecutors said that Beulah had said. Here are the words that the paper represented as a quotation:

> I have been fooling around with Harry for two months. As soon as my husband left for work, Harry called me. I told him I would not be home but he came over anyway. We sat in the bedroom for some time drinking liquor I gave him money to buy, and then I told him in a joking way that I was going to quit him. "Oh no you are not," he said, "I am going to quit you," and then he got up to go out. I went to the dresser, got the revolver and shot him.

The first sentence was factually accurate. So was the second. Neither, however, was a verbatim quotation from the after-midnight statement, and the rest of the quotation flatly misrepresented it. The *Post* probably relied on what police and prosecutors told the night-shift reporters who were present at the Hyde Park police station when Beulah was brought in for questioning.[22]

The practice of paraquoting also explains why Beulah's speech patterns differ between the verbatim transcript of her after-midnight statement taken down by a court stenographer and the newspaper quotations of that statement.

The court stenographer's record captured her idiomatic speech in expressions such as "I says," "I don't remember very little," "there was children playing," and "we both beat it for the bedroom." The papers replaced her colloquial style with proper grammar and more formal prose. Some made her sound like a character in a melodrama.

Not all paraquoting distorted a subject's meaning, even if it was typical for reporters to alter a subject's style. Sonia Lee of the *Chicago American* interviewed Beulah at Cook County Jail on Saturday morning and appears to have been generally careful to represent Beulah's own thoughts, although in more polished prose than Beulah would have used. Lee's article about her visit included Beulah's answer to the question of whether she was sorry for what she had done. Lee rendered Beulah's response as a little morality speech. "Sorry? Who wouldn't be? But what is there to do? My husband says he'll see me through. I wouldn't blame him if he didn't. We can all be sorry after it's done. If only we could go back! If we only could. It's so little we get out of cheating. But the pleasure looks big, for the moment, doesn't it? The only thing on earth then. But worthless afterwards. Not a single memory." One may suspect that when the Beulah of this speech shifts from the personal *I* to the generalized *we*, the words are more Lee's elaboration than a paraphrase of Beulah's reflection. A sign, however, that Lee conveyed the *spirit* of Beulah's words and did not simply make things up is the fact that although on Friday the *American*, Lee's own paper, had described the shooting as a murder, Lee's Saturday paraquotation represented Beulah as expressing guilt only for the affair and not admitting to murder.[23]

"We kept on drinking and quarreling," Lee's article continued to quote. "He called me names and I cursed him. He made a dive for the bedroom. He had a terrible light in his eyes. And I knew he was going to kill me. I grabbed the gun lying on the bed. I had never shot a gun but once on New Year's Eve. Every day, I'd pick it up so carefully. I was afraid of it. I don't know how I happened to kill him. I don't know." One should assume that this, too, is Lee's paraquotation, a post-interview reconstruction of what Beulah had said, based on Lee's memory. Yet here, as well, there is good reason to think that Lee hewed rather closely to Beulah's meaning and even reproduced some of her wording. The reference to a "dive" for the bedroom echoes what William Wilcox heard Beulah say in the kitchen, and so does the reference to the gun being on the bed. Moreover, it is hard to imagine that Lee invented the idea that Beulah was in the habit of picking up the gun every day. Significantly, that detail suggests that when Beulah made the bed, she always put the gun back in its appointed place, assuming that she took the time to make the bed (a bed that police found *un*made). Lee did not press Beulah about this or ask her how Kalsted knew that there was a gun on the bed. Reporters were a generally non-confrontative lot, and Sonia Lee's aim was to elicit feelings from Beulah, not to test her account of the shooting.[24]

The police had already begun referring to Beulah as "the prettiest woman ever accused of murder in Chicago," and the papers called her "the prettiest murderer," "the beautiful slayer," and so forth. Sonia Lee was the first reporter to mention the possibility that this might work in Beulah's favor with a jury. While a weepy Beulah lamented her predicament, Lee wrote, an inmate named Sabella Nitti said, "You pretty, pretty—you speak English. They won't kill you. Why you cry?" Lee then drew a contrast. "Sabella, stocky, with a baffled aged fury in her eyes, muttering about beauty and its worth, passed with an armful of wet laundry. Her apron was hiked up showing the short brown legs. Her heelless slippers, a slosh-slosh, a hopeless sound. Beulah Annan looked after her. 'Poor thing. She's a lost soul—nobody cares about her!'" These were clichés of sympathy, but the reporter quoted them only to draw a contrast between Sabella's looks and Beulah's. "Beulah's was not a mouth that drew back from discolored teeth, but one perfectly formed. Her hair was glossy and not dry. Her figure was perfectly modeled and her suit was impeccable."[25]

In reporting on people accused of capital crimes, the major newspapers tended to mention their ethnicity in cases where they happened to be immigrants from non-Anglo countries, a tendency that was typical of the times and often carried demeaning overtones. Sabella Nitti was the "Italian woman" and "Senora Nitti." Tillie Klimek was "the squat little Polish storekeeper." If the accused was an African American, that, too, was always noted. Minnie Nichols and Rose Epps were distinguished as "colored." The papers never referred to Beulah's ethnic background. Beulah had been born and raised in Kentucky and was Scotch-Irish on her father's side, probably English on her mother's. In short, she was quintessentially "white." But no paper called her white. It was not necessary. Silence about her ethnicity implied that she was white and that she enjoyed all the rights and privileges of whiteness.[26]

Italian immigrants generally also counted as white in America, and Sabella Nitti was referred to in the news as the "first white woman" to be given a death sentence. Yet 1924, which saw the passage of the Johnson-Reed Immigration Act, was a year of high anti-immigrant sentiment, especially toward immigrants from southern and eastern Europe. By quoting Nitti's broken

English and referring to her skin as dark, Sonia Lee made clear to readers of the *American* that Nitti belonged to the unwanted class of immigrants. An even uglier version of this same assessment could be heard over at the *Chicago Tribune*, where Genevieve Forbes told her readers that Nitti was "a dumb, crouching animal-like Italian peasant."[27]

Sonia Lee was one of six reporters who went to the county jail that day to conduct a "human-interest" interview with Beulah. Four of them saw her in the morning, perhaps with some overlap. Their quotations of Beulah's description of the shooting are substantially the same, but each one's account offers some unique material about her life reflections. Their stories also show variety about where their interviews took place. The *Post* has Beulah "in her cell," while the *American* at first pictures her in her cell but later has her fingering the dial of the radio (which was kept in the sixth-floor common area), and the *Daily Journal* places her at one of the dining tables on the fifth floor.

An article written by a fourth reporter who visited her that morning does not mention where the interview took place. According to the *Daily News*, Beulah was burdened by "sober thoughts" and mused, "Well, thinking it all over now, I think I would rather have been shot myself. Of course, it all happened so quickly, I didn't have time to think then." She denied that she was the one who started the quarrel. Kalsted was drunk and got angry, she said, and "he sprang for the bed. There was a revolver under the pillow. I got it first. If he'd got it he'd have shot me."[28]

Ione Quinby of the *Chicago Evening Post* visited Beulah around 10:00 A.M. Quinby was the *Post*'s sole female reporter and covered any cases of women tried for murder that the paper deemed worthy of newsprint. In an article published that same day, she pictured "the red-haired beauty" as anxious, her hands "clasping and unlocking," her eyes "rimmed with deep purple shadows." The *Post*'s initial story about Beulah had stated that she had confessed to murder, and Quinby's Saturday story began with the declaration that "forty hours of questioning and cogitation have burned the red-hot coals of remorse and repentance into the soul of Beulah Annan." Yet Quinby's quotation of Beulah's own account of the shooting, like Lee's and that of the *Daily News* reporter, did not contain any confession of murder:

> I am just a fool. I'd been married to Albert four years. I haven't any excuse except that Harry came into the Tennent laundry, where I worked as a bookkeeper, and I fell in love with him. I met him last October. He seemed fairly to worship me. Then I found out he had served a term in the penitentiary and all my dreams were

broken. He knew I was thru and that I had found out he wasn't worth the cost. I was ashamed of the way I had fooled myself. He knew I was going to quit him and words led to words. We both ran to the bedroom where a revolver was kept. I got there first.

The style of this quotation is too polished to be Beulah's exact words. Still, there is reason to credit key points of the quotation's content. First, Quinby was an experienced, serious, and responsible reporter who had studied news craft at Northwestern University's Medill School of Journalism. She cared about getting facts right and honoring the gist of someone's words. Second, even though Quinby herself probably assumed that Beulah had confessed to murder in her after-midnight statement, as Quinby's own paper had reported on Friday, she did not insinuate that assumption into her paraquotation. Instead, she represented Beulah as remorseful about her adulterous affair.[29]

Beulah also talked to Quinby about her job at Tennent's Laundry as though it were the main cause of her troubles and needed explaining. Quinby had the impression that Beulah was simply thinking out loud. "Her mind works vagrantly." Beulah was not the first person in a predicament to indulge in backward-looking fantasies of how things would have turned out differently if only they had made other choices. "If I hadn't been working, I'd never have met Harry," she told Quinby. "We were trying, I mean my husband, Albert, and I, to get ahead. We paid $75 a month rent on our apartment and $75 a month on our furniture. We planned to get a car. Albert makes only $65 a week and we needed money. . . . I love to cook and keep house and go marketing. Oh, why did I ever take that job!" She meant the job at Tennent's that brought her and Harry together; nonetheless, the Annans needed her income, and Beulah liked to work. "It's lonesome to be in the house all alone," she told another reporter. "The days go so slowly. But when you work, it's lots more fun." "I have always worked since I've been married." "Book keeping is rather hard work, though. Sometimes when I come home at night I'm completely worn out, and then I always have to get supper. No, I really don't care for housework."[30]

Beulah's reflections suggest she wished to think of herself as both a traditional wife and a modern woman. Her statement that she loved to cook, keep house, and go marketing was not a pose. Nor was it a pose when she said that these things were exhausting and that she did *not* like housework. Her opposing thoughts were not really contradictory. She wanted to be a good wife but more than a housewife; she wanted to have her own set of friends and earn her own money.

Many of the *Post's* women readers may have sympathized with Beulah's musings about liking to have a job but finding it difficult to prepare meals and otherwise keep house while working full-time. If Beulah was of two minds about these things, it was partly because 1920s culture sent conflicting signals to women. Leading cultural voices, including mass entertainment, heralded a new age of women's independence and equality, yet society also expected women to fill traditional roles as wives and mothers. Not many wives worked outside the home in 1924. Specifically, about 23 percent of all women of working age were part of the paid workforce, but only about 8 percent of married women whose spouses were present in the home were gainfully employed.[31]

Moreover, many Americans thought that a married woman should not work outside the home, especially if she had the support of an able-bodied husband. If a woman did work, it was thought to reflect poorly on her wifeliness, since a married woman was supposed to focus her energies on making a home for her husband and raising children. It was not only conservative *men* who believed this; many women did, too, or at least had divided feelings about the subject. A national women's advice columnist remarked that the question most often posed to her was "Should a woman work outside the home after marriage?"[32]

No one suggested that a working man like Al was selfish because he put in extra hours at work to provide a better life for himself and his family. But it was a "pet theory" of some people that "'erring wives and mothers' whose place so obviously is in the home" seek outside employment merely so that they can enjoy "unnecessary comforts and a sociable life." The author of these words was Willystine Goodsell, a leading feminist and educator of the era. Goodsell did not criticize a woman's interest in comforts and a social life but instead remarked that it was usually the inadequate earnings of working-class husbands that caused wives to take outside jobs.[33]

The Annans needed the extra money, and Tennent's Model Laundry also afforded Beulah a chance to make friends who were more or less her own age. Beulah's diary shows that in 1923, after she and Al had lived in Chicago for nearly three years, they regularly changed jobs, were sometimes out of work, and moved out of their living quarters every several months, occasionally making do with a sleeping room between moves. This was the pattern during the first nine months of that single year. It was only in late 1923, when Beulah went to work for Tennent's and Al started working at the Cudahy garage, that the couple began to enjoy the benefits of steady employment and stable residence in the same apartment. Not a single friend is mentioned in Beulah's 1923 diary, except her mother's friend John. But after she began working full-time at the laundry, which postdates her diary entries, Beulah found a social life at work. These were *her* friends, not Al's. As Al explained it, Beulah thought of herself as "modern" and "believe[d] in having her own set of friends."[34]

It is possible that Beulah had embraced some version of the "companion-ate marriage" philosophy, which held that the central purpose of marriage is a couple's mutual happiness, not procreation, and that mutual happiness requires that the wife enjoy equality with her husband and not merely bend to his authority. It is also likely that Mary's marital career and influence shaped Beulah's conception of her own freedom as a wife. Yet side by side with her notion of herself as a modern woman was her idea of Al as her strong fatherlike man. She called him "Daddy," which sounds very unmodern. She probably used that word when she wanted something from Al. But she also used it as a term of sincere affection, for it appears in her diary references to him. Most young women of the 1920s conformed, to one degree or other, to the prevailing cultural trends, and sometimes the competing pressures of the old and the new led a person into contradictions or at least idiosyncratic ways of behaving and understanding themselves. Beulah was a mixture of old and new ideas about being a woman.[35]

Was Beulah a flapper? The 1920s flapper was above all an expression of consumer culture "invented by the 'merchants of cool.'" Young women of any social class could be flappers, or at least flapperish, including "working girls" like Beulah, who had not figured among the avant-garde progenitors of flapperism in the 1910s but became consumers of the flapper style in the 1920s. The papers did not call Beulah a flapper, however, perhaps because she was married and perhaps because her attire did not strike them as flap-perish: the fawn-colored suit dress she is shown wearing in all photos taken of her up to the second day of her trial. Beulah did own some flapper-style dresses. Her younger cousin Thelma Marksberry recalled that in 1926 or so, she received some hand-me-down dresses from Beulah and wore them to her rural high school. "I might have looked funny," laughed Thelma, looking back from the age of ninety-two. "One was black satin with a fringe. I wore it with my old brown oxfords. I was only 14 or 15 years old. I thought I was something." Apparently, Thelma's mother permitted it, with whatever degree of eye-rolling, and the school did not send her home to change clothes. Nor would there have been anything racy about that dress when twenty-four-year-old Beulah wore it in Chicago in 1924. The flapper style, shocking when it first appeared before the war, was no longer shocking in 1924. There was far more entertainment value in calling Beulah "the prettiest woman ever accused of murder in Cook County" than in referring to her as a flapper, one of millions.[36]

Beulah's attorney, William O'Brien, also visited her at the jail on Saturday morning. He was with Beulah when Quinby arrived, and after consulting with his client, he went out into the hallway and told Quinby and any other reporters who may have been present that Beulah planned to plead self-defense. "Kalsted was an ex-convict," added O'Brien, "and served five years in Minnesota on a serious charge."[37]

O'Brien had no doubt seen the morning papers in which Beulah's after-midnight statement was characterized as an admission to murder. He hoped to get the trial judge to exclude this so-called confession on the grounds that it had been improperly obtained and that its details about Beulah's extramarital affair would prejudice the jury. As O'Brien saw it, a jury would more likely

Beulah Annan playing solitaire in Cook County Jail. *Chicago Tribune* archive photo/TCA.

acquit her if she claimed that she knew Kalsted only casually and had resisted his attempts to rape her. As it turned out, this version of the shooting was the defense that Beulah presented at her trial six weeks later, a mixture of fact and fiction that the prosecutors claimed had been cooked up by her lawyers. It had almost certainly been cooked up by O'Brien.

It was no doubt O'Brien who told Beulah that the reason for Harry Kalsted's time in a Minnesota penitentiary was a "criminal attack on a woman," a phrase Beulah used with reporters on Saturday morning. Not all of what O'Brien told Beulah about Kalsted was true, however, since the actual criminal charge against him had been wife desertion.[38]

Beulah's use of the expression "criminal attack on a woman" appeared in the *Daily Journal*. The *Journal*'s reporter had found Beulah sitting at the dining table outside her cell, perhaps already speaking to one or more other reporters. Beulah said she wished she was dead instead of Harry, although she had not felt that way in the moment. "You know, if a fellow pulled a gun on you, you wouldn't stand there and let him shoot you. My one idea was to put my hand on that gun first." "Pulled a gun" was a figure of speech. Beulah did not mean that Kalsted brought the gun to the apartment.

The *Journal* reporter also recorded Beulah's description of how she and Al had been robbed while they slept in their hotel room during a vacation in Michigan. "My hubby bought a revolver and kept it under his pillow all the time after that," she said. "And then I had to go and use it in this way."[39]

"We were sitting like this," she said. "He was here and I was there." She used two fingers to show they had sat side by side. "And he was so angry. You know, he had been drinking an awful lot. He was so angry that I couldn't help but get that way a little bit myself. And I swore at him. He said I couldn't get away with that, and I told him I knew he had served five years in the penitentiary in St. Cloud, Minn. for criminal attack on a woman. Was he furious then? We both ran for the gun. I tried for it, of course, when it occurred to me that he would try to kill me."[40]

Although it was undoubtedly from O'Brien that Beulah had gotten the idea that Harry had served time for a rape, the account of the shooting she gave to the reporters on Saturday was *not* the one O'Brien wanted her to tell. In fact, he wanted her to stop talking to the press. Before the afternoon was out, she followed his advice and refused to speak to a reporter from the *Herald and Examiner*—but not before she agreed to talk with Maurine Watkins.[41]

7. MAURINE WATKINS'S NEWS WITH WIT

When Maurine Watkins visited the women's wing of Cook County Jail on the afternoon of April 5, 1924, she had been working for the *Chicago Tribune* for just a month, having been hired with no prior professional experience as a reporter. Since graduating from college in 1919, she had been engaged, off and on, in graduate studies in classics at Radcliffe College, all the while pursuing her true passion—writing plays. That passion had led her to enroll in George Pierce Baker's English 47, a playwriting workshop at nearby Harvard University.[1]

Watkins had been writing and acting in plays since childhood, and at some point she had formed a relationship with actor-playwright Leo Dietrichstein. Dietrichstein had accepted two or three plays from her over the years but had not followed through to seeing them produced. Watkins remained hopeful, however; and in the fall of 1923 she made a brief trip to Pittsburgh to see Dietrichstein. Nothing came of the effort.[2]

The Pittsburgh trip took place during a hiatus in her graduate studies. Watkins had moved to Chicago and was working for the advertising department of Standard Oil. During this time, she began considering a shift to newspaper work. She had acquired some limited experience serving as a reporter and editor for her school newspapers in high school and college; hence, a liking for journalism may have been one of her motivations for exploring a change in employment. It is also possible that she wanted to enlarge the scope of her "real world" experience more directly than by using the method her teacher George Baker encouraged. He used to tell his students to read the newspapers to find "dramatic episodes in real life," which they were to clip and paste into a scrapbook. Going directly into newspaper work itself would give Watkins a more immediate look at "dramatic episodes." She later told interviewers that she had been especially eager to cover murders.[3]

Near the end of February 1924, the city editor of the *Chicago Tribune* granted her a job interview. Within weeks, she was covering the case of accused murderer Belva Gaertner, and in the beginning of April she was assigned to the Annan case.[4]

Three years later, when Watkins looked back on her days as a newspaper reporter, she noted that the *Chicago Tribune* "doesn't use sob stories," a style of sentimental or "tear-jerking" journalism, usually associated with a certain type of female reporter called a "sob sister." *Sob sisters*, the *sympathy squad*, and similar expressions, all of them meant to demean, had begun to appear around the turn of the century when an increasing number of women were entering the field of journalism. The stereotype certainly did not do justice to the range and variety of their reporting, and it was not only female but also male reporters who occasionally turned out melodramatic prose. Moreover, it was newspaper owners and managing editors who insisted on the style and tended to assign women to stories that, in the editors' opinion, invited the sentimentality of a woman's touch. This was especially true at the tabloids. Reporters either conformed or left a paper that demanded too many tear-jerking adjectives from them.[5]

Watkins's accounts of how she happened to become a reporter make no mention of any job interviews besides the one she had with the *Chicago Tribune*. One suspects that she applied to the *Trib* because she had been a regular reader of the paper. During the weeks or months when she was still toying with the idea of becoming a reporter, she would have paid attention to the style and structure of *Tribune* articles, especially those that carried a woman's byline.

To what degree Watkins's editor expected her to write "straight news" is unknown. In the 1920s, the term *straight news* referred to what was by then a well-established trend in journalism toward more "objective," neutral reporting. Although straight news was not in fact free from bias, it did have a distinctive, recognizable style. At the *Chicago Tribune*, straight news was informational and matter of fact, sometimes enhanced by vivid descriptions but rarely containing insinuations of opinion or clever remarks. Straight-news articles were almost always unsigned and represented the routine collaboration of reporters and rewrite staff. By contrast, human-interest stories and topical articles sometimes did include opinion and wit, notably those penned by Genevieve Forbes, a highly regarded *Tribune* reporter who wrote under her own byline.[6]

Forbes wrote compellingly, entertainingly, and sometimes glibly, even mockingly, depending on the subject. Even when giving straight-news coverage of a homicide, she occasionally included notes of humor or insinuated a slant through her characterizations of defendants. And sometimes she was quite direct. Since Forbes regularly wrote under her own byline, she felt free to inject some of her own wit and attitude when reporting on criminal trials.[7]

The use of wry mockery in the coverage of certain kinds of homicides, especially cases of gangster violence, was something of a hallmark of the crime reporting of Chicago presswomen in the late 1920s and 1930s. Its first hints appeared in articles by Maude Martin Evers in 1919, a *Tribune* reporter who covered all kinds of rather inconsequential subjects and occasionally enlivened her stories with wit and doses of light sarcasm. She also brought this reporting style to the handful of murder cases to which she was assigned. Perhaps Forbes was inspired or emboldened by Evers's example to write in a similar style when she was assigned to cover women accused of murder in 1923, and presumably Maurine Watkins was influenced by Forbes and Evers. Remarkably, although Watkins's career as a reporter lasted only six months, she ended up being something of a pioneer in the development of this new trend in women's reporting—the use of "sarcastic humor, a cynical viewpoint and slang-infused prose" to cover certain kinds of violent crime, especially where defendants struck the reporters as self-assured, nonchalant, and cavalier.[8]

Watkins did not follow a formula. The stylistic variety in her homicide coverage suggests that she engaged in a degree of experimentation. She began her first article about Belva Gaertner—who had been charged with murdering her lover Walter Law while the two of them were sitting in his parked car—by characterizing Gaertner as "a handsome divorcée of numerous experiences with divorce publicity." This was a somewhat surprising opening to what purported to be a straight-news story about a homicide. Later, in her background description of Gaertner's marriage to William Gaertner, Watkins called the couple's courtship "a romance of the south park bridle paths," a phrase that evoked the idiom of the society pages. Watkins repeated the expression when she wrote that, just when the Gaertners' divorce proceedings had gotten under way, they were back together "and once more took to the bridle paths of Jackson park." The conclusion of her article mentioned a subsequent divorce action and settlement, which she characterized with a pair of droll formulations. "It developed at the divorce hearing that they both had hired so many detectives that their home was filled and life was just one sleuth after another"; and, when the divorce was final, Belva, having "received $3,000 and a lot of household furniture," used the settlement to "set up an establishment in Forrestville avenue." This establishment was merely her

Undated publicity photo of Maurine Watkins. Vandamm collection, New York Public Library, image ID 485274.

apartment, but Watkins managed to make even that fact mildly entertaining by using a somewhat grandiose word.[9]

Absent from Watkins's account of the Gaertner case were two details reported by the *Chicago Daily News*. The *Daily News* story (which contained no clever descriptions of Gaertner) mentioned that Gaertner's face showed a bruise and that the crystal of her watch had been smashed, stopping the watch at what police had determined was probably the time of the shooting. Whether these injuries resulted from Walter Law trying to fight off Gaertner in a struggle over the gun or her trying to fight him off, they showed that some sort of physical altercation preceded the shooting and that determining just how it unfolded would be necessary before guilt could be assigned. Watkins may have been unaware of these facts. Or she left them out on purpose, whether because they would spoil her otherwise glib portrait of Gaertner or because she had already absorbed the *Tribune* policy of favoring the prosecution's perspective. "We were a real hanging paper," she later remarked to an interviewer, "out for conviction always."[10]

While the Gaertner case was pending, a *Tribune* editor assigned Watkins to the Annan case. It is unlikely that Watkins was on assignment at the Hyde Park police station when Beulah was brought in for questioning. The first *Tribune* article about Beulah was an unsigned account in straight-news style, and it lacked the sort of humorous touches that Watkins had used in her reporting about Gaertner. This unsigned article appeared on Friday, April 4, the day after the shooting, and it reflected in every respect what police and prosecutors were claiming, including their misleading characterizations of Beulah's statements (Beulah herself not being available for an interview).[11]

The next *Tribune* article about Beulah carried Watkins's byline. She had been assigned to cover the inquest, and her article began with a prosaic rehearsal of the chief facts of the case. Then it drew a damning contrast. "Thursday afternoon, Mrs. Annan played 'Hula Lou' on her phonograph while the wooer she had shot during a drunken quarrel lay dying in her bedroom at 817 East 46th street. And yesterday afternoon the chapel organ at Boydston's undertaking parlor played 'Nearer, My God to Thee' for an old soldier's funeral, while she waited for the inquest to start." This was a maudlin touch, but Watkins's aim was not to engender sympathy for Beulah. She meant to draw a sharp contrast between worthy music for a worthy subject and the jazz music preferred by a woman of dubious character.[12]

Watkins's account of the inquest testimony included a somewhat ambiguous and perhaps even misleading rehearsal of O'Brien's questioning of William Wilcox. Lacking a copy of the transcript of the inquest for comparison, one might easily infer from Watkins's abbreviated account—as later re-tellers of Beulah's story have in fact inferred—that it was Beulah's

DEMAND NOOSE FOR 'PRETTIEST' WOMAN SLAYER

Mrs. Annan Held on Murder Charge.

BY MAURINE WATKINS.
(Pictures on back page)
Beulah May Annan, the 23 year old wife who shot "the other man" Thursday afternoon to the tune of her husband's phonograph, was held to the grand jury yesterday afternoon by a coroner's jury, which charged her with the murder of Harry Kolstedt.

Maurine Watkins's first bylined article about Beulah. Chicago Tribune, April 5, 1924, p. 1. Newspapers.com.

attorney, William O'Brien, who first suggested that "both went for the gun" in order to supply Beulah with a self-defense claim. In fact, it was Beulah herself, in her after-midnight statement, who had said that she and Harry both reached for the revolver.[13]

Watkins also implied that Beulah's demeanor during the inquest reflected poorly on her. When her after-midnight statement was read aloud, Beulah seemed nonchalant, Watkins insinuated. "Calmly she played with a piece of paper and whistled softly through it" while the prosecutor read William Wilcox's testimony. "She cupped her chin in a slim white hand, with its orange blossom ring, and didn't blanche" as he quoted her description of the moment when she shot Kalsted. "She played again with the paper" as he read her admissions of intimacy with Kalsted, and she "laughed lightly as the lawyers quarreled over the questioning." The story concluded with Beulah's reaction to the delivery of the verdict by the coroner's jury and a detail about Al borrowing five dollars so that Beulah would have cash for sundries in jail. "When the finding of murder was announced," Beulah "powdered her nose, took the money her husband borrowed, and went back to jail to await developments." The reference to the nose-powdering suggested that despite the charge against her, Beulah remained blasé or even arrogant in her primping.[14]

Watkins's references to Beulah's demeanor resembled the sorts of character-impugning observations that Forbes had made about the female murder defendants she covered the year before. Tillie Klimek giggled and groaned mirthfully in court, Forbes had written. Accused killers Anna McGinnis and her sister Myna Pioch were cool and collected in the face of mounting evidence against them. During jury selection, McGinnis remained poised, "coyly" resting her head on the shoulder of a male codefendant, all the while maintaining a fixed "sneer" behind her widow's veil. Pioch sat "motionless, almost superior, as if she were tolerantly bored." And during another day's trial testimony, when Pioch herself was in the witness chair, "she registered her discomfort by glaring at the jury," Forbes had said, and "twisted up the corners of her memory as much as the lines of her mouth as she tried to 'remember' facts to back up her assertions that the man she killed was a 'drunken fiend' given to beating his wife [Myna's sister Anna] and threatening to kill her."[15]

Since *Tribune* readers knew nothing about the demeanor of Tillie Klimek, Anna McGinnis, Myna Pioch, Belva Gaertner, or Beulah Annan, except what Forbes and Watkins told them, they were in no position to doubt that these accused women revealed their arrogant guiltiness in the ways described. Moreover, the third-person mode of straight-news reporting lent an air of objectivity to what was in fact tendentious.

Photo of Beulah Annan at the inquest (with a misleading caption). *Chicago Tribune*, April 5, 1924, p. 34. Newspapers.com.

STATE ASKS LIFE FOR LIFE. Mrs. Beulah M' Annan calmly told a coroner's jury she killed lover when M tired of her. State will ask death penalty.
(TRIBUNE Photo.)   (Story on page one.)

Beulah's gestures were open to more than one interpretation. Did she play with the paper because she was bored in her lofty indifference or because she was anxious and afraid? Did she laugh arrogantly or nervously? Did she powder her nose because she was shallow and self-absorbed or because nose-powdering was a habit, even a comforting act, like so many self-grooming reflexes of people in anxious circumstances? A reporter for the *Daily Journal* also noted the nose-powdering at the inquest and called it "fastidious."[16]

Watkins's next article about Beulah drew on the reporter's visit to the county jail on April 5th. Watkins arrived in the afternoon, when the inmates were free to move around in the common areas. For a while, some were led in song by Belva Gaertner, who played the piano. A *Tribune* photographer posed Beulah and Belva sitting together at a dining table, Beulah still attired in the fawn-colored suit she had been wearing since her arrest on Thursday evening.[17]

Although a caption, supplied for the photo by a *Tribune* editor, referred to Beulah as an "admitted murderer," Watkins's article lacked any insinuation of guilt. It also differed in tone from her previous piece, giving a seemingly sympathetic and accepting description of Beulah's account of the shooting. After mentioning the singing of the inmates, Watkins described Beulah's frame of mind: "It jars on her horribly—the laughter of the girls, their constant talking, the music. 'How can they!' she said, shivering." Watkins then drew a contrast between Beulah and Belva:

> But unlike Mrs. Gaertner, who waits cheerfully and philosophi-cally, protesting her innocence and disclaiming all recollection of the killing, Mrs. Annan remembers.
>
> "I'll never forget it." She shuddered. "That white silk shirt—all covered with blood. He never spoke or moved, just lay there—I know he died as soon as he fell. And I was with him—dead," her eyes widened with horror, "for two or three hours. I never thought of a doctor until the policeman came, and when they said he might be alive, oh, it was the happiest moment in my life!"
>
> She remembers, too, just how it happened.
>
> "I had learned that morning—just before I came home—that he had been in the penitentiary, and I accused him of it. And he grew angry—but it wouldn't have happened if we hadn't been drinking; and he had had quite a lot before he came over. We both lost our heads, saw the revolver lying there under the pillow, for I hadn't made the bed that morning, and grabbed for it. I can see him now, that look in his eyes! He was perfectly wild, and I know he would have killed me if I hadn't reached it first."[18]

These paraquotations are probably a condensation, containing at least some of Beulah's own phrases. Watkins also paraquoted Beulah's assessments of how she had been represented in the press:

> I listened when they read the statement at the inquest. Some of the things were right, but the newspapers are all wrong. They say I killed him rather than have him leave me. Why, I was the one who was going to quit him. You see, I realized that we wouldn't go on, that we never could really be anything to each other. I never loved him as much as I did my hubby and besides he had nothing to offer me, no inducement to make me leave Albert. It had gone on as long as it should. I knew no good could come of it.[19]

Beulah's insistence that she had never loved Harry as much as she loved Al was probably calculated to fend off the prosecutor's claim that she shot Harry in a passionate rage as a woman scorned.

But Beulah sounded quite frank in her response to a question about what she planned to do if she were acquitted: "I don't know. There's not much use to think about that. Al probably won't want me back—my life's ruined anyway. I can never live it down. Even if I went away where nobody knew, you can't get away from yourself." This was a very different image of Beulah from Watkins's portrait of her as the cool and callous killer who had listened with bored indifference to the inquest testimony about her crime. It was also as sympathetic a picture of Beulah as Watkins would ever offer, the article's only jab being a wry remark about how Beulah and Belva had "not yet talked over their common interests. A man, a woman, liquor, and a gun."[20]

Watkins visited Beulah again the following day and turned in an article with a different tone. Chicago's "prettiest killer" was "lonesome behind bars" and was finding jail "a trifle monotonous." The other inmates had tuned the radio to "a sacred concert instead of Hawaiian fox trots." Beulah missed her cold cream, cosmetics not being allowed. Al was unable to visit her, but admirers were "helping to while away the hours for Beulah." "A group of young men, admittedly after having 'a few drinks,' sent flowers with a note." Having been apprised that meals could be catered in to an inmate, Al had arranged for a dinner to be sent in to Beulah from a local restaurant. But "she didn't eat the chicken dinner he had planned for her; for a 'friend' sent in a juicy steak, French fried potatoes, and a cucumber salad."[21]

After visiting Beulah at the jail, Watkins took a streetcar to Forty-Sixth and Cottage Grove and walked the remaining block to the Annan apartment in hopes of interviewing Al. He was in no mood to talk to another reporter. Standing in the doorway of his flat, he told Watkins he had "nothing to say." She waited. "Tell her I'll stick," he said; "that's all—that I'll stick." He planned to see Beulah's lawyer about a bond. "We've got to get her out."

Unable to get more from Al, Watkins walked ten blocks to the rooming house where Beulah's mother had been living. There she learned that Mary Neel had moved out the night before, leaving no address. Beulah's mother was probably tired of being pestered by the press, but she had found an ally in one reporter—Leola Allard of the *Herald and Examiner*.

8. BACK IN OWENSBORO

Leola Allard had become convinced that Beulah was innocent. She had heard from Harry Kalsted's brother Richard and from Harry's brother-in-law William Wilcox that when it came to women, Harry was a "dangerous man." In the days following the inquest, Allard befriended Mary Neel, and Mary, recognizing that Allard might be of help in efforts to persuade John Sheriff and other relatives to come to Beulah's aid, asked Allard to accompany her on her trip to Kentucky. The reporter agreed.[1]

Meanwhile, the story of the shooting was hitting out-of-town papers with headlines ranging from "Vampire Plays Jazz Over Body After Killing Man" to "Another Death Dealing Blond" and "Phonograph Records Drown Sorrows of Repentant Slayer." In Beulah's hometown of Owensboro, the *Messenger* shouted, "FORMER OWENSBORO WOMAN IS HELD FOR MURDER IN CHICAGO," and mentioned Beulah's local origins.[2]

Perry Stephens did not see this Owensboro headline. Now thirty-one years old and recently remarried to an Owensboro woman named Alice Brown, he had been living in Chicago for the last year or two, working at one of the Chicago papers. He would have learned about the shooting on Friday from the Chicago papers, perhaps even while sitting at his linotype in the composition rooms of a Chicago daily. In later years, when

Divorced Wife of Perry Stephens and Daughter of John Sheriff Slays Her "Great Love."

Chicago, April 4 (*AP*)—Mrs. Beulah Annan, divorced wife of Perry Stephens, of Owensboro, Ky., and daughter of John Sheriff, of Daviess county, Ky., cried and laughed almost in one breath today as she declared she killed her "great love" and added that "I'm glad I did it; the affair was wrecking my life."

The news breaks in Owensboro, Kentucky. Associated Press story, *Owensboro Messenger*, April 5, 1924, p. 1. Newspapers.com.

87

Perry was back living in Owensboro and Beulah's name happened to appear in the papers—"usually in the magazine section"—he "would go to every news stand, buy every paper, and personally destroy them." Just how literally one is to take this family anecdote is uncertain. In any case, Perry was in no position to do any newspaper destroying in Owensboro that Saturday morning in April when the *Messenger* hit the newsstands and doorsteps of his hometown.[3]

P. W. was seven years old and still lived with his grandparents in Owensboro. In that household, it was as if Beulah had never existed. When the news of her arrest was emblazoned in the headlines, no one spoke about it in front of him. If William and Margaret Stephens worried that he would hear gossip about his mother at school or play, that did not happen either. Owensboro parents did not talk about Beulah in front of their children, and any children who got wind of the story were instructed in severe tones not to speak of it. A bubble of silence enveloped the boy—in the neighborhood, at church, and, by some miracle, even among his playmates. It was not until he was twelve that the silence was broken. Not ever having heard of a mother, he later joked to his wife, Ruth, "I thought I had been hatched."[4]

Beulah's father, John Sheriff, saw the news in the Saturday *Messenger,* although he had almost certainly heard it from Beulah's mother on Friday. Besides wanting John to know what had happened, Mary had called to get his help. The lawyers who had taken Beulah's case were still waiting for a commitment to their fee, which may have been as much as several thousand dollars. Mary certainly could not pay it. Nor could Al. Only John Sheriff and certain other men of his extended family were in a position to provide for Beulah's defense. When her efforts by telephone went nowhere, Mary made the trip to Kentucky to see John and other family members, traveling with reporter Leola Allard.[5]

The two women journeyed all night by train and arrived in Owensboro on Tuesday morning, April 8. After checking into the Rudd Hotel, they hired a car and went to see John at his farm in Moseleyville. According to two subsequent descriptions by Allard, John and Martha received them in the front room of their farmhouse. Mary stated her appeal, and John answered, "Beulah has chosen the gay life, and I don't think my wife and I, in our old age, should die in the poorhouse to pay for her folly. I'd do even that if I thought it would change her. I don't. It wouldn't do any good." Allard described how John had looked "straight into the fire that crackled in a rickety gate" and said, "If I could go there and help a good daughter, I'd go. I don't want to see her where she is. She's been in lots of trouble. I've lost faith in her." Martha added, "These city butterflies always pay in the end." Allard noted that Martha wore a "voluminous blue apron," while Mary was "in pleated georgette, a blue hat and a string of city pearls." Mary countered Martha's observation by pointing out that "even in the country they sin, where there are only land and hogs and no temptations."[6]

If these paraquotations reflect the substance of what John, Martha, and Mary said to one another, they reveal that John and Mary were in agreement about Beulah's wrongdoing and that they disagreed only about whether she deserved help. Their agreement implied that the wrongdoing was Beulah's lifestyle and especially her extramarital affair in sordid circumstances. Apparently, neither parent could imagine that Beulah had murdered Kalsted, which is why John spoke of Beulah's "gay life" and her "folly," a 1920s euphemism for infidelity, and why Mary's response referred to sin and temptations.[7]

"John, you always lived on a farm," Mary said, "and you know too little about the world." John did not disagree with her. Instead, still staring at the fire, he countered, "And you, you two"—meaning Mary and Leola Allard—"know too much."

A terrific storm was raging outside, beating loudly against the small Sheriff farmhouse. John's eyes remained fixed on the fire. Then he said, "Mary, I'm through. The night the phone rang as late as 10 o'clock, I knew it must be Chicago and Beulah and trouble. I didn't sleep or eat the first few days, and then my mind settled. It's no use."

"They may hang her," Mary said. She was weeping now.

Beulah Annan's father, John Sheriff. Courtesy of Sharon Watts.

"No they won't," John tried to reassure her. "She's too pretty." John Sheriff struck Allard as a hard, almost heartless man. But it was only the circumstances. Although two of the Chicago papers reported that John was a "wealthy farmer," he was in fact only land-rich, in a certain measure, and his land was his only security for his old age. If he helped Beulah, he would have to mortgage his farm. He was confident a jury would not sentence Beulah to death, and he had to think of Martha.[8]

Allard finished her story by remarking that "as we drove away John stood upon a doorstep like a statue in a park, a straight, fine figure against the gray frame house."

Ten days later, John changed his mind and agreed to help Beulah.[9]

9. POPULAR OPINIONS ABOUT JURY BIAS IN FAVOR OF WOMEN

John Sheriff believed that twelve Chicago jurymen would not vote to hang Beulah, but he worried that her gender and good looks would not prevent them from convicting her. What counted with a jury when they faced a woman accused of murder? Maurine Watkins posed this question to her readers after making a second trip to the women's wing of Cook County Jail. The occasion was a verdict in the trial of another woman. Elizabeth Uncapher had been sentenced to life in prison for murdering her former boarder and love interest, a streetcar conductor named Sam Bischoff. Watkins had covered the trial, and in the final sentence of her article she had used a familiar prosecutorial trope. "Bischoff was killed after he declared he was 'through with' her."[1]

When Watkins paid her visit to the jail on the day after the Uncapher verdict, she found the inmates of "Murderess' Row" engaged in "worried analysis" of their trial prospects. There were eight of them: Elizabeth "Lizzie" Uncapher, Beulah Annan, Belva Gaertner, Sabella Nitti, Katherine Malm, Minnie Nichols, Rose Epps, and Leila Foster. Six were still awaiting trial. Besides Uncapher, Malm had already been tried and was waiting to be transferred to the Joliet penitentiary. Sabella Nitti was awaiting a new trial. The newspapers had run stories about five of these women but had remained silent about the three African American women—Nichols, Epps, and Foster. Just as the white press generally ignored Black life in its society pages and took little notice of the achievements of African Americans, it also showed little interest in telling the stories of African Americans from their own perspective when they were in trouble with the law. The papers over-reported allegations of criminal behavior by Black people, doing so in a disproportionately greater degree compared with their reporting about white people accused of crimes;

but it was rare for any of the papers' reporting to include a personal interview or human-interest story about accused African Americans.[2]

One of these rarities was press coverage of two African American men who were hanged in Cook County Jail two weeks after Beulah arrived there. Although the papers devoted scant space to the arrest and trial of Lucius Dalton and Henry Wilson—the men were not interviewed, nor were their attorneys or their relatives—the two Hearst papers gave melodramatic accounts of their executions and let the men speak in their own words. Perhaps it was assumed that some white readers, even if they were generally uninterested in the feelings and life stories of African Americans arrested on murder charges, would nonetheless empathize with fellow human beings facing death. The accounts in the Hearst papers were dignified and sympathetic; and they included Dalton's declaration to the executions' witnesses that he had not received justice because, had he been white, he would have been given a life sentence. He was almost certainly correct. In Chicago, no white person was ever sentenced to death for killing a Black person, but nearly every Black person convicted of murdering a white person was eventually executed.[3]

Every inmate of Cook County Jail heard the pounding of hammers when the gallows were erected for Dalton and Wilson. The sound must have increased the anxieties of the jail's white women who were facing murder charges, even though, statistically speaking, it was extremely unlikely that any of them would receive death sentences. Yet they all knew that Sabella Nitti's first jury had sentenced her to hang.[4]

Moreover, the prosecutors in Beulah's case had declared their intention to seek the death penalty. In Illinois, it was juries, not judges, who rendered sentences. When prosecutors planned to ask for capital punishment, they typically "qualified" jury prospects during voir dire to weed out any who would hesitate to inflict the death penalty. They had done that in the Nitti case, and they meant to do so in Beulah's. Then Beulah announced that she was pregnant. The press asked whether that would cause the prosecutors to alter their plans. A former state's attorney commented that if Beulah were sentenced to death, execution would simply be postponed until after the birth of her child.[5]

Nothing in Watkins's initial reporting about Beulah's pregnancy hinted that Watkins doubted the claim. Yet Beulah never did give birth. It is possible that stress caused her to miss her period, leading her to mistakenly believe that she was pregnant. Or she might have had a miscarriage at some point after her trial. It is also possible that she made the whole thing up to win sympathy.

Watkins asked her readers to consider whether juries were more lenient to women and whether a woman's youth, beauty, or expectant motherhood influenced them in a woman's favor. (She omitted mention of race as a factor.) Motherhood had not prevented juries from convicting two other inmates, Katherine Malm and Sabella Nitti. Prospective jurors in the Malm case had been asked whether they could impose a death sentence on the mother of a toddler. All said that they could. In the end, they had sentenced Malm to life in prison. The jury at Sabella Nitti's first trial had confronted a woman with two small children. They sentenced her to hang.[6]

Beulah was in little danger of being hanged, not so much because she was pretty but because the infliction of the death penalty on a woman was extremely rare. When Sabella Nitti was sentenced, the papers reported that she was "the first white woman to be sentenced to die" in Chicago. Her sentence was subsequently reversed, and the case was eventually dropped. Moreover, from 1900 through 1924, it is likely that fewer than ten women were executed in the whole of the United States. None of these executions occurred in Illinois.[7]

The more pertinent question in Beulah's case was not whether she was likely to be hanged but whether someone like her was likely to be convicted in the first place. "A jury's not blind," one of the inmates interviewed by Watkins declared, "and a pretty woman's never been convicted in Cook county." "Gallant old Cook county!" Watkins added. That line would end up in her play.[8]

The inmates had no basis for their opinions except their own common sense and what they read in the papers. The papers, for their part, quoted prosecutors making declarations in trial speeches and in post-trial complaints about all-male juries acquitting good-looking women. "It's the same old story," said assistant state's attorney Lloyd Heth after Cora Orthwein was acquitted in 1921. "You can't convict a woman if she is good looking. That's all there is to be said." Two years later, prosecutor Edgar Jonas lamented that "no matter how well a case is presented, the verdict is not guilty if there is a woman in it that can be called even passably good looking." Later that same year Sabella Nitti's lawyer chimed in. He blamed the guilty verdict in her case on her lack of good looks and refinement. The more than thirty women charged with murder who were acquitted in the past several years, he said, were young or pretty "or at least subtle and cleverly feminine."[9]

There were no scientific studies of jury decision-making in the 1920s, but a large body of jury research has been conducted since the 1970s. According to some interpretations of these investigations, perceived attractiveness does indeed play a role in jury leniency, yet the tendency "is moderated by the seriousness of the crime and the strength of the evidence against the defendant." Moreover, one of the leading specialists in the field concludes that the research results suggest no more than "a modest leniency bias in favor of physically attractive defendants that probably depends on other variables and appears to be somewhat stronger for judgments of punishment as opposed to guilt"; moreover, "some of the inconsistency in research findings is likely due to the fact that physical attractiveness is not an objective quality."[10]

In a 1927 *Tribune* article, occasioned by a not-guilty verdict in the case of accused murderer Cora Orthwein, Genevieve Forbes suggested that claims about a long string of pretty female murderers passing unscathed through the judicial system was something of a myth. She did not doubt that all the accused women were guilty, but she thought that few of them were actually pretty. Instead, the press hyped them as more attractive than they really were. Almost every female murder suspect is touted as "beautiful," Forbes wrote. No one will let her remain "just average." "If she has the usual number of teeth and a not bad smile, presto, she emerges from the coroner's inquest a raving beauty." Forbes granted that this transformation is due in part to "reporters' pencils," but she opined that the reporters were influenced by the fact that every woman tends to look lovely by contrast with the drab circumstances of a jail cell, inquest room, or gray courtroom, where the comparison with perspiring men in circumstances dingy and dotted with cuspidors favors her. Nice clothes make a female suspect shine in those same settings. Or, if she happens to own a book, she is immediately dubbed a "literary killer," and if "a mauve colored volume of poetry . . . be found within a city block of the corpse, the literary lady becomes also an aesthete." Even if she is "just terribly plain" and lacks any other feminine virtues but "is not too dumb to talk, the public will herald her as the plaintive, the wistful, the childlike murderess." And "if she's just ugly," she must still be "a creature, inevitably, of superlatives," someone "O, so hard working and home loving."[11]

The public had no direct access to defendants. What the public saw instead was the sometimes-grainy black-and-white newsprint photograph, often of uncertain date. It was the press that told them what to look for in the photo. It was the press that conveyed impressions of a defendant's appearance and quoted observations by prosecutors, who tended to emphasize a woman's good looks when they wished to admonish the potential jury pool not to be taken in *or* when they needed to account for their own lack of success at trial. When assistant state's attorney Lloyd Heth tried Cora Orthwein, he told the jury that she killed her lover when he broke off their relationship because she was getting "old" and "fat" and lacked "pep." But when the jury acquitted her, Heth's boss, the state's attorney, declared, "You cannot convict a pretty woman." Two years later, a story on the topic, "Can a Beauty Be Convicted?," made the same claim and described Orthwein as "dashing, handsome and young." Forbes squared the circle by declaring that while Cora was "not a raving beauty," she was "mighty good looking in an abundant way"—not "fat" but "fleshy." Two years later, when Bernice Zalimas was convicted, a *Tribune* writer expressed surprise because Bernice was young, blonde, and pretty. The writer's explanation: although Zalimas had faced "a jury of young men," she had been "unable to cry convincingly enough to get their sympathy."[12]

Katherine Malm was convicted of murdering a watchman during a holdup with her common-law husband, Otto Malm. Young and slim, she had what Forbes described as a "pretty, well-molded face." A photograph of her seems to confirm this. Malm also had a young child. Moreover, she cried genuine tears at her trial, Forbes wrote, and she spoke with surprising candor, her emotions oscillating back and forth "from the primitive mother to the product of the underworld." It struck Forbes that Malm seemed "unconscious of her badness and unmindful of her goodness." This observation was as complex an analysis as Forbes ever offered in describing a female murder defendant.

Katherine Malm, an inmate of Cook County Jail who was convicted of murder in 1924. *Chicago Tribune* archive photo/TCA.

Usually, her assessments were absolute and unnuanced. But Malm's youth, good looks, motherhood, and genuine tears did not prevent her from being sentenced to a life term in the state penitentiary at Joliet. She was still awaiting transfer when Watkins visited the women's cellblock in May of 1924. Watkins explained Malm's conviction by observing that, although Malm was youthful, she "wasn't—well—quite 'refined.'"[13]

One female murder defendant whom reporters made no effort to describe as pretty, sympathetic, or good-hearted was Sabella Nitti, an immigrant from southern Italy who, before her arrest, had been eking out a meager living as a truck farmer. Nitti was tried for the murder of her husband, Francesco, who had gone missing a year before. Suspicions were thrown on Nitti and a farmhand named Peter Crudelle, the assumption being that Nitti was sexually involved with Crudelle. When a body turned up in a catch basin on Ridgeland Avenue, about a mile from the Nitti farm, neighbors and a resentful son identified it as Francesco and accused Sabella and Peter of murdering him.[14]

Nitti spoke almost no English, and she did not speak much Italian, either. Her native language was Barese, which made it especially difficult for her to communicate with police, prosecutors, the court, and even her own lawyer. The Italian translators brought in to facilitate at the judicial proceedings laughed out loud at her speech, earning themselves a reprimand from the judge. Nitti's original defense attorney, an inexperienced and incompetent fellow named Eugene Moran, was so inept that the judge felt compelled to advise him, at more than one point during trial testimony, that his line of questioning was detrimental to his client. The jury convicted Nitti and sentenced her to hang.[15]

There was an immediate backlash in certain segments of the public. The wife of the jury foreman was incensed by the harsh sentence, as were other women who wrote letters to the papers. But even some of the sympathizers showed their prejudices. "What did this ugly-looking Italian woman do," one Chicagoan asked, "that she should receive extreme and unusual punishment never urged against other women charged with crimes as atrocious as this one?"[16]

Nitti's jail mates also weighed in, complaining in a letter to the *Tribune* about the way the jury, prosecutors, and reporters had treated Nitti. They criticized Genevieve Forbes in particular for referring to Nitti as "dumb" and "crouching" and for calling her a "dirty disheveled woman," since Nitti was in fact neat and clean. Moreover, in her character, they said, she was "motherly" toward all the inmates, not "repulsive" as Forbes claimed.[17]

A new attorney named Helen Cirese took over Nitti's case. Cirese gave her a makeover (modern coiffure, new clothes, makeup), coached her on how to appear "ladylike" according to prevailing middle-class standards, and taught her how to interact with the press. Cirese believed that it would aid Nitti's chances of receiving fair treatment at her second trial if she appeared "familiar," not "foreign," to the men of the jury.[18]

Maurine Watkins offered a cynical take on makeovers for trial. Every female defendant was supplied with the same "weapons of defense," as she described it, "powder, rouge, lipstick, and mascara." These were not allowed in jail, but an exception was made when a woman went to court. "Then the fashion show begins. . . . Shops send dresses on approval, friends bring in frocks of their own, and anxious lawyers borrow from their wives for their clients. They study every effect, turn, and change." Watkins seemed to imply that it was somehow unethical for a female defendant whose best street clothes were shabby to make any effort to appear as presentable in court as better-off defendants. Was the "fashion show" a deceitful ploy, or did it help to overcome jury bias? Lawyers such as Helen Cirese thought the latter. Cirese and her team also revealed the flimsiness of the state's evidence against Sabella Nitti and exposed malfeasance by Cook County deputy sheriff Paul Dasso. The Illinois Supreme Court reviewed the case and granted Nitti a new trial. The prosecutors dithered but eventually decided that a jury was unlikely to convict Nitti, and they dropped all charges.[19]

10. BEULAH ANNAN GOES TO TRIAL

Although Sabella Nitti's "makeover" removed a potential cause of jury bias against her, it was a sharp analysis of the evidence by her attorneys that eventually secured her freedom. Beulah was represented by equally capable attorneys—William W. O'Brien and William Scott Stewart. By spring of 1924, this pair had built themselves a reputation for winning every case they tried. Their practice was still young, however, and none of their cases had made headlines. That changed in early April when Mary Neel asked them to represent Beulah Annan. O'Brien handled the case in its initial phases. It was he who told Beulah that Kalsted had gone to prison on a rape charge. Hence, it was probably O'Brien who coaxed Beulah into lying about her relationship to Kalsted. By the time of the trial, this lie was a given, and the lawyers hoped to persuade the judge to exclude Beulah's after-midnight statement, in which she admitted to her affair with Kalsted.[1]

Although Beulah's lawyers saw her affair as a potential weakness for her defense, they must have concluded that the state's case was vulnerable, especially at two points. First, there were no witnesses to the shooting other than Beulah herself. Second, as O'Brien had discovered at the inquest, the state's best evidence, the after-midnight "confession," was open to more than one interpretation. Given that Stewart and O'Brien ran a risk of spoiling, in a very public way, their perfect record of courtroom successes, should they take a case that they could not be confident of winning, they probably saw the deficiencies of the state's evidence with clearer vision than the prosecutors did. In fact, the state's attorney's office had begun to over-prosecute women accused of murder, pressing forward with cases throughout 1924 where the state lacked convincing evidence. Stewart, who had recently left the state's attorney's office, was cautious. As he would later write in his book on trial strategy, "It is difficult to catch a good lawyer on the wrong side of a case.[2]

Beulah's original trial date was Monday, May 19th, but she felt sick that day. Her lawyers petitioned the court for a postponement, which was granted until Thursday, May 22nd. Beulah's symptoms may have been morning sickness. At least that is what Beulah believed or claimed. She had been on a "milk diet" for the past few weeks, a common method of treating morning sickness in the 1920s.[3]

When the new trial date arrived, Beulah's makeup was returned to her. A hairdresser had already come to the jail to cut and curl her hair. She went to court attired in her fawn-colored suit and georgette hat, an ensemble that was familiar to reporters. Thus far, every photo of her in the papers and every description of her attire—in detention after her arrest, at the inquest, behind bars in Cook County Jail, and at her arraignment on April 21—depicted her in the tan suit. A report about the clothing that Al brought her for her jail stay implies that she possessed only three outfits: this tan-colored suit dress, a checked flannel frock, and a black crepe dress. The continuing reappearance of the suit dress led the press to declare that although Beulah was the

Beulah Annan's attorney William Scott Stewart (*left*) with Beulah and her husband, Albert Annan. DN-0076803, *Chicago Daily News* collection, Chicago History Museum.

"prettiest killer" to grace Cook County Jail, the costume-rich Belva Gaertner was the "most stylish." The hefty fee Beulah's lawyers charged would pay for two additional dresses for Beulah at subsequent days of the trial.[4]

Shortly before 9:00 A.M., guards appeared and escorted Beulah from the hallway outside the women's cellblock to the jail's sixth floor, where they conducted her through an elevated corridor that connected the jail to the courthouse, "the bridge of sighs," reporters liked to call it, borrowing the nickname of a famous bridge in Venice that condemned criminals crossed on their way to prison. Beulah's attorneys were waiting for her in judge William Lindsay's courtroom.

Jury selection commenced. More than a dozen men were excused for having already formed fixed opinions about Beulah's guilt or innocence. Of these, eleven said they were confident that she was guilty; only one thought she was innocent. Several were removed when they admitted a bias against a woman who drank. One was struck after he grunted, "Too damned many women getting away with murder." "I'd have given her the rope, I would," another said. He, too, was excluded.[5]

By the time of Beulah's trial, the idea that Chicago juries almost always acquitted women accused of murder, especially pretty ones, was regarded as a truism. So familiar was this commonplace that when Anna McGinnis and her sister Myna Pioch were brought to trial in June of 1923, McGinnis complained that "[so] many really bad women have beat the rope in this state that men are scared of bein' called mollycoddles unless they're severe with all of us, no matter what we do." Her sister added that "men have been kidded for fallin' for good looks, so now any woman who's under sixty and white can't move without some fellow thinking she's trying to vamp him." This reference to whiteness was a rare instance in which race was singled out as a factor in criminal justice, although Pioch's comment implied the absurdity that being a white woman was somehow a liability.[6]

State's attorney Robert Crowe had to be pleased that the public believed that male juries were soft on "lady murderesses," since that perception served to exonerate his office from blame for failed prosecutions of female defendants. Moreover, prosecutors could also use the idea preemptively. At voir dire in Belva Gaertner's trial, for example, the prosecutor asked one prospective juror whether a "stylish hat" would influence his verdict; the man promised that "sex" would play no part in his judgment. William McLaughlin, who led the state's questioning of prospective jurors at Beulah's trial, made a point of asking each man whether the fact that the defendant was pretty would make any difference in his verdict. Each denied it. In response to the insinuations of this line of jury questioning, defense-attorney Stewart went out of his way to stress that the defense had no intention of resting its case on Beulah's good looks. "We do not want this woman freed because she is pretty," he said. "We want justice done." Maurine Watkins called the jury for Gaertner's trial "hat-proof" and "sex-proof." Reporters called Beulah's jury "beauty proof."[7]

The following morning, Beulah donned one of the new outfits her at-torneys had ordered, a dress of brown satin crepe with a matching fur piece delivered the day before from a downtown shop. She applied a bit of makeup, draped the fur over her arm, and proceeded with the bailiffs to Judge Lind-say's courtroom.[8]

The place was already filled with spectators, as if the trial were an enter-tainment event. The first order of business was an evidentiary hearing. Judge Lindsay dismissed the jury and heard arguments about the admissibility of Beulah's two recorded statements, the one made in the kitchen of her apart-ment on the evening of her arrest and the one given under questioning by Assistant State's Attorney Woods at 12:30 A.M. in the Hyde Park police station.[9]

In the first statement, Beulah claimed that she knew Kalsted only casually and shot him when he tried to rape her, having grabbed a gun from the bed when she retreated to the bedroom and he followed. In the second statement, she admitted to her affair with Kalsted and told how they had drunk wine together, had sex, and then quarreled, which led to their joint rush to the bedroom, where both reached for the gun.

McLaughlin and Woods wanted to place this second statement in evi-dence as the foundation of their case. Stewart and O'Brien wanted it excluded. They intended to argue a version of the first statement, and they did not want the jury to hear Beulah's confession about the affair, the wine-drinking, and the consensual sex. Therefore, they moved to have the after-midnight statement excluded, arguing that it had been improperly obtained through unlawful third-degree tactics and promises of immunity.[10]

When the judge ruled that the after-midnight statement could come in as evidence, the defense did not change course. Beulah, who had probably been influenced by hints from O'Brien when he first visited her at Cook County Jail six weeks earlier, continued to deny that she and Kalsted had been having an affair. She planned to testify that Kalsted made unwanted sexual advances when he showed up at her apartment. It did not occur to her to admit to the affair but claim that his advances were nonetheless unwanted. The reason was probably that "date rape" was not a recognized concept in 1924, legally or culturally. Therefore, taking O'Brien's clue that Kalsted had gone to prison for raping a woman, she probably felt she had to deny the affair and claim that

Kalsted had tried to do the same thing to her. She would explain that when she refused him, he referenced the gun and headed toward the bedroom. She followed and grabbed the gun from the bed just as he was reaching for it. Then, as he came toward her, she shot him. How did he know about the gun? She had an answer for that, and it may have been an honest one. When Kalsted came to her apartment, she would say, one of the first things he did was go into the bedroom. He must have seen the gun, which happened to be lying in plain sight on the unmade bed.[11]

Over the course of the second and third days of the trial, the prosecutors and defense attorneys presented their evidence and arguments. Coroner's physician Dr. Joseph Springer described the path of the bullet through Kalsted's body and testified that "in his opinion death had been instantaneous." William Wilcox testified that Beulah had tried to get Woods to "frame" the shooting to "look like an accident." Wilcox and stenographer Elbert Allen both testified that Woods had made no "promises of immunity" to Beulah to induce her to give her after-midnight statement. Even Woods himself was called to testify about this, which required that he withdraw from the case, since he could not serve as both a prosecutor and a witness (which left McLaughlin to handle the prosecution by himself from that point on). Officer Malachi Murphy told the court about what police found at the apartment, and he said that when he asked Al where he kept his gun, Al said "in the bureau drawer." These witnesses and Beulah's two transcribed statements, which McLaughlin read out loud, formed the basis for the state's case.[12]

The centerpiece of the defense's evidence was Beulah's testimony. Stewart led her through it. In retrospect, it is possible to identify the elements that were fabrications, those that were probably true, and those that elude definite judgment. Stewart began as follows:

> STEWART: Did you shoot this man, Harry Kalstedt [*sic*]?
> BEULAH: Yes.
> STEWART: Why did you shoot him?
> BEULAH: Because he was going to shoot me.[13]

When Woods had questioned Beulah at the station, the one most relevant question he had failed to ask her was why she shot Kalsted. As a result, her answer to that question was not in the transcript of the after-midnight statement, the state's chief exhibit. Now, Beulah had supplied an answer.

Stewart then asked her to describe what led to the shooting. She told the court about Kalsted's visit in the morning to borrow money, but she omitted the fact that the two of them agreed that he would bring her some wine in

Beulah Annan on the witness stand at her trial. *Chicago Tribune* archive photo/TCA.

the afternoon. And when she described how he appeared at her apartment around 2:00 P.M., she claimed that the visit was a surprise. He was drunk, she said, and he pushed his way in, put on a record, coaxed her into drinking wine, tried to dance with her, and then made unwanted sexual advances. She resisted, warning that her husband might come home at any minute, and she threatened to call him. When that did not work, she tried to talk Kalsted out of raping her by telling him she was pregnant. "You'll go back to the penitentiary if you don't leave me alone," she said, and he said, "You'll never send me back there." Then he asked her whether she was "afraid," and she repeated, "I'm going to call my husband. If he comes home and finds you here, he'll shoot you." And that is when Kalsted said, "Where is that goddamn gun." This was all fiction to the extent that it turned Kalsted into a casual acquaintance who tried to rape her.[14]

Then Kalsted jumped up, Beulah recounted, and said, "Where is that damned gun," and they both headed to the bedroom. "We were almost at the bed. He grabbed for the gun and I reached round him and grabbed it. Then he yelled, 'Damn you, I'll kill you!' and he raised his hand to grab the gun. I pushed him on the right shoulder with my left hand. He struggled for the gun and I shot him."[15]

This testimony about Kalsted's words and actions in the bedroom may have been a complete fabrication, but it cannot be tested through comparison to anything in the relevant context in the after-midnight statement, since Woods never asked Beulah what Kalsted did or said just before he reached for the gun or what he did or said immediately after.

When Assistant State's Attorney McLaughlin cross-examined Beulah, he asked her whether she had heard what Sergeant Murphy had testified—that Al had told him the gun was kept in the dresser drawer. Beulah simply denied having heard that. It was an important point for the prosecution, and Beulah's attorneys decided to ignore it, even though they might have been able to raise certain doubts about it. For example, they might have asked Murphy on cross-examination why it was that in the statement that he himself had taken from Al, there was no mention of Al saying that the gun was kept in the dresser drawer.

In fact, the first mention of the gun being kept in a drawer did not appear in the record until ten days after the inquest, in a police report filed at that time by two other officers. Moreover, when the prosecutors had Al on the stand at the inquest, they did not ask him where he kept his gun; and when they had Officer Torpy on the stand at the inquest, they did not ask him whether Al had told him where the gun was kept. Chicago police did not always tell the truth about evidence, and they may have made up the statement by Al about the gun. In any case, Stewart and O'Brien must have thought that a debate at trial about the household routine with the gun was a distraction and also a dead end, since Al himself, as Beulah's spouse, could not be called to testify. As for the prosecutors, they were faced with the problem that in all Beulah's accounts, she had spoken of the gun being on the bed—in her private conversation with Wilcox, in her kitchen statement (where the gun's location was an incidental detail), and in her after-midnight statement, which the prosecutors represented as her honest confession.[16]

McLaughlin's cross-examination also included questions about Kalsted's movements when he arrived at the apartment:

MCLAUGHLIN: When he first came, where did he go?
BEULAH: In the reception hall.
MCLAUGHLIN: Where next?
BEULAH: In the bedroom.
MCLAUGHLIN: Did you go in the bedroom?
BEULAH: No.[17]

The prosecutor did not pursue this subject any further. Perhaps he realized that Beulah's answer had, in effect, given the jury an explanation of how Kalsted could have known about a gun lying on the bed in the bedroom. Her answer also explained why police found Kalsted's hat and coat in the bedroom. And it explained why, when Woods had asked her where Kalsted's hat and coat were, she had said "in the bedroom" but had not been able to specify whether they had been on the chair or on the bed. In other words, if one assumed that Kalsted was Beulah's lover, which was true, Beulah's response to McLaughlin's questions implied that shortly after Kalsted entered the apartment, he had put his hat and coat on the bed in the bedroom, which is where the gun may have been.

When McLaughlin asked Beulah about the rush to the bedroom, her answers essentially agreed with what she had just testified in her answers to Stewart's questions:

MCLAUGHLIN:	Did you go to the bedroom?
BEULAH:	Yes.
MCLAUGHLIN:	Who was first?
BEULAH:	He was one step ahead of me.
MCLAUGHLIN:	Why did you go to the bedroom?
BEULAH:	He was going to shoot me.
MCLAUGHLIN:	How did he know where the gun was?[18]

The jury must have been eager to hear the answer to the last question. But Stewart objected, and the judge sustained the objection. Asking a witness what was in the mind of another person was improper. McLaughlin might have rephrased his question, however, by asking not how Kalsted knew something but whether he had made any reference to the gun after he first went into the bedroom or whether Beulah had told him where the gun was or had shown it to him. But, of course, McLaughlin did not want to travel down any of these paths. His question had been purely rhetorical, a hint to the jury.

McLaughlin next focused on Beulah's and Harry's movements to the bedroom:

MCLAUGHLIN:	Did he get to the door first?
BEULAH:	One side of it.
MCLAUGHLIN:	Was the gun in plain sight on the bed?
BEULAH:	Yes.
MCLAUGHLIN:	How did you beat him to it?
BEULAH:	He lunged for it and I grabbed it.
MCLAUGHLIN:	Where was the gun?

BEULAH:	Two or three feet from the head of the bed.
MCLAUGHLIN:	Did you push him?
BEULAH:	Not when he grabbed for the gun.
MCLAUGHLIN:	How did you get past him?
BEULAH:	The gun was the same distance from both of us.
MCLAUGHLIN:	What did you do?
BEULAH:	I grabbed the gun.
MCLAUGHLIN:	Did he grab your wrist?
BEULAH:	No.
MCLAUGHLIN:	What did he do?
BEULAH:	He put his hand up and said, "I'll kill you yet."
MCLAUGHLIN:	What next?
BEULAH:	He came toward me with both hands up.
MCLAUGHLIN:	Where were you?
BEULAH:	Near the foot of the bed.
MCLAUGHLIN:	Where was he?
BEULAH:	East of me.
MCLAUGHLIN:	What did you do?
BEULAH:	I put my hand on his right shoulder or arm and pushed him.
MCLAUGHLIN:	Have you remembered that since the day of the shooting?
BEULAH:	Yes.
MCLAUGHLIN:	Did you ever tell anyone about it?
BEULAH:	I don't remember.
MCLAUGHLIN:	What happened next?
BEULAH:	I shot him.[19]

The details about Kalsted saying he would kill her, his coming toward her with his hands up, and her pushing on his "right shoulder or arm" were not in the after-midnight statement. McLaughlin insinuated that Beulah had recently made up these details to fit her defense. That is certainly possible. Nevertheless, these specifics did not contradict anything in her after-midnight statement, and some might have been honest recollections.

By the time McLaughlin had finished cross-examining Beulah, the prosecutors may have realized that their case was in trouble. Even if the jurors discounted Beulah's testimony about Kalsted being an intruder who had tried to rape her, if they simply accepted the after-midnight statement as the closest version to the truth—as the prosecutors said it was—they might well reason as follows. Beulah and Harry had been having an affair. A revelation about Harry's past (his stint in a penitentiary) caused a heated argument between them as they sat, both very drunk, on the couch in Beulah's flat. Harry became enraged when Beulah caught him in his lies and called him names. There was a gun on the bed that Harry already knew about, because he had seen it there when he put his hat and coat in the bedroom. He might even have asked Beulah about it. So, when Beulah and Harry, both highly intoxicated and angry, rushed to the bedroom more or less simultaneously and ended up at the bed together, they both reached for the gun. The only question was why.

The lawyers made their closing arguments, and McLaughlin, who had the last word, concluded his appeal by telling the jury, "The verdict is in your hands, and you must decide whether you will permit a woman to commit a crime and let her go because she is good looking; you must decide whether you want to let another pretty woman go out and say, 'I got away with it.'"[20]

It was now long past sundown. The tall windows of the sixth-floor courtroom were black; the collars of electric light encircling the large white pillars blazed brightly as the judge charged the jurymen and sent them off to deliberate. Beulah, who had kept her composure throughout the proceedings, now broke down and began to cry audibly. Mary, seated in the first row of the spectators' seats, also began to cry.[21]

Assistant state's attorney William McLaughlin, who prosecuted the Annan case. *Chicago Tribune*, April 29, 1922, p. 17. Newspapers.com.

Gathered in the privacy of the jury room, the jurors elected as their foreman the distinguished-looking Harry Dunham, president of the Wolff Dunham Melum Company, a tailoring business that occupied the seventh floor of the Brand Building at Dearborn and Jackson. Dunham suggested an initial ballot to see where everyone stood. The outcome was a lopsided division—eight favoring acquittal and four supporting conviction. The men settled into a discussion of the evidence. Perhaps some of the jurors posed questions such as the following. Did Kalsted reach for the gun in anger or simply to prevent Beulah from getting hold of it? Did Beulah reach for the gun because she meant to threaten or shoot Kalsted or because she saw him reaching for it? Were they perhaps both so drunk that they misinterpreted each other's intentions? And did the bullet pass laterally through Kalsted's body because he was turning to escape or because he was reaching toward Beulah? Did she try to keep him away by pushing his right shoulder or arm, causing his body to turn sideways? Or did she make that up for her trial testimony?[22]

An hour later a second ballot showed the jurors closer to agreeing that the prosecution had not proved its case. After further deliberation, they took a third ballot. This time it was unanimous.[23]

Around 10:30 P.M., Judge Lindsay reconvened the court and received the jury's verdict. When the words *not guilty* were read out by the clerk, the court fans cheered. Al and Mary rushed to Beulah, and she embraced them. Members of the jury wandered over, and she patted their hands, saying, "Oh, it was so fine of you—it was wonderful—still it couldn't have been other—Oh, I can't thank you, you don't know, you can't know—but I felt sure that you would." Photographers then took charge and posed the jurors with Beulah and Al.[24]

The jury that tried Beulah may not have been confident that she was innocent, only convinced that the prosecution had not proven its case beyond a reasonable doubt. In courts of the State of Illinois, when judges instructed juries, they often used a traditional formulation to define what reasonable

Beulah Annan between Albert Annan (*left of her*) and her attorney William Stewart (*right of her*) thanking the jury. Jury foreman Harry Dunham is second from the left. *Chicago Tribune* archive photo/TCA.

doubt meant, explaining that it was a doubt "arising from a candid and impartial investigation of all the evidence, and such as, *in the graver transactions of life, would cause a reasonable and prudent man to pause or hesitate.*" In the end, faced with the grave matter of a murder trial, the jurymen who tried Beulah were hesitant to find her guilty on the basis of a so-called confession that was open to more than one interpretation.[25]

Beulah Annan and her mother, Mary Neel, following the verdict. *Chicago Tribune* archive photo/TCA.

11. WATKINS'S TENDENTIOUS REPORTING ON THE ANNAN TRIAL

Whatever Maurine Watkins's original motivations may have been for seeking a job at the *Chicago Tribune*, she gave the impression in a retrospective remark that she had approached newspaper work with a keen sense of moral vocation. She wanted to expose wrongs and improve society. But the *Tribune* did not assign their inexperienced reporter to cover political corruption and social ills. Criminal trials were as close as Watkins came to covering matters of consequence. Her moral targets became criminal defendants, the lawyers who represented them, and the juries who acquitted them. Yet she felt constrained. "In news articles," she explained, "you are not allowed to write editorials—to my everlasting regret." Therefore, as long as she remained a reporter, Watkins had to find some other way of expressing opinions. She chose the path of witty insinuation.[1]

Feeling confident and high-minded in her belief that Beulah Annan was guilty, Watkins wrote three subtly scathing articles about Beulah's trial, beginning with Thursday's jury selection and concluding with Saturday's late-night verdict. In previous articles, she had injected bits of humor and clever turns of phrase into her coverage of Beulah. Now she suffused her trial reportage with a consistently mocking tone that shifted back and forth between eye-rolling comment and laughing sneer. She made clear to her readers that Beulah was a calculating faker. No tear was genuine; no tone or glance was motivated by authentic feeling. When prospective jurymen were interviewed, Watkins said, Beulah "smiled and pouted, sighed and turned r.s.v.p. eyes on the jury." As the trial got under way, "she leaned wearily on one white hand—with Raphaelite profile turned toward the jury—and pensively sighed now and then." Yet "she revived sufficiently to powder her nose and pose for some pictures while she chatted of her recent illness." Later, when the jury was excused so that the judge could hold a hearing about the admissibility of her after-midnight statement, "Beulah, frankly bored by such technicalities, stared around the room like a wide eyed kitten." When the jury returned, however, she "'pepped up' a bit and tried to register contrition and regret at the proper intervals."[2]

Watkins insinuated that Beulah had postured as a helpless female innocent, shedding crocodile tears on the witness stand in a calculated effort to manipulate the jurors' emotions. "She answered the questions in her childlike southern voice and turned innocent, pleading eyes to jury and attorney." When one of her lawyers gave an "impassioned account of the police and assistant state's attorney who questioned her for statements," "the tender hearted slayer . . . broke down in tears." When her other lawyer presented his closing argument, "she was overcome with emotion." And when McLaughlin cross-examined her, she was "childishly petulant" and left the witness chair "with the settled complacency of a school girl who had said her piece."[3]

A number of papers commented on Beulah's reaction to the presence of cameras in the courtroom. At various points during the trial, the photographers took pictures, and each time they did, they had to put magnesium powder in the trough of their flash lamps and set them off with a pop and a brief eruption of bright light and smoke. The *Chicago American* observed how Beulah "seemed to shrink back in her chair as a flashlight went off with a bang," and the *Herald and Examiner* noted occasions when "several photographers set off their flashlight powders in a series of explosions," causing Beulah "to cringe and blanch." Watkins said nothing about these moments but instead depicted Beulah as an actress performing for motion-picture cameras in full command of her role.[4]

It was not the first time that a reporter had compared a trial witness to a stage or movie actor. But that analogy could mean different things, whether dissembling, maintaining a composed demeanor under great pressure, communicating effectively to the jury, or some combination of these. In 1907, more than one newspaper suggested that Evelyn Nesbit's testimony in the murder trial of her husband was a tribute to her "histrionic ability." Evelyn was a model and a stage actress. In 1909, the *Philadelphia Inquirer* said of non-actor Catharine Beisel that "like an actress portraying an emotional role, she sprang from her chair on the witness stand and with gestures, depicted how she wrested the revolver from Captain Ebb and shot him." The paper did not insinuate that this was all a fiction. The implication was different when the *New York Sun* told its readers that a certain Mr. Mellen's "performance on the witness stand" missed the mark because he had failed to devote the "careful attention to small details of verisimilitude which is one of the marks of the truly great artist." Skepticism was also the point when a prosecutor who cross-examined non-actor Madelynne Obenchain during her well-publicized 1922 murder trial asked her whether she had "ever studied for the stage." *Tribune* correspondent Edward Doherty, by contrast, spoke more admiringly about Obenchain's demeanor, observing that "she was sparkling, sure of herself, playing a dramatic role." Nowhere did Doherty imply that her emotional displays were all an act. He may have believed they were genuine, for in describing the conclusion of her testimony, he noted, sympathetically, that she had been on the stand for four hours and that "it had been a terrible ordeal."[5]

In addition to flash cameras at Beulah's trial, there were also motion-picture cameras. Movie cameras were rather new to the American courtroom. One finds few references to them in earlier news coverage of trials. In Chicago, they had been permitted for the proceedings of a bank-fraud case in the mid-teens; the defendants complained. In 1917 the Illinois Supreme Court declared that "it is not in keeping with the dignity a court should maintain, or with the proper and orderly conduct of its business, to permit its sessions to be interrupted and suspended for such a purpose." This wording seemed to allow that movie cameras could operate in a courtroom, so long as the judicial proceedings were not disturbed. Yet they must not have become a fixture of highly publicized Chicago criminal trials until the latter half of the 1920s, for the movie cameras at Beulah's 1924 trial surprised veteran court watchers. A *Daily News* reporter noted that "it was the first time, according to regulars, that movie men ever got into a criminal court here," although "they enjoyed a freedom as ample as if they had always existed."[6]

The presence of motion-picture cameras at Beulah's trial made her testimony seem all the more thespian. The movie men "ground away, their 'spots' on the witness stand," the *Daily News* said; and "in a manner that an actress might have envied," Beulah "lifted her eyes toward the jury box" and murmured that she was "going to have a baby." Watkins was even more direct. A smartly dressed Beulah, she wrote, took the witness chair "under the glare of motion picture lights" and *made her debut as an actress.* The *Daily News* did not suggest that Beulah was lying, but that was Watkins's implication—that Beulah's testimony was all fiction, a bit of contrived theater calculated to deceive a gullible jury. In fact, much of it *was*, in particular Beulah's claims about the nature of her relationship with Kalsted and his attempt to rape her. The difference between Watkins's coverage of the trial and that of papers such as the *Daily News* was that Watkins went on to draw the inference that Beulah was guilty of murder, saying so explicitly, which broke a tacit rule of straight-news reporting.[7]

Watkins made fun of the jury, too, describing how they listened "fascinated" as Beulah's attorney led them "down the path" of his tale about how Kalsted had pressured Beulah into taking sips of wine and had then tried to attack her sexually. When O'Brien described "this frail little girl, gentlemen, struggling with a drunken brute," the jurors "shook their heads in approbation and chewed their gum more energetically," Watkins wrote. In other words, the jurymen were dupes. McLaughlin implored them not "to let another pretty woman go out and say, 'I got away with it'"—but "they did," Watkins declared in the final sentence of her article.[8]

Ten days later, the trial of Belva Gaertner began. Watkins wrote three engaging and at points amusing accounts of the proceedings, which took place from the third through the fifth of June. The state produced the gin bottle that had been found on the floor of the dead man's car, where the shooting had taken place. At the sight of this bottle, Watkins wrote, "Belva's jury, selected for their lack of prejudice in favor of the Volstead act, pepped up a bit at the sight of this, and Belva herself leaned forward. But it was empty." Watkins also made a witty reference to "the 'one more struggle and I'm free' dress" that the prosecution put into evidence as the garment Gaertner had worn on the night of the shooting, and she described how the self-assured, fashionable Gaertner "fastened her 'choker,' gathered up her white kid gloves as court was adjourned, and swept out," which suggested that Gaertner left the courtroom the way a well-heeled society woman might leave a social function. When the jury reached a not-guilty verdict the following day, Watkins commented that "another of those women who messed things up by adding a gun to her fondness for gin and men" had been acquitted. This implied that Gaertner was guilty and should have been convicted. The judge, however, agreed with the jury. He had already told the attorneys, outside the jury's hearing, that he was certain the Illinois Supreme Court would reverse the verdict if Gaertner were found guilty, since "the evidence is only circumstantial: strong enough to arouse suspicion of guilt but not to convict." The defense attorneys shared this opinion. They had even waived opening and closing arguments and had not put a single witness on the stand.[9]

All told, Watkins penned sixteen articles about women tried for murder during the months of March through June of 1924. She had cause for pride in her success as a female reporter who had reached the front pages of a major city newspaper within weeks of being hired. She did not, however, send copies of her articles about Annan and Gaertner to her conservative parents in Crawfordsville, Indiana. She felt too self-conscious. She had reason to believe that her parents would not appreciate the tone of her pieces, the breezy humor that suggested her own "worldliness" or lack of seriousness about a matter as sober as homicide.[10]

In fact, she felt ambivalent. She enjoyed writing about homicide, as she later admitted in an interview. Echoing the remark of one of her dramatic characters in *Chicago*—Jake the reporter, who says he's "been prayin' for a nice, juicy murder"—Watkins declared to an interviewer, "Don't you love a good murder!" She also confessed that although, as a "conscientious person," she "never prayed for a murder," she used to hope that "if there was one, I'd be assigned to it." Yet she also wanted to treat her subjects seriously and with moral purpose. She had "a preacher's mind." This was no casual turn of phrase. Watkins was the daughter of a Protestant minister. She had attended the college of her religious denomination, and she had gone on to Radcliffe with the intention of studying ancient Greek so that she could read the New Testament in its original language. She remained convinced throughout her life that the only cure for the world's moral ills was "a real application of Christianity." In an era of social reform movements, Watkins wanted to advance her own moral vision for society through her writing. When a professor at Yale Divinity School named John Archer called *Chicago* "too vile to put before the public," she responded that he had "missed the point entirely." What she had done was no different from what ministers do when "they preach on life, all its shortcomings." She expressed surprise that "he of all people, a divinity professor, should condemn the action of calling attention to evil." Did he imagine that "the way to combat evil was to ignore it?"[11]

She was also surprised that at the *Tribune*, "a murder assignment doesn't put anyone in a flurry." The casual joking about homicides in newsrooms offended her moral sense and contradicted her notions of policing and news reporting as righteous work. The newspaper-reading public was eager for anything that contained "gore and action," she observed, and court fans want "something hot." Yet, if she was disturbed by the news industry's tendency to treat crime as a subject for entertainment, she was surely also aware that she was a rather willing participant, given the cheerful ways in which she spiced up her articles. She must have believed that the attitude she brought to her stories, especially the mocking tone and bits of sarcasm that she directed against defendants, together with the sympathy that she sought to stimulate for victims, served a purpose greater than mere entertainment; that she was, in her own way, engaging in social critique.[12]

Insinuating an opinion about a homicide case was not the same, though, as reporting on societal ills in the way that investigative reporters of the era did, "muckrakers" such as Ida Tarbell, who were sticklers for fact and wrote devastating exposés of political corruption and the harms that big business and industrialization were inflicting on ordinary workers and citizens. Muckraking was not the passion of reporter Watkins. Instead, her chief wish was to be assigned to murders. She loved murder stories. Hence, there was a certain mismatch between her avowed wish to "write editorials" and her actual interests as a working reporter.[13]

12. A PLAY IS BORN

Had Watkins made a career for herself at the *Tribune*, it is likely that she would eventually have been granted the freedom enjoyed by Genevieve Forbes to write opinion pieces on topics of her own choosing. It is remarkable that even during Watkins's brief tenure at the paper, she was given bylined assignments. Following the Gaertner trial, she wrote both signed and unsigned articles on a variety of subjects, including the "latest methods" used in anesthesia, the murder trial of Leopold and Loeb, the case of a check-bouncing actor, a blind beggar's lawsuit, and an "alienist's" advice about child-rearing. She also wrote a string of movie reviews. Her last bylined article for the *Tribune* was published on August 7, 1924, just six months after she was hired. Soon after, she left the paper. She had had her "fill" of newspaper work and feared she was getting a "murder story complex."[1]

It is possible that an idea for a play based on her news reporting had begun to germinate in her mind three months earlier, in May, when she had sat with inmates of the women's cellblock at Cook County Jail—at the white tables strewn with newspaper coverage of the Uncapher trial—and had listened to their opinions about "what counts with juries." If, by August of 1924, she was already thinking about writing a play inspired by the women of "Murderess' Row," advancing that plan by re-enrolling in Baker's class was not an option for the fall because Baker had taken a sabbatical. Watkins settled in New York and found a job as an editor for the *American Yearbook*.[2]

By late November 1924, Baker had accepted a position as head of the newly established Yale School of Drama. A year after that, Watkins enrolled in a master's program in fine arts at Yale and resumed her studies with Baker, commuting from New York City to New Haven. It was during this semester that she wrote a play called *A Brave Little Woman*, which she eventually renamed *Chicago*.[3]

When Baker was asked what he knew about the origins of Watkins's play, he said that "when she worked with me at Radcliffe, she hadn't the remotest notion of that play. After she had been working for a time with me here [at Yale], she told me of this play, which had its inception in her work as a reporter on the Chicago *Tribune*. . . . The play was written and polished here." Watkins told one interviewer that the play's characters were composites, including Roxie Hart, who was based on "six or seven women I have encountered who committed homicides." But she told another reporter that Roxie "was drawn from one of our leading lady murderesses," meaning Beulah Annan. When the play opened in Chicago, after its New York run, Belva Gaertner told

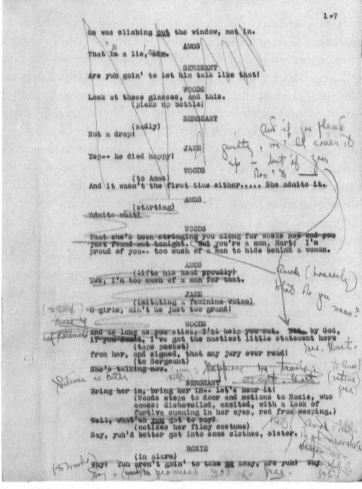

Page 1-7 from a typescript of the 1926 play *Chicago*, with Maurine Watkins's own handwritten revisions. Beinecke Rare Book Room and Manuscript Library, Yale University.

reporters that she herself was Velma and that Roxie was Beulah. And when Genevieve Forbes imagined who deserved a block of theater seats as special guests for the play, she suggested that "Beulah Annan ought to have the aisle-seat. For it was she—too beautiful to work in a laundry but a sufficiently good shot to get her man with one bullet in the back—who is the Roxie of the piece." "Of course," Forbes added, "Beulah went free: else, there might have been no play."[4]

The *case* of Roxie was clearly drawn from that of Beulah, even if Roxie's *personality* was a composite or a pure invention. Velma and the other inmates were also based on women accused of murder whom Watkins had covered or knew of as a reporter. Velma Kelly was inspired by Belva Gaertner. Liz, whose lawyers in the play try to defend her by proving her insane, had parallels with Elizabeth Uncapher. Lucia, "the Eyetalian woman," was partly modeled on Sabella Nitti. Kitty Baxter, the "Tiger Cat," resembled Katherine "Kitty" Malm. Moonshine Maggie was based on "Moonshine Mary" Wazniak and also had features of Sabella Nitti.[5]

Watkins fashioned the play's reporters as types. Mary Sunshine is a sob sister. Jake is her opposite, a cynical but cheerful male reporter, who is always accompanied by a photographer named "Babe." Roxie's lawyer, Billy Flynn, is a version of William O'Brien. Flynn warns Roxie about a newswoman from the *Ledger* (who never actually appears on stage), and Roxie complains about her. This *Ledger* woman represents Watkins herself, and she is quoted in words that recall Watkins's own first signed article about Beulah.[6]

Watkins modeled the physical settings of the play's action on the Annan apartment, the women's wing of Cook County Jail, and the Cook County courthouse. Many details in the play came straight from her reporting, from small ones such as a "white enameled table" in the common room of the women's jail to primary elements of the plot, such as a shooting that takes place to the music of a jazz record and a lawyer who proclaims to a jury that "they both reached for the gun."

The plot is not conventional. The play opens in a bedroom where Roxie ends her affair with Fred Casely by uttering a few coarse words and shooting him in the back. This scene was contrived to last no more than thirty seconds: at first a few moments of silence while Roxie watches Casely put on his coat, then ten angry words, a quick reach into a bureau drawer for a revolver, a gunshot, Casely's body dropping to the floor, voices of children outside. Then the curtain falls.[7]

This was an extraordinary way to begin a drama, almost completely unprecedented. It announced to the audience that the play was a kind of crime drama but not a murder mystery. The opening scene not only shows the murder but makes plain who does the shooting and why. The woman with the gun kills the man pulling on his coat because he is a "tightwad" and "louse" who has just declared that he is "through" with her. To the extent that the ensuing dramatic action follows a plotline, it is nothing like the usual crime-drama formula. There is no crime-solving, and the story does not conclude with the usual satisfaction of justice. And as for structure, one of the first reviewers noted that "the play was written more after the fashion of a good news story than in the accepted style of the theatre," inasmuch as "the action begins with what should have been the climax [the shooting]."[8]

There was something of a plot-type parallel in the "inverted" detective stories of R. Austin Freeman, who designed plots where the first part of the story narrates the crime, from the murderer's point of view, and the second half follows the detection work of one Dr. Thorndyke, who eventually solves the mystery. It is doubtful, however, that Maurine Watkins's plot construction for *Chicago* was in any way inspired by Freeman's stories, which she had probably never read. *Chicago* is not about a clever detective who figures out what an audience has already been shown. It is a satire in which not only the audience but also all the characters are in the know from beginning to end, apart from a bumbling jury that fails to mete out justice. In structure, the plot reflects Watkins's own experience of the Annan case. The first *Tribune* story about the shooting had reported the basic details and a confession. After that, as Watkins saw it, almost everyone knew or should have known that Beulah was guilty, that her subsequent change of story was a sham, and that the jury failed to see through her phony act on the witness stand or did not want to.[9]

The play tracks Roxie's progress from arrest to jail to court and depicts various people helping her or seeking to thwart her. Along the way, Roxie is inducted into the ways of the criminal-justice system, both its public face and its behind-the-scenes machinations. The audience, too, is given an inside look at the ways of newspaper reporters, police and prosecutors, murder defendants, jail matrons, defense attorneys, and all-male juries charged with trying female murder defendants. Of these players, the only group that is shown exclusively in its public aspect, not in its behind-the-scenes operations, is the jury.

The opening revelation of the facts of the crime is for the audience's sake, but it also has an internal counterpart in the investigation shown immediately afterward. An inept attempt by Roxie's husband to take the blame collapses, and Roxie herself confesses to the murder in the hearing of a police officer, a prosecutor, and a reporter. "Yes, it was me!" she says. "I shot him and I'm damned glad I did! I'd do it again." It is essential to the play's satirical message that not only the audience but also everyone involved in preparing Roxie for her trial—her attorney, the reporter Jake, and even the jail matron—knows that Roxie is guilty. More precisely, the audience has to be shown that each of these characters knows that Roxie is guilty.[10]

The action of the two central acts takes place in the women's wing of Cook County Jail, where inmates, the jail matron, defense lawyers, and even certain insider reporters engage in frank talk outside the hearing of police and prosecutors. The play makes clear that each of the inmate characters is guilty. Roxie admits to murder. So does Kitty. Jake and the matron declare that Maggie is guilty. Liz, who killed her husband, Jim, gives a speech, as "God's Messenger," in which she says that she herself, Roxie, and Velma are all murderesses. When Velma protests that "you're not [a murderer] unless you're *convicted*," Liz corrects her. "Oh yes, you are! It don't take no trial. I was a murderess the moment Jim fell."[11]

In the jail scenes, the matron, Velma, and defense-attorney Flynn tutor Roxie in the way to freedom. The matron is a sympathetic confidante who does not betray secrets. When Roxie admits to killing Casely because she was mad at him, the matron makes an observation that seems to be a maxim of the women's jail: "I never hear of a man's bein' killed but I know he got *just* what was comin' to him. . . . But you mustn't *say* it." This is lesson number one: admit nothing. Velma then explains that what matters in court is not the *reason* but the *grounds*, "just like divorce." It has to be "accordin' to law, dearie," the matron adds, "like he threatened or attacked you or somethin'." That's lesson number two: make up a story that fits one of the defenses provided by law. And when Roxie asks whether "bein' drunk" is "grounds," the matron tells her not to worry. Her lawyer "will take care of all that." When Billy Flynn arrives, he coaches Roxie on how to behave in front of reporters so that she can win sympathy from the public. He also provides her with a sympathetic life story—his "secretary is typing it up this afternoon"—and tells her exactly what to say when she is asked about the shooting. This is lesson number three: defense attorneys provide clients with fabricated stories that will serve as their defense. "Whenever they ask 'why,'" Flynn tells Roxie, "all you remember is a fearful quarrel, he threatened to kill you. You can see him coming toward you with that awful look in his eyes—that *wild* look! And get this, now—you both grabbed for the gun. See? Self-defense. Whatever else we weave in afterwards, *that's* there from the start."[12]

Jake the reporter provides a wider view. This is evident not only from a close analysis of his role in the play but also from comments made by Maurine Watkins. Three weeks after *Chicago* opened, Watkins interviewed the actor Charles Bickford, who played the part of Jake, and asked him whether he was enjoying the role. Bickford answered, drily, "What there is of it." To her readers, Watkins commented, "Can you beat it? After we've spent hours explaining that it's Jake who gives the slant to the play, that it's really through his eyes that the audience sees 'Chicago.'"[13]

Jake's slant is set forth right away. During the initial police investigations in the prologue, Jake has the run of the crime scene and at one point reminds Sergeant Murdock, "You're one of our men, ain't yuh?" That is, Murdock is one of the police officers paid by Jake's paper, the *Gazette*, to feed scoops to its reporters. Murdock had better "play ball," Jake reminds him, meaning that he should let the reporter and the *Gazette* photographer get whatever information and photos they need.[14]

Having established the press's rights to the crime scene, Jake turns to Roxie, from whom he hopes to obtain a "sweet story," the "nice, juicy murder" he's been praying for. As it dawns on Roxie that she is in big trouble, it is Jake who reassures her: "gallant old Cook County never hung a woman yet," he tells her, and he is almost certain that she will be acquitted. "It's 47 to 1 you'll go free," he declares, even "a hundred to one—that's straight goods." He then explains that Cook County Jail will provide the beauty treatment for the "big show" (the trial) in which Roxie will star (testify) as "leading lady." And if that fails, she can always count on a pardon from the governor. As a bonus, Jake will make her famous. She will get more publicity than a movie queen. When the *Gazette*'s photographer arrives and wants to photograph Roxie with Amos, her husband, in sympathetic poses, Jake overcomes Amos's resistance by explaining that he, too, has "gotta play ball," if he wants Roxie to get friendly press coverage.[15]

The two main lessons that Jake teaches Roxie—that the press is going to make a show of her case and that the trial itself will be a show that leads to her acquittal—raises the question of how these two things are connected. According to some 1927 reviews of the play, one of its main themes was that good press influences juries, encouraging them to render not-guilty verdicts. "It seems that Miss Watkins," wrote one New York theater critic, "plying her occupation as a police reporter, discovered that ladies who kill gentlemen in the capitol of the Middle West are never hanged for that rudeness; and that the press, neglectful of its star-eyed purpose, aids them in their escape." A reviewer writing for the *Chicago Tribune* offered a similar analysis. "Told that publicity will save her from hanging, Roxie goes to it, and is saved." In fact, the play gives mixed signals on this subject. Jake explains to Roxie that he himself would rather see her hanged, since that would make bigger headlines;

yet she need not worry, because the jury will be kind to her. And when Roxie complains about what the papers are saying about her, the jail matron tells her not to worry about it. "It's only the papers, and the jury's all you care about." Neither statement implies any influence of press coverage on the jury, and the matron's remark seems to exclude it. Yet Roxie's lawyer advises her that *bad* press coverage might lead to a guilty verdict. Perhaps Watkins was not careful to ensure that the matron's opinion about the influence of pretrial publicity agreed with that of Roxie's lawyer, since the playwright's main purpose in portraying the press was, in her own words, to expose "the thirsty desire of all involved to 'play ball' with the papers for the sake of publicity."[16]

A desire for publicity is one thing that prosecutor Harrison and defendant Roxie share in common, albeit for different reasons. Harrison hopes that good press will smooth his way to a more lucrative job as a defense attorney. Roxie wants publicity for its own sake: "Why, it's just like I was president or some-thin'." Yet the media spotlight is fickle and quickly shifts away from Roxie, and the play ends with Jake informing an acquitted but unhappy Roxie that she is yesterday's news, now that a new sensation—"Machine-Gun Rosie"—has captured the press's interest.[17]

An equally prominent theme is the idea that the murdering women of Chicago routinely elude justice. The main purpose of the play is to assert this "fact" and to explain it. Jake tells Roxie that as a matter of "cold hard statistics . . . it's 47 to 1 you'll go free." This is a reassuring ratio, and since Jake is not given to say "50 to 1," the unrounded "47 to 1" suggests an actual statistic derived from the records of Chicago's criminal-justice system. In fact, an earlier manuscript version of the play shows that Watkins had originally made Jake say "100 to 1." The final change to "47 to 1" was clearly intended to give an impression of realism.[18]

Curiously, however, three of the inmates in the play's jail scenes do not win jury acquittals: Lucia, Liz, and Maggie. The matron claims that Liz and Maggie were convicted because they did not "doll up" for the jury, but the audience is left mostly to guess why these three did not fare as well in court as Jake's ratio should have guaranteed. In any case, these characters were inspired by three convicted woman whom Watkins encountered in Cook County Jail, and their function in the play is chiefly to create atmosphere and to reveal unappealing sides of the more important characters. We learn that vain Velma Kelly has made Lucia her servant. Moonshine Maggie, whom Jake calls a "hunyak" (as does Watkins's list of characters), speaks broken English with a thick accent, has trouble grasping what she is told, weeps for the baby from whom incarceration has separated her, and is told by the matron, who is kind and reassuring to Roxie and Velma, that "nobody cares about you and your baby." A protracted interchange in which the matron and Jake join forces to make fun of Maggie does not seem at all funny today and was criticized by one of the play's original reviewers. Moreover, while neither Jake nor the matron faults Roxie for her emotional outbursts, the matron tells Maggie to "shut up."[19]

Hunyak is not the only ethnically derogatory term in the playscript. When Roxie's husband is slow to give her money so that she can have restaurant dinners sent in, Roxie retorts, "All right then, I'll eat with the wops and the n——s." The humor of this remark depends on the audience agreeing with Roxie's white racist sentiment and finding it funny that someone as unworthy as she should assume such air of superiority among her fellow inmates in jail.[20]

Roxie's remark about undesirable dinner companions is one of two references in the dialogue to Roxie's whiteness. The other appears in Jake's statement to Roxie that, for the sake of a bigger headline, he would be happy to "put a hemp rope around your nice white neck." Yet nowhere does the play directly acknowledge that whiteness is an advantage to Roxie. Moreover, Jake is emphatic that what counts *most* with juries is "just being a woman." Gender is enough, effective so long as the defense attorney is competent. Even Maggie would have been acquitted, Jake says, if she had had a decent attorney. And Liz might have done better at her trial if she had "dolled up," the matron observes. This is consistent with the play's message that female defendants win acquittals by putting on a show for the jury. Any woman can do it.[21]

There was nothing new in the idea that a defendant's words and demeanor on the witness stand might be dramatic, like the work of an actor. But Watkins was perhaps the first to suggest not only that defendants sometimes play-act fictions scripted by their defense attorneys but also that members of the press operate like stage managers of the drama in which those scripts are performed. Twice, just before Roxie goes into the courtroom to take the witness stand at her trial, Watkins has reporter Jake speak to her as if she were an actress waiting in the wings: "That ain't your cue. . . . I'll call you when the stage is set"; and then, "Come on, Cinderella, the stage is set." Thus, a cliché applicable to any preparation is refurbished and repurposed. Roxie is next shown in the courtroom as an actress dressed for her part and ready to play her scripted role. And the whole proceeding takes place like a movie shoot, with motion-picture cameras grinding away under Klieg lights.[22]

In contrast to the play's damning portrayal of murder defendants and their attorneys, *Chicago* implies that prosecutors are reliable defenders of truth and justice. Although the play pokes fun at a certain police officer for his gull-ibility, it casts no aspersions on his honesty. Nor does it impugn the integrity of the assistant state's attorney. It pictures prosecutor Harrison as an honest but demoralized man engaged in an often-futile pursuit of justice. Harrison is worn out from toiling "like a dog for 'justice and society'" and hopes that by convicting a woman of murder, he will make a name for himself so that he can become a defense attorney, because "that's where the money is." He intends to fulfill this ambition by finally getting a guilty woman convicted by proceeding in his usual way, by the book, not by trumping up charges against an innocent defendant. It is defense-attorney Flynn who concocts a phony story about the state's use of threats, even physical violence, to extract a false confession from Roxie. The audience knows the truth about all of this, for the play's prologue depicts Harrison's very above-board questioning of Roxie, which leads to her confession; and act I shows Flynn supplying Roxie with a phony story. It is a premise of the play that Harrison serves justice, while Flynn undermines it.[23]

The version of the play that Watkins completed and submitted to George Baker in the fall semester of 1925 carried the title *A Brave Little Woman* (echo-ing an expression that Flynn applies to Roxie at one point in the play). Shortly thereafter, sometime between January 1 and February 26, 1926, Watkins changed the title to *Chicago* because, as she later explained to the *New York World*, the play described Chicago's particular ways of subverting justice.[24]

The copyright registration, playbill, and ads for *Chicago* called it a "satir-ical comedy." In the early 1920s, satire was well established in literature and had begun to appear increasingly in English and American drama. *Webster's*

Catalog card for the copyright registration of Maurine Watkins's play *Chicago*. U.S. Copyright Office.

New International Dictionary of 1909, fresh off the press when Watkins entered high school, defined *satire* as "a literary composition, originally in verse and still generally so, holding up public or private abuses, errors, vice, or folly to reprobation or ridicule; as, the *Satires* of Juvenal." The words "and still generally so" may have overstated the degree to which poetry was still the primary form of satire. In any case, there was a widespread consensus in the nineteenth and early-twentieth centuries that satire addresses contemporary reality and aims to tell the truth about that reality in order to elicit a disapproving response.[25]

The use of satire in *realistic* styles of narrative had entered English literature as early as the novels of William Makepeace Thackeray and Charles Dickens. The trend continued, and dramatists eventually followed suit, first in the English theater with George Bernard Shaw and Oscar Wilde. Their plays crossed the pond to become hits in the United States. Plays described as "satirical comedies" had been advertised and summarized in American newspapers since the 1890s, when dramas of this sort had first become popular. Most satirical comedies of the period poked fun at social conventions. Few addressed weighty social and political topics. Of the latter subjects, "the modern woman" and suffragism seem to have been favorites. Maurine Watkins's *Chicago* was notable, perhaps even pioneering, as an American satirical comedy about the interaction between two powerful *institutions*, the press and the courts. To that extent it was more ambitious than Arnold Bennett's 1922 play, *What the Public Wants*, which made fun of the sensationalist press but did not treat its relation to any social institution and focused more on the vapid pretentiousness of the main character than on the power of the news business.[26]

Dramatic satire tended to work in the realist tradition that was typical of modern novels. One might think that satirical realism was a contradiction in terms, since satire's typical techniques included exaggeration and distortion, while realism aimed at the opposite—verisimilitude. But the blend of satire and realism was not so mysterious. Setting, dress, manners of speech, and the like were portrayed realistically in this type of satire; and the dialogue and action contained enough realism to make clear which contemporary social reality was the target.

Watkins established a realistic feel in the opening scene of her play. Her instructions called for a bedroom with working-class cheapness, which she spelled out in detail. This authentic-looking setting, Roxie's two shouts in the vernacular, the man pulling on his coat to leave, the pistol shot that sends him to the floor, the sound of children playing outside as a clock begins to chime—all combined to suggest the beginning of a melodrama in a starkly realistic mode. And although the play soon turned humorous, it retained realistic elements in both staging and manner of speech.

Theater critics found reporter Jake to be one of its most realistic characters, and his assertion about jury acquittals ("47 to 1") may have sounded plausible to 1920s audiences or at least not too exaggerated. The strategic lessons taught to Roxie by the matron, her attorney, and Jake were also meant to be taken as fact. Phrased in colloquial language, they were supposed to sound realistic and plausible, and they provided the explanation for Jake's claim about the mercy of Chicago juries toward women charged with murder. The play's satire lay in humorous depictions that purported to be revelations of how things really operated in Chicago's criminal-justice system. As Watkins herself put it, she wrote the play "all straight, without any idea of exaggeration."[27]

Undated publicity photo of Maurine Watkins. Beinecke Rare Book Room and Manuscript Library, Yale University.

Chicago debuted on Broadway at the Music Box Theatre in early winter of 1926 and enjoyed an impressive run before going on to other cities. The reactions from theater critics were generally positive and suggested that both critics and audiences generally understood the play to carry a social message critiquing the city of Chicago. Yet there was disagreement about the style of that critique and its degree of realism. A critic at the *Baltimore Sun* summarized mixed audience reactions. A "burlesque painted too broad" was the verdict of some, but other Baltimoreans liked what they saw. One declared that *Chicago* was "the cleverest play he had seen since Beggar on Horseback," a highly acclaimed realistic-expressionist satire of American business and platitudes about personal happiness.[28]

Ad for *Chicago. New York Daily News,* January 2, 1927, p. 14F. Newspapers.com.

John Daly of the *Washington Post* noted "highly realistic character sketches" in an over-the-top burlesque of the way things actually proceed in the American criminal-justice system. Daly was among the reviewers who saw the production with some or all of its original cast, led by Francine Larrimore in the role of Roxie Hart; and he thought its satirical edge was blunted by mistaken choices on the part of the actors. It seems that Larrimore was especially comic in her role as Roxie and that other cast members followed suit. They "have thrown caution to the four winds," Daly wrote, playing "with such abandon" that one might think they operated with no sense of limits at all. Offering similar comments, Brooks Atkinson of the *New York Times* blamed the cast for transforming "a firm, compact satire, deadly in import" into nothing more than a bit of "diverting entertainment." Instead of "hard, earnest, and brittle" performances, the actors, with their knowing smirks and tongue-in-cheek deliveries, gave the impression that it was all a joke. And in Boston, a reviewer for the *Daily Globe* concluded that Chicago, "though penned as a satire," was played as "nothing more than burlesque."[29]

When *Chicago* was staged in Los Angeles with a different actress in the role of Roxie, the playwright and Hollywood screenwriter Rupert Hughes declared that Maurine Watkins "has contributed to the American theater the most profound and powerful satire it has ever known. . . . [S]he makes the audience howl with laughter, but with spine-chilling laughter that is the sanest thing in this wide world." It was sane and salutary because its aim was "to put an end to the ghastly business of railroading pretty women safely through murder trials by making fools of solemn jurymen." *Los Angeles Times* theater critic Marquis Busby agreed, calling the play a "caustically biting satire" that will make audiences "roar with laughter" at its namesake but also get "the uncomfortable feeling that the same conditions might hold true in New York, Los Angeles, Cleveland, and Oshkosh." Neither commentator used the word *burlesque* or *farce*, perhaps because the acting was more restrained.[30]

Like Busby's, one of the first New York reviews also emphasized that the message of *Chicago* was pertinent to other cities. New Yorkers might laugh at the play as a "parody of Chicago," wrote Frank Vreeland, "but just the same it is nationally applicable to the current tendency to turn a trial into a rousing free show rather than a sober quest for justice." Vreeland had Hearst's brand of yellow journalism especially in mind and understood from the play's message that the problem lay not only in what the yellow press printed about trials but also in the way the press and cameras at trials influenced the proceedings themselves.[31]

Light on the question of the play's nature and purpose is shed by a letter that Watkins's teacher, George Baker, wrote to the New York Theatre Guild and its director, Maurice Wertheim. Baker may have hoped to dissuade the guild from misunderstanding the play, given how it was being performed on the New York stage with over-the-top performances that made it seem like a burlesque or farce and not a realistic satire:

> It is a comedy, intensely satirical, treating the sentimentalization of the criminal in this country by the public, newspapers, lawyers, and even the courts. . . . Whatever happens to the play, I know it was written with honest intent and with knowledge of facts existing for Chicago, though not perhaps for other cities to the same extent.[32]

Baker also wrote to Watkins herself:

> You wrote a play with commendable purpose. It was well character- ized and actable. Don't let any willingness on the part of anybody to turn it into a play to force as many laughs as possible change you from your original purpose. You wrote something that might have an effect on the conditions you ridicule. It may well be turned into something which will have no such effect.[33]

Baker regarded the play as satire and thought that the inherent comedy of a serious satire should not be turned into farce by a producer or director whose vision differed from that of the author.

Watkins herself explained her intentions in public clarifications. She told one paper that the play depicted "conditions as I actually found [them] during my newspaper work" and that although it "may sound like burlesque or travesty in New York, it would pass for realism in its home town." She told another that she was surprised at the many claims that she had written a satire. It was Sam Harris, the producer, who had put the catchphrase "satirical comedy" in the playbill, she explained. "But I didn't think I was satirizing anybody or anything. I thought it was real, all through." It was "all straight, without any idea of exaggeration," "an honest attempt to say something I believe terrifically."[34]

Despite Watkins's claim that she had not composed a satire, the title page of a typescript for the play under its original name, A Brave Little Woman, carried the subtitle "a satirical comedy in a prologue and three acts." To this same title page, Watkins had applied her own pen to cross out the ironic title "A Brave Little Woman" and write "Chicago," but she left undisturbed the subtitle, "a satirical comedy". She also included this subtitle when she submitted the play for copyright, according to the registration, dated February 26, 1926.

No author has ever hesitated to mix elements of different genres. Moreover, genre categories themselves are understood differently by different critics. Both the genre mixing and the differing conceptions of genres are well illustrated by another acclaimed play of the 1920s—The Front Page by Ben Hecht and Charles MacArthur. Producer Jed Harris billed The Front Page as a "farce," and some critics followed suit, but not all. A review in the Asbury Park Evening Press avoided that term and instead dubbed the play "an interesting story of the 'hard-boiled' newspaper life," which exaggerated its subject only modestly to heighten the drama. New York Times critic Brooks Atkinson called the play a hilarious comedy with no more than the bit of exaggeration typical of many realistic dramas. Burns Mantle drew a parallel with Watkins's play, suggesting that The Front Page blended "the satirical quality of 'Chicago' with the bold frankness of 'What Price Glory,'" the latter being a realistic war play. A Chicago reviewer also found a layer of satire in the play, and many reviewers emphasized the drama's realism. The Chicago Tribune's Fanny Butcher called the play a "veritable and veracious drama" of life as lived by the authors when they were reporters. Butcher's colleague Frederick Donaghey objected to the playbill's label, "farce," but allowed that The Front Page included farcical elements of the physical-comedy variety. Meanwhile, leading drama critic George Nathan opined that Hecht and MacArthur had attempted to write "a straight newspaper story" but had ended up creating a farce. Commentators in later decades applied a similar range of terms to the play, and in 1972 the director of the first London production offered the following solution to the riddle: act I is realistic drama; act II, comedy; and act III, farce.[35]

Owing to some combination of dramatic content and actors' choices, Watkins's *Chicago*, like Hecht and MacArthur's *The Front Page*, struck some 1920s reviewers as farce, others as realistic drama, and still others as satire or a combination of all three. The various terms may have been understood differently by different reviewers, and it is possible that Watkins herself became uncertain about just what the word *satire* was supposed to mean as applied to her play. Having initially called *Chicago* a "satirical comedy," she was given pause after certain theater critics found farce and buffoonery in it. When she protested that she had written the play "straight" without "satirizing," she may have used the word *satirize* to mean "exaggerate and distort," thinking that this is how certain critics were using the word. Apparently, she wanted to clarify that the play's method of mocking its character types was not to exaggerate their shameful traits but to make them speak shamelessly, with shocking honesty. In that case, the humor and the social critique arose from the play's purported realism and truth-telling, its realistic mimicry.

The damning revelations in the play, however, were clearly Watkins's inventions, her way of having the characters say out loud what she believed to be the truth about them. There were no examples of shocking honesty, much less any confessions of murder, in the real-life inmates' conversations in Cook County Jail as Watkins had reported on them for the *Tribune*. Beulah never admitted to reporter Watkins that she had murdered Harry Kalsted, yet Roxie confesses the murder to prosecutor Harrison in the presence of reporter Jake and again to the matron in the presence of Velma. Reporter Watkins never heard William O'Brien counsel Beulah to claim that Harry "reached for the gun," but playwright Watkins has lawyer Flynn tell Roxie, "Get this, now—you both grabbed for the gun. See? Self-defense." In other words, Watkins modeled Roxie's case on her own theory of Beulah's case, and that is what Watkins meant when she insisted that it was "straight, without any idea of exaggeration," with the further implication that cases like Roxie's were typical. Such cases explained why the odds of a woman being acquitted of murder in Chicago were "47 to 1."

According to Rupert Hughes, the play was "a tremendous denunciation of the sacrilege by which the juryman, who should be the wisest and sanest of our guardians, is easily turned into a blithering come-on" because men pay "false homage to women" and engage in "silly efforts to protect her while

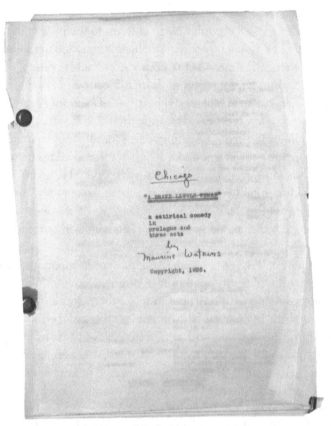

Amended title page for *Chicago*. Beinecke Rare Book Room and Manuscript Library, Yale University.

she dupes them." Hughes told readers that Watkins, who "reported murder trials and saw them from the inside, was inspired to turn them inside out and show the public the whole works." Burns Mantle, the *Chicago Tribune*'s New York correspondent, used similar language. Watkins had told "a front-page murder story *from the inside out*" that "exposed the loose ways of the courts in dealing with lady murderesses and stressed the danger in which the country stands from susceptible juries." Another *Chicago Tribune* writer objected to characterizations of the play as a farce: "it looked like realism to us." The same paper's "Armchair Playgoer" reported that *Chicago* would keep on "tell[ing] the world the truth about 'lady murderesses'" for two more weeks at the Harris Theater in its namesake city. And *Tribune* theater critic Frederick Donaghey declared that *Chicago* was "a stage-piece whereby and wherein aphrodisiacal murderesses, stunt-crazy newspapers, and cash-down jury-pleaders are made to seem nearly, if not quite, as funny as they are in the mess generally referred to as 'real life.'" Watkins, wrote another critic, described the methods by which "shrewd Cook County lawyers," interested only in money, "turn heartless but beautiful feminine murderers into heroines" who escape justice with the help of tears, sob sisters, and sob-sensitive juries. Other pundits also opined that the play contained a factual message. *Chicago*, wrote New York correspondent Alexander Woollcott, was a look "behind the scenes" of the criminal-justice process, a drama with details so exact they must reflect "an inside job." A widely published feature magazine story declared that the play was a retelling of "Beulah Annan's story almost exactly as it happened"; another paper asserted that the play's main character was "almost identical" to Beulah; a review published by United Press called it a news-like satire that gave "the straight stuff;" a review in the *Owensboro Messenger* reported that "according to Chicago newspaper men who have seen the show, it is actually a photograph."[36]

The eleven commentators just quoted—five of them from Chicago—agreed that *Chicago* showed the truth about its subject and disagreed only about whether *satire* was an apt term for it. Donaghey's comment helps explain this. Sometimes satire, whether called that or not, simply mimics its subjects because no hyperbole is needed to make an audience laugh at them. Likewise Hughes, who called *Chicago* a burlesque, believed that the elements of burlesque in the play derived from *reality*, from the *actual* farce that the press and defense lawyers made of the courts. The hokum was no invention by Watkins. She had simply told the truth.

Mantle was one of the few critics who offered an opinion about how *Chicago* compared to other plays that dealt with the same or similar subject matter. In his first review of *Chicago*, he noted that the playwright William Hurlbut had treated some of the same themes as Watkins in his play *Chivalry*, which Mantle had reviewed in December of 1925. *Chivalry*, Mantle had written, "relates the story of one of those murder trials in which the young and attractive heroine is carefully coached and for which she carefully stages her courtroom appearances and is acquitted by a sentimental jury despite the evidence." The play "offers nothing unusual in the way of either theme or content." In December of 1927, he said the same thing about *Chicago*. "Basically it offers nothing new." "The coddled and dramatized criminal and the tricked jury have been fair game for the satirists these many months. The omnipresent camera men, the human hounds for publicity, the enterprise of the tidy little tabloids have all frequently been the subject of comic exaggeration in the revues."[37]

Mantle gave no examples of other satires of recent memory that dealt with these subjects. Another serious drama besides *Chivalry*, though, had treated the matter of jury verdicts from the perspective of gender differences. In *The Woman on the Jury* by Bernard K. Burns, a young woman, stirred by anger at her man for ending their relationship, shoots a gun at him but misses. Some years later, she finds herself on a jury where she and eleven men must decide a similar case, except that in this instance the bullet had hit its mark. The eleven men want to send the defendant to the electric chair, but the female juror, who shares her personal story with them, persuades them to acquit the woman. Worth noting is the assumption of this play that male jurors tend to be overly *tough* on women who kill lovers who ill-use them and that more jury deliberations ought to include the empathetic voices of women. This was opposite to the view that male jurors tended to be too soft on women defendants.

The Woman on the Jury was a serious play and not at all satirical. According to Mantle, *Chivalry*, likewise, was "a serious and studied drama." Audiences found it depressing. Comparing it to *Chicago*, Mantle suggested that *Chicago* succeeded where *Chivalry* failed because *Chicago* was "equally revealing" but "much lighter on its feet." The play's "value and its hope," Mantle opined, "centers in its author's skillful and amusing exposure of shameful practices that have become common." Watkins "blasts her way through many walls and the exploding laughter that follows the blast should prove cleansing." "No one has before taken the case of a beautiful first-page murderess and carried it and her through from crime to acquittal, mercilessly exposing the progressive stages of their carefully staged journey, as cleverly as Miss Watkins had done."[38]

Newspapers let the public know that *Chicago* was based on Watkins's own crime reporting. When *Chicago* was in its second month in New York, a press report out of Chicago revealed the connection between the play and the Annan case. Moreover, Watkins herself made clear in interviews that the play reflected "what I had seen in covering murders and murder trials" and that Roxie Hart was based on "one of our leading murderesses" in Chicago. Meanwhile a newspaper magazine story about Beulah Annan, which appeared in papers across the country, told readers that Watkins had turned Beulah's case into a play and that "if you saw it you must realize that she told Beulah Annan's story almost exactly as it happened."[39]

The theater critics who believed that *Chicago* offered a realistic, factual picture of its subject matter had no firsthand knowledge of what went on behind the scenes in the women's wing of Cook County Jail, what female murder defendants had confided to their fellow inmates or attorneys, what sorts of coaching defense attorneys had given to the defendants, or what factors had influenced the jurymen who tried them, much less which of the acquitted women were in fact guilty. But they had their suspicions, and *Chicago* seemed to confirm them.

Respecting the role of the press in the criminal-justice process, the reviewers *did* have some degree of inside knowledge. Perhaps the typical theater critic did not know firsthand what went on at a crime scene or in a police station when the criminal authorities gathered information about a homicide with one or more crime reporters close at hand, but all reporters were familiar with the way the sensationalist papers hyped crime stories. Moreover, one of the reviewers seems to have had at least some crime-beat experience. Percy Hammond had been a reporter and theater critic for the *Chicago Tribune* from 1909 to 1921, where he carried "a pad and pencil with which to record the violences of life on the Lake Shore." In his two reviews for the *New York Herald Tribune*, Hammond described the play as mostly *un*realistic, calling it a mere "cartoon," a "flighty panorama in burlesque, depicting Chicago as a merry pleasure ground for murderesses." Yet Hammond granted the verity of the play's message as social satire. "If the corrective art of the Drama has any influence at all upon Chicago, more nooses hereafter will encircle the white throats of the female assassins."[40]

If the play was a farce with no other purpose than to make its audiences laugh, then it did not matter one whit whether anything in it was realistic or socially revealing, so long as it was funny. If the play was a satire, however, it did matter, because it was widely agreed that satire purports to criticize social ills. Watkins's own statements and those of her teacher make clear that her purpose was indeed satirical in this sense, and most of the critics and others who commented on the play also understood that *Chicago* carried a social message. Even Hammond, who concluded that the play's subjects and its action were so unhinged from reality that the play was better described as burlesque or farce, agreed that the play's claim about Chicago juries letting women get away with murder was accurate and, as "corrective art," socially salutary. There was no contradiction in Hammond's views, given the long tradition of farces and fantastical stories that carried serious social messages, Apuleius's *Metamorphoses* and Jonathan Swift's *Gulliver's Travels* being two famous examples. This type of serious-minded farce would be produced in later generations as well, an especially striking example being the 1964 movie *Dr. Strangelove*, with its scene where Major T. J. "King" Kong bronco-rides a nuclear missile.

13. THE TRUTH ABOUT CHICAGO'S CRIMINAL-JUSTICE SYSTEM

Chicago, Watkins declared, was "an honest attempt to say something I believe terrifically." The play said something that others believed, too, as it "blast[ed] through many walls" to show audiences what many already suspected. But a close look at facts that were publicly available might have raised important questions, had an investigative reporter thought to assemble them. At the very least, a close look at an important 1922 report on race relations in Chicago might have put the question of criminal justice in a more revealing light for Chicagoans who bothered to read it. This exceptionally fine report was ignored by Chicago politicians, however, and seems not to have made any impression on the Chicago press. Instead, the press reported what police and prosecutors told them.[1]

For more than two decades, the people of Chicago had been periodically informed that juries were practically incapable of convicting women charged with murder. In 1912, the *Tribune* referred to a "long list of acquittals and mistrials of women for murder" and gave the names of seven women set free by juries "during the last few years." That same year, Walter Burns of Chicago's *Inter Ocean* declared that "it is next to impossible to convict a woman of murder" in Chicago, the proof being that "thirty-nine women charged with murder have been set free in the last nine years." "Sentiment and chivalry" were said to be the causes. Burns did not report the number of convictions for that same period or the rate of conviction. Nor did he compare the women's rate of conviction to the men's. Readers might have inferred that scarcely any women were convicted of murder during these years.[2]

It was usually the outcome of a particular trial that prompted comments on the topic. When Marie Carbonara was acquitted of murdering her husband, the *Tribune* described Chicago as "a place where it is impossible to convict a woman of slaying her husband." When Tillie Klimek received a life sentence for killing her husband, Genevieve Forbes rehearsed the prosecutor's statement that only four women had been convicted of murder "in recent years" and that the Klimek verdict showed that the time had come for "the chain of immunity for women" to "be broken." Clearly, there was a contradiction between these statements, unless the number of cases was very high, making the four acquittals a mere drop in the bucket. But the number of cases was not high, although the press seems not to have noticed that. After the acquittals of Annan and Gaertner, a reporter in Chicago wrote that "out here males are sacrificed right and left to the whims of the 'deadlier sex.'"[3]

The history of Chicago homicides prior to the 1920s is the subject of a penetrating 2006 study that helps put the 1920s discussion in perspective. The author finds that within the small subset of women's acts of homicide in the period from 1875 through 1920, about a third involved women killing their husbands. Some of these women acted in the context of a physical altercation; others planned their killings. Anecdotal evidence suggests that a sizable number in both categories justified their acts as self-defense against an abusive spouse and thus challenged the traditional right of husbands to beat or otherwise "discipline" their wives. Other women claimed that they had acted with forethought to avenge mistreatment by a man who had misused them. Both types of justification were classified as a new "unwritten law," similar to the right claimed by many men to kill in defense of family honor when a wife or daughter had been raped or somehow mistreated. It is unknown how many of the women's self-defense claims met the legal standard for justifiable homicide and how many were essentially appeals to the new unwritten law. One can presume, however, that both types of defenses were argued to juries in the *relatively small* number of these cases that were prosecuted through to trial.[4]

By the early 1920s, any avid newspaper reader who had consumed the Chicago dailies for the past twenty years was familiar with alarmist pronouncements by prosecutors and pundits about a dramatic increase in husband killers and the scandal of jury failure to convict them, a trend said to pose a danger to men and to law and order generally. Prosecutors attacked the new doctrine of a woman's right of self-defense against a husband who physically abused her. In 1906 an assistant state's attorney named J. R. Newcomer told a group of jurors that if they "set the precedent that any woman who is attacked or beaten by her husband can shoot him, there won't be many husbands left in Chicago six months from now." In 1912 a prosecutor implied that a wife had no right to use a gun on her husband just because he was in the habit of coming home drunk and beating her. "What if [her husband] did get drunk once in a while?" the prosecutor asked the jury. "A glass of beer is the only consolation some men have." In 1914, judge Marcus Kavanaugh declared that "a mock sense of chivalry" lets "a good-looking woman kill any man she wants," which implied that jury acquittals bestowed a public license. Later that same year, the *Chicago Tribune* seemed to vindicate the judge's implication by noting that when Belle Benson killed her husband after he "started to beat me up again," she had in her possession a newspaper article about a string of fourteen women who had been acquitted of killing their husbands.[5]

Newspaper reports about women killing men with impunity became conversation topics in the many places where Chicagoans gathered to socialize. Hence, one can assume that the reporter's comment in 1924 that "out here males are sacrificed right and left to the whims of the 'deadlier sex'" was regarded by many as a truism. Yet in that same year, during the handful of months when Watkins was reporting on murder trials where Chicago prosecutors supposedly pleaded in vain with juries not to acquit guilty women, state's attorney Robert Crowe gave *Chicago Tribune* reporter Oscar Hewitt some numbers. Hewitt composed an article commending Crowe for his prosecutorial successes, telling *Tribune* readers that the number of "unpunished 'lady killers'" had stood at forty-two but that in just over three years in office, Crowe had won guilty verdicts for thirteen women charged with murder. Hewitt listed them by name.[6]

Hewitt gave out only raw numbers, not the percentage of women who were acquitted or a comparison of that rate to the acquittal rate for men. This was typical. One cited an absolute number as though it spoke for itself. In fact, what stands out from an analysis of cases brought to trial during the years 1920 through 1923 (three of which were part of Crowe's term) is that the murder conviction rate for women in these four years was comparable to the rate for men. Then, in 1924, it took a dive.

The specifics are as follows. In 1920, the year before Crowe took office, the state's attorney's office tried only two women for murder; both were convicted. In 1921, when Crowe was in charge, the office tried four women for murder; two were acquitted and two were convicted. In 1922 his office tried ten women for murder; five were acquitted, five were convicted. In 1923, his prosecutors tried twelve women for murder; seven were acquitted, five were convicted. Taking these four years together, we find that fourteen women were convicted and fourteen acquitted, a 50 percent conviction rate that was not much less than the men's 54 percent rate. But in 1924, Crowe's office doubled the previous year's number of cases brought to trial, prosecuting twenty-four women for murder. The result was that the number of convictions increased by only two over the prior year, while acquittals more than doubled, increasing from seven to seventeen. Since the number of homicides committed by women in 1924 was essentially the same as the number in 1923, and was scarcely larger than the number in 1922, it appears that Crowe became overzealous or overconfident in 1924. A reasonable inference is that by doubling the number of cases he brought to trial that year, he ended up prosecuting too many cases where the evidence was insufficient to convict.[7]

An alternative possibility is that juries became softer on female defendants in 1924. This is a less likely explanation, since there is no conceivable reason for it. On the contrary, negative media coverage about supposed jury favor toward female defendants gave jurymen a reason to prove that they could not be duped by good looks or swayed by a false sense of chivalry. Moreover, each man interviewed for jury service in a case involving a woman was screened for any such tendencies. Hence, it is unlikely that jury bias in favor of women suddenly spiked in 1924.

The topic of women getting away with murder was communicated to the public in terms that were rhetorically and politically calculated, not sociologically informational. It was in the interest of prosecutors to generalize in raw numbers, without comparison or context. It was likewise in the self-interest of state's attorney Robert Crowe to encourage his assistant state's attorneys to insinuate to juries and to the public that too many murderous women were going free, while he himself told the press that he was the first state's attorney to succeed in stemming the shameful tide of acquittals.

Undoubtably, some number of women probably *were* getting away with murder but not to any alarming degree or in a measure that posed a serious social problem. To recall the percentages already given, in the four-year period from 1920 through 1923, the murder conviction rate for women was 50 percent. The men's was 54 percent. Then, in 1924, the women's acquittal rate dropped to 29 percent for the year, when Crowe doubled the number of cases he brought to trial. As a result, the conviction rate for the five-year period from 1920 through 1924 ended up being 40 percent. (The incarceration rate was slightly higher, since two of the women found not guilty in 1924 were committed to insane asylums. That was not thanks to the prosecution, since these two could have been committed without trials.) In raw numbers, fifty-two women were tried for murder in these years, nearly half of them in Crowe's year of misjudgment, 1924. Although some of the acquitted may have been guilty, surely not all of them were.[8]

There was, then, some rather gross hyperbole in *Chicago*, despite Watkins's claim that her play was "all straight, without any idea of exaggeration." In fact, she put a whopper of an exaggeration in the mouth of the character who served as the audience's primary guide to the play's point of view, reporter Jake. It is Jake who makes the crucial plot-explaining declaration that the odds of a woman tried for murder going free were "47 to 1," or 98 percent. Watkins may have believed that this assertion was only modestly hyperbolic and that it contributed a valid point to the play's social messaging. In reality, it was way off and gave a misleading impression. In the five-year period from 1920 through 1924, the ratio of acquittals to convictions was 31:21, and the ratio of those "set free" to those denied their freedom was 29:23.[9]

A report by the National Commission on Law Observance and Enforcement puts these statistics in perspective. The task force, chaired by George Wickersham and often called the Wickersham Commission, was established in 1929 by president Herbert Hoover in response to the pervasive and violent lawlessness that had developed in U.S. cities under Prohibition. A final straw in the public mind was the St. Valentine's Day Massacre in Chicago, where a group of Al Capone's gunmen, disguised as police officers, raided a garage on North Clark Street and executed members of rival George "Bugs" Moran's gang.[10]

The commission's 1931 reports looked back over the prior decade with special attention paid to certain major cities, including Chicago. One of these publications, the *Report on Prosecution*, sought to dispel public misperceptions about the role of jury trials in the criminal-justice system. The report described how the publicity given to certain jury trials influenced public perceptions. Since "the hardest fought and the most difficult cases result in acquittals to a greater degree than other cases," the public, which mistakenly imagines that juries are the chief arbiters of justice, ends up with the false impression that "acquittals by juries constitute the predominant mode or method whereby men accused of crime escape conviction and that the jury trial is the weak spot in the administration [of justice]." In fact, the report explained, jury trials decided the fates of very few criminal defendants. In Chicago in 1926, for example, juries dealt with only 3.8 percent of criminal cases (the figure for New York was 4.7 percent). In other words, "the jury trial plays a relatively minor direct part in the disposition of offenders or in the results of criminal cases."[11]

A report by the Illinois Crime Survey drew a similar conclusion. It, too, found that only 3.8 percent of felony charges filed in 1926 were handled by juries. "It is, therefore, plain," the report commented, "that the results of jury trials, while of psychological importance in determining public opinion upon the whole process of judicial administration," are *"relatively unimportant* so far as the number of cases disposed of is concerned." The report also reflected the authors' awareness that the public was mostly concerned about miscarriages of justice through acquittals. "Assuming that each acquittal by jury is a failure of justice, which of course is not the fact," the report pointed out, "this would still account for only two per cent of all felony charges." The anecdotal fallacy, reinforced by newspaper amplification through stories relating to violent crime and criminal trials, must have contributed to distorted impressions of the societal significance of jury acquittals.[12]

None of the reports of the Wickersham Commission discussed the subject of *women* tried for murder, no doubt because these cases were only a small part of homicides that went to trial and an even smaller fraction of felonies that did. The reports of the Illinois Crime Survey were also silent on the subject, except for an incidental observation by report writer Arthur Lashley. "So much is made of killings of husbands by their wives, in the columns of the daily press," Lashley wrote, "that the fact [shown in a table] that there were more than four times more wives killed by husbands in 1927 as there were husbands killed by wives is rather interesting." "The record is very little different for the previous year," Lashley added.[13]

In summary, since holding jury trials was only a small part of the way capital cases were dealt with and since the percentage of women's murder cases was only a small subset of those murder trials, the failure of juries to convict some handful of guilty female killers each year was a minuscule social problem in 1920s Chicago, not a statistically significant part of the city's criminal-justice problems or even of its murder problem. Hence, Watkins's supposedly straight play not only grossly exaggerated; it misdirected.

The play also made no mention of what were probably the most significant factors in jury acquittals: the high standard of proof in a criminal case and the requirement of a unanimous verdict. These two pillars of American law reflected the principle that it is better for a guilty person to go free than for an innocent person to be convicted and punished. Those who subscribe to this philosophy believe that under-prosecution is better than over-prosecution and that bias is worse when it harms the innocent than when it benefits the guilty. Watkins's play operated on an opposite set of assumptions. The premise of its satirical message was that bias that benefited the guilty was the more serious problem. At the same time, the play implied that bias against the innocent was not a problem in Chicago since police and prosecutors do not charge innocent people.

The play further implied that Black women enjoyed the same privilege as white women as beneficiaries of jury leniency. The facts were otherwise. In the five-year span from 1920 through 1924, Cook County juries, almost all of them in Chicago, convicted 35 percent of white women tried for murder and 48 percent of Black female murder defendants. In that same period, they convicted 48 percent of white men tried for murder and 67 percent of Black men. Hence, whiteness was as at least as influential a factor in diminishing a defendant's chances of conviction as gender was.[14]

There was further widespread bias toward Black people in the process by which homicide cases were handled from the point of arrest forward, and this bias touched many more persons than jury bias did. Coroners, coroners' juries, grand juries, prosecutors, and judges played their respective roles at each juncture in defendants' paths through the system. From 1920 through 1924, the police logs show arrests of 1,118 persons for criminal homicides (not including arrests connected with automobile accidents, abortions, and shootings by police officers in the line of duty). Most of these people were exonerated by coroners, discharged by judges, or released when the state dropped charges or let the case languish unprosecuted. About 35 percent of white men processed through the system were eventually brought to trial, and half of those tried (47 percent) were convicted, which means that only 17 percent of white men arrested for murder were eventually convicted. In the case of Black men, about 54 percent of those arrested on suspicion of murder were brought to trial, and 66 percent of those tried were convicted. Hence, 36 percent of Black men arrested on murder charges were eventually convicted, a little more than twice the percentage of white men.[15]

In 1922, the governor's Commission on Race Relations published a report of its three-year study following the 1919 "race riots." Among other things, the commission called for greater police protection of Black citizens and observed that "Negroes are more commonly arrested, subjected to police identification, and convicted than white offenders; that on similar evidence, they are generally held and convicted on more serious charges, and that they are given longer sentences."[16]

Another part of the story of the criminal-justice system in early-twentieth-century Chicago was the pervasiveness of police and prosecutorial misconduct in securing confessions. One routine practice was to beat suspects above the kidneys with a rubber hose called a "goldfish." This technique left no marks but inflicted excruciating pain. The Chicago police had a "goldfish room," and when extraordinary discretion was desired, they took suspects out of town for goldfishing and other forms of torture. Police called these methods "sweating."[17]

By 1917, reformers' efforts had succeeded in persuading the Illinois legislature to pass a bill outlawing the use of third-degree methods, but the governor sided with the Chicago police department and vetoed it. Similar legislative efforts also failed. One Illinois senator remarked about an antisweating bill that "there is too much sentiment for those accused of crime." The courts finally acted where legislation had failed, but they, too, were met with resistance from the police. When an appellate court ruled against the legality of third-degree practices, a representative from the Chicago police department was quoted as saying that "95% of the work of the department will be nullified" if the decision was upheld. The Illinois Supreme Court did uphold the appellate court's ban, but the practices continued, sustained by an institutional culture that viewed violence in the handling of criminal suspects as necessary and justifiable. When faculty at Northwestern University established a crime laboratory in the late 1920s and proposed to the police that they make use of the lie detector, a "leading official" of the Chicago police department declined, holding out his extended fist as "the best lie detector."[18]

Alarmist claims that juries were letting women get away with murder sounded high-minded, and Maurine Watkins's *Chicago* effectively amplified the opinion that doing something about this travesty ought to be a high priority, whether that meant reforming the jury system or somehow changing the attitudes of the male segment of the public that made up the jury pool. The play's righteous message was in fact tendentious and reflected the perspective of Chicago prosecutors, most of whom, it seems, were happy to rail against the failure of juries to convict some handful of female murderers, while ignoring the problem of racial bias and the police department's routine use of violence to coerce confessions.

There was, in fact, talk of making changes to the jury system. Two unrelated concerns, which were sometimes conflated in obfuscating ways, precipitated these discussions. One had to do with the alleged failure of juries to do their part in deterring crime. The other was an administrative problem. Regarding the first, those who wanted higher conviction rates for women charged with murder argued that if women were permitted to serve on juries, there would be fewer acquittals of guilty female killers. Others in the law-and-order category, concerned about the crime problem more generally, criticized the "better" citizens for begging off jury service.[19]

The administrative concern was taken up by judges, who found that it sometimes took an inordinate amount of time to seat a jury. One of the most striking examples was jury selection in a 1925 trial of two men accused of holding up the Drake Hotel and killing a hotel staff member in the process. It took a court nine days to interview 333 men and assemble a jury. According to Cook County judges, too many men called to jury service gave phony jury-disqualifying statements to get themselves excluded—claiming to have a fixed opinion about the case or to be opposed to the death penalty or biased against drinkers in a case involving the use of alcohol, for example—when the real reason, which would not have disqualified them, was that they did not want to miss work. Hence, judges considered how to make jury service less onerous for working-class men. A proposal had already been made by a Cook County judge to base the schedules of jury summonses on the seasonality of certain types of labor, the work of "carpenters, bricklayers, painters, and farmers," for example, who might more easily serve on a jury during the winter.[20]

The law-and-order jury blamers, which included newspaper editors and various pundits, along with a few judges, seized on the problem of protracted jury selection as somehow evidence of poor jury quality. So-called jury slackers were alleged to be "one of the causes of the shocking miscarriages of justice" in the criminal courts. A certain Judge Hopkins criticized the "cleanly-shaven" men "wearing clean linen" who demand justice in the courts but shirk jury duty when summoned. Kickham Scanlan, another judge, complained that businessmen in particular were evading jury service. An editorial claimed that since the better class of citizens was eager to avoid jury service, it was easy for defense attorneys with guilty clients to get the juries they wanted. The Chicago Crime Commission—a project organized by Chicago businessmen, bankers, and attorneys who wanted to improve the city's business climate and reputation through increased policing and punishment of offenders—claimed that people of "lower average intelligence and capability" were ending up on juries and that too many men who were "property owners, experienced in business, intelligent and apparently qualified" were not being called to jury service or else were managing to evade service. A Chicago attorney, quoted by the Chicago Crime Commission's Committee on Juries, declared that the present system let the "better" prospective jurors avoid service, with the result that juries were composed of "riff-raff and persons unfit in every way for jury service." This was all cant with probably more than a hint of class bias. Jury selection in the Drake Hotel case ended up seating a group of ordinary Chicagoans, even if they did not include any of the so-called superior men of property and business experience: a chauffeur, a motorman, a truckman, a waiter, a civil engineer, a department-store salesman, a clerk, a yardmaster, an automobile mechanic, a garage man, and two firemen.[21]

There were no systematic post-trial interviews of jurors in the 1920s or scientific studies of jurors in mock trials. We do know, however, that judges almost always advised juries that the standard of proof in a criminal proceeding was "beyond a reasonable doubt." This reflected the long-standing principle, already mentioned, that it was morally better that a guilty person go free than that an innocent person suffer. This dictum of Anglo-American law was famously formulated by the influential English jurist William Blackstone in what came to be called Blackstone's ratio: "The law holds that it is better that ten guilty persons escape than that one innocent should suffer." The American legal tradition honored this principle not only with its reasonable-doubt standard but also with the requirement, in most jurisdictions (including Illinois), that a jury verdict be unanimous in criminal trials. Whatever the average Chicagoan thought in the abstract about crime and punishment, when he sat on a jury, he invariably felt the weight of having to decide a concrete individual's fate, involving loss of freedom or even life. Hence, although many Chicagoans may have worried about crime and believed that there ought to be more guilty verdicts in criminal trials, the men of Chicago tended to be cautious when they themselves sat on juries and had to consider facts that were ambiguous, as was often the case, being acutely aware that it fell to them alone to decide the outcome for the accused. As newspaper readers they cared about justice and public safety generally; as jurors they had to care about justice in the particular case before them and what the verdict meant for their own consciences.[22]

No one asked the jurors in Beulah's case why they found her not guilty. At least there is no record of any of the jurors' explanations of their verdict. But a group of New York jurors explained their verdict in a murder trial after they were publicly tarred by the prosecutor as "unintelligent," blasted by the trial judge as stupid, and further insulted by an official order that their names be stricken from the rolls of eligible jurors. They responded by saying that they had only followed the instructions of the judge himself, who had charged them, in the usual way, that if reasonable doubt remained in their minds as to the guilt of the accused woman, they should acquit her. That is what they had done.[23]

The reasonable-doubt standard and Blackstone's ratio did not go unchallenged in the early twentieth century. In a survey of "criminal justice in America," a prominent attorney and politician named Herbert Hadley told fellow members of the legal profession that although "the right of a defendant to be presumed innocent and not subject to conviction unless shown to be guilty beyond a reasonable doubt would seem to be so thoroughly imbedded in our jurisprudence as not to be open to question . . . this rule was devised in a time of tyranny," whereas "today in the ordinary criminal case, after the police, the coroner's jury (if it is a homicide case), the examining magistrate, the prosecuting officer and the grand jury . . . have declared on their oaths, after investigation, that a crime has been committed and the defendant is guilty of it, it is almost an insult to intelligence to assert with the force and reiteration usual in criminal trials that the defendant must be presumed to be innocent of the offense charged." Hadley's sanguine confidence in the honesty and accuracy of criminal prosecution in the United States was not supported by the reports of the Wickersham Commission and the Illinois Crime Survey. Moreover, a twenty-first-century student of the subject would be justified in suspecting that evidence that was accepted with a good deal of confidence in the 1920s, such as eyewitness testimony, may have led to a considerable number of wrongful verdicts, especially given the state of forensic science a hundred years ago.[24]

None of the theater critics and commentators who reviewed *Chicago* quoted any statistics about conviction rates according to gender or race in Chicago or anywhere else. None noted that the number of women tried for murder was a minuscule part of the homicide statistics for Chicago in a given year. None brought up the high standard of proof in a criminal trial or thought to cite Blackstone's dictum. Nor did any reviewers challenge the play's insinuation that it was routine in Chicago for defense attorneys to help their defendants lie but that prosecutors were as a rule honest and built their cases on the facts. Nor did any suggest that it might be impossible to assess the satirical message of *Chicago* without specific factual knowledge of conviction rates and the complexities of the criminal-justice system, including its full range of biases and odious practices. None of these silences is particularly surprising. Theater critics were not expected, after all, to cite commission reports, rehearse statistics from police logs, or discuss philosophies of criminal justice. Nor were they investigative reporters, much less jurists. Moreover, they faced immediate deadlines.

Like the general public, theater critics got their picture of the faults of the criminal-justice system mostly by reading the newspapers, and what the newspapers purveyed bore distortions as well as grave omissions. Although newspapers in various parts of the country printed summaries of findings by investigative crime commissions, information of that sort tended to be drowned out by all the other crime reporting and editorializing in the news.

Moreover, when *Chicago* debuted in New York, the Wickersham Commission had not yet been established. Theoretically, *Tribune* correspondent Burns Mantle, who wrote some of the first reviews of the play, might have recalled the Illinois governor's Commission on Race Relations, had it occurred to him that the revelations in that report had bearing on the wider social context of the play's message. But it did not occur to him.[25]

Newspaper reporting on crime and criminal justice created the conditions of public knowledge in which Watkins's play seemed plausible as realistic satire. *Chicago* perpetuated public misperceptions about criminal justice, and when the play purported to reveal and explain, its revelations and explanations gave a flawed picture of what was wrong with the system by foregrounding a socially insignificant problem, distorting it, saying nothing about the serious problems, and giving the impression that the most honorable actors in the system were the police and prosecutors.

Not that Watkins intended to mislead. In fact, when she read a review in the *New York World* that questioned why a play should be called "Chicago" when it was about "the prostitution of justice in a pretty murderess' trial" and, to the extent that its story was meant to represent a larger problem in the criminal-justice system, might as well have been called "America," she wrote to the drama editor to defend the title of her play. She granted that subversion of justice can be found in other metropolises, but she insisted that no place besides Chicago was "quite such a conspicuous example" of conditions that conduced to the subversion of justice: a lack of handgun regulation, boot-legging in the county jail, entanglement of the prosecutor's office in politics, Illinois statutes that were too protective of defendants, juries composed of "inexperienced men," a court of appeals that was too lenient toward convicted criminals, and a governor who gave out too many pardons. Apart from the comments about handguns, bootlegging, and the entanglement of the state's attorney's office in politics, this list rehearsed the play's message, and so did a rhetorical question that Watkins posed in conclusion: "Is it any wonder [that] one charming murderess told me, 'I always said if I wanted to shoot a man I'd come to Chicago to do it'?"[26]

This anecdote was meant to shock, but women were not in fact coming to Chicago to find a man and murder him. Nor were female killers guaranteed to be acquitted by juries if brought to trial. Nor did acquittals of women tried for murder amount to more than a drop in a bucket compared with Chicago's annual murder number—not to mention that some of the women acquitted were probably innocent. The idea that women were getting away with murder in alarming numbers was a canard.[27]

One Chicagoan who appreciated the play's misdirection was corrupt Chicago mayor William Hale Thompson, who was back in office in 1927, having defeated reformist mayor William Dever. When Thompson emerged from the Harris Theater after seeing *Chicago*, he told the press that Maurine Watkins "was excellently suited to tell the world *all it need know* about the city of Chicago." He must have been happy that the play contained no veiled references to gang wars or graft—or to *himself*. His praise of Watkins as a savvy Chicago expert was a wily bit of spin. Watkins was in fact poorly suited to inform the world about Chicago, after having spent but a year as a writer in the advertising department of the Chicago office of Standard Oil and a mere six months as a cub reporter for the *Chicago Tribune*. She had no inside experience of the state's attorney's office, no real knowledge of how the Chicago police operated, much less any adequate grasp of racial dynamics in Chicago. But Thompson, who *did* know just about everything there was to know about internal corruption in his city, was happy to commend the author of a play whose thesis was that the problems with the criminal-justice system resided in lying defendants, unethical defense attorneys, and dumb juries, *not* in the machinery of the state—its police, prosecutors, and judges.[28]

14. THE UNHAPPY FINISH TO BEULAH'S SHORT LIFE

While *Chicago* was regaling New York audiences with 172 performances at the Music Box Theatre, Watkins went to work on another play. The initial reviews of *Chicago* had led the play's producer, Sam Harris, to invite Watkins to write a theatrical script based on Samuel Hopkins Adams's 1926 novel *Revelry*, which was a *roman à clef* about Washington and the Harding administration. Still living in the West Seventies of New York City, Watkins continued to commute to Baker's class at Yale in New Haven. She also paid a visit to Washington, DC, to conduct interviews and visit the relevant sites in preparation for her new play, and she made other occasional trips, including winter jaunts to Atlantic City to work on *Revelry* by the seaside.[1]

Watkins remained in demand as a journalist as well. In April of 1927, she wrote several articles about the highly publicized New York trial of Ruth Snyder, who, along with her alleged lover and accomplice Henry Judd Gray, was charged with murdering her husband. In one piece, Watkins assured her readers that the so-called gentle sex would not hesitate to convict Ruth and that admitting women to juries "would remove the present curse of sentimentality." In an article about a judicial hearing on the admissibility of statements made by Snyder and Gray while in police custody, Watkins explained that, according to the law, a confession "obtained under duress, violence, threat, or promise of reward or immunity" is invalid *"however true it may be."* The last comment was her own, and it revealed her impatience with the ways in which the law safeguarded defendants' rights and her disdain for defense attorneys who sought to turn what she called "impoliteness" on the part of police and prosecutors into evidence of "the third degree." She sneered at the objection of the defense counsel in the Snyder-Gray trial that Snyder's and Gray's admissions had been obtained after the defendants had been denied their request to have their lawyers present during the questioning. And she added a jab at juries who tend to be "liars, illiterates, [or] eccentrics." She was now free to make remarks of this sort in newspaper articles because she was writing opinion pieces. It was no longer necessary for her to merely hint and insinuate. She had, of course, already shouted her opinions on these subjects in *Chicago*.[2]

Revelry opened at Philadelphia's Garrick Theater on August 29, 1927, and suffered quite a few boos from the critics. The Garrick managers closed the play after a week; the paying audience had dwindled to fewer than a hundred. The producers then brought *Revelry* to the Masque Theater in New York, where it received mixed reviews and closed after five weeks.[3]

The failure of *Revelry* must have been a blow to Watkins and may have shaken her confidence. Had *Chicago* been a fluke? Yet she remained in demand for articles about criminal trials, and magazines were accepting her short stories. She also remained a minor celebrity and continued to be interviewed about *Chicago*. Hence, a rainy March morning in 1928 found her talking to a reporter in New Orleans over "several cups of coffee." She had gone to the Crescent City to take in the sights, write magazine articles, and, presumably, contemplate ideas for her next play. As it turned out, she never did enjoy another great success like *Chicago*. But on that rainy day in New Orleans in 1928, she was still in her early thirties and full of interest in her work. Questions about her professional history led her to tell her interviewer that she had a special "liking" for murders. She had been eager to cover them when she was a reporter in Chicago, and she was still fascinated by them, in an intellectual and philosophical way, which was why she was looking forward to covering a certain murder trial that was about to begin in New Orleans.[4]

That same day, the 10th of March 1928, Beulah Annan died in Chicago. She was 28.

Beulah and Al had tried to make a go of it after the trial, but eventually they separated. As was so often the case in press coverage of Beulah, the newspapers gave different and conflicting accounts. The only firsthand information is testimony in a divorce proceeding initiated by Beulah two years later, in the summer of 1926. During the hearing, Beulah told the judge that Al "refused to live with me" after the trial. Her mother testified that Al "felt he could not live with her after all this trouble which has caused him so much humiliation." This explanation, coming from Mary, who was ever Beulah's defender, sounds honest, since it implies that Beulah was to blame. A witness named Park Nelson, who was probably Mary's boss, testified that he had known both Mary and Beulah since sometime in 1923, hence before the trial. According to Nelson, Beulah went to live with her mother after the trial, and she and Al did not live together after that.[5]

Not many months after her divorce, Beulah met Edward Harlib, an ex-boxer who owned a small taxi concern called the Big Four Motor Livery. Probably on an impulse, the two rushed off one afternoon to get married at Crown Point, an Indiana town where a marriage license could be obtained on the spot. Harlib promised a honeymoon in California and a house in the Chicago suburb of Barrington. The honeymoon came off, but the house never materialized. Instead, the couple settled into an apartment in Uptown on Chicago's far north side.[6]

Harlib had a violent temper and sometimes hit Beulah. One night, when she arrived home later than she had promised, Harlib struck her in the face, blackening one of her eyes. On another occasion, after she refused to run him a bath, the ex-pugilist hit her in the jaw and punched her in the ribs, knocking her down. The punch in the ribs turned out to be serious. For three days the pain intensified. Finally, Beulah called a doctor, and an X-ray revealed a fractured rib. The physician wrapped her chest in bandages and told her to stay in bed. Her mother moved into the flat; Harlib moved out; and Beulah filed for divorce.[7]

Harlib's side of the story was not told during the divorce proceedings, in which he did not participate. But many years later, when asked about Beulah, he said that she drank herself to death. Since he had known her only six months and was not married to her when she died, his diagnosis was only a guess. But his remark showed that her tendency to overdrink, which had earned her two fines in 1919 and was noted at several points in her 1923 diary, was not something she outgrew as she got older. At least one diary entry implies that she used alcohol as an escape from unhappiness.[8]

Her divorce from Harlib was briefly delayed when the judge learned that a woman named Mrs. White was suing Harlib for non-support, claiming that she was his lawful wife and that their marriage had never been dissolved. She had married him, she said, when he was a boxer going under the moniker "Boston Red," but his real name was Edward White. Apparently, to escape supporting his family, White had skipped out on them and changed his name to Harlib. When the papers published a photo of White as Beulah's husband, Mrs. White recognized him and swore out a complaint.[9]

After divorcing Harlib, Beulah moved into an apartment in a large three-story apartment building on the 2400 block of North Albany near Logan Square. By July of 1927 her rib was healed, but she did not feel well. In fact, she had been having difficulties with her digestion and bowels for several months. Her appetite was poor, she suffered fevers, and her abdomen was somewhat swollen and tender.[10]

A man named Abel Marcus was now in love with her. Like Perry and Al, Abel became devoted to her.[11]

That September, *Chicago* began its run at the Sam Harris Theater in Chicago. Back in January, someone had told Beulah that she resembled Francine Larrimore, the actress who played Roxie. Beulah said that she hoped to see the play. When the play arrived in Chicago, Belva Gaertner was present for the opening and so was William O'Brien. Beulah was not.[12]

In October she was diagnosed as suffering from peritoneal tuberculosis, tuberculosis of the abdomen, and in January she was admitted to Chicago Fresh Air Hospital in West Ridge on Chicago's north side. Her father helped pay for her expensive care, which cost about twenty-five dollars a day.[13]

Since her divorce from Harlib, Beulah had resumed her maiden name— Beulah Mae Sheriff. But now, to preserve her anonymity, she told the sanitarium's admitting clerk that her name was Dorothy Stevens (or Stephens). The clerk asked "Dorothy" her age. "Twenty-five," Beulah said. She was in fact twenty-eight.[14]

Her father was with her when she died. It was the first time in twenty-one years that Beulah, Mary, and John had been together for any common purpose as a family. That the business was Beulah's dying was a sad thing. Beulah, "thin and faded," told her father that she was sorry for how she had lived. The end came on March 10, a Saturday afternoon. Beulah said, "I'm ready to go." She was pronounced dead at 3:05 P.M.[15]

The family had Beulah's body prepared in Chicago, then brought back to Owensboro, where, on Tuesday evening and Wednesday morning, throngs of people descended on the James H. Davis undertaking parlors. By noon on Wednesday, as many as three thousand had processed past the open, flower-banked coffin.[16]

At 1:00 P.M., the casket was loaded into a black hearse, and John, Mary, Abel Marcus, John Lydon, and several Sheriff relatives climbed into four additional automobiles provided by the funeral parlor. The somber procession wound its way out of the city, then headed south along Calhoun Road into the countryside of Beulah's childhood, eventually stopping at a small, white country chapel called Mount Pleasant Cumberland Presbyterian Church.[17]

Perry Stephens was now back in Owensboro and working once more as a linotype operator for the *Owensboro Inquirer*. When he learned of Beulah's death and where the services were to be held, he decided to take P. W. to her funeral. It was the first time in the boy's life that anyone had ever spoken to him about his mother, and it was his schoolteacher who informed him that he would not be attending school the next day because he was going to his mother's funeral. Many years later, he recalled his experience, standing beside the flower-laden coffin at the front of the sanctuary. Although everyone else who had known Beulah saw an emaciated shadow of the girl and woman of memory, for twelve-year-old P. W., the whole scene was overwhelming in its splendor: the gleaming casket, the masses of fragrant fresh flowers, the sparkling dress worn by his mother, and a tiara that he took to be a crown. He thought, "Isn't she beautiful."[18]

After the service, Beulah's remains were buried in the church graveyard near the edge of a broad, winter-yellowed field. Nearby were the graves of her grandparents, Samuel and Agnes Sheriff, and her stepmother, Martha, who had died from a sudden stroke three years earlier. John's name was already presumptively inscribed on Martha's tombstone. He had assumed that he would never remarry after Martha's death, but he had remarried. His third wife was a widow named Sue Malda Ralph, "Sue-Mal" as the family called her, whose first husband had perished in a fire.

The day turned chilly and overcast. The funeral crowd quickly dispersed. P. W. went home with his father without being introduced to any of his Sheriff relatives, not even his grandfather. The Sheriffs understood that they were not to approach him.

In the evening, thunderstorms threatened, and Sue-Mal thought of the many pretty ribbons tied to the flowers on the grave. She hated to think that those satin ribbons would be ruined, so she made John take her back to the graveyard, where they untied the ribbons and carried them home in their pockets as the rain descended.

John went to bed early that evening and slept deeply. The next morning, he told Sue-Mal it was the first good night's sleep he'd had in years.

15. BEULAH REMEMBERED AS ROXIE

Notices of Beulah's death appeared in newspapers across the country and invariably mentioned her murder trial and the play *Chicago*, thus cementing a link that was already well known to some but, from that point on, became part of the public information that newspapers and magazines often rehearsed when they spoke of Beulah or Maurine Watkins. Reference to the one often led to mention of the other, and it was almost always Watkins's version of Beulah, overlaid with features of the fictional Roxie Hart, that was repeated for public consumption.

Several reports of Beulah's death took the form of lengthy articles, and one writer used the occasion to compose a retrospective on all that had been wrong with the 1920s, calling Beulah a "prototype" of young people who had rejected the old values. A jaded generation, thinking it no longer possible to be both virtuous and successful, went in for "jazz, gin, and free love." After the war, which the author called a debacle born of greed and selfishness that left a pall of cynicism over the country (a common opinion at the time), young men "rejected marriage" and substituted the "fling." Woman got the vote. Young women bobbed their hair, donned knickers, and wore extremely short skirts. And Beulah Annan, the inspiration for the "play which astounded even blasé Broadway" was both "the effect" and a "symbol" of all the lamentable cultural influences "upon modern, childless femininity." Perhaps the jury at Beulah's trial, bearing its own sense of guilt for what the world had become, "felt that it could not afford to cast stones." The author concluded by warning that only when people returned to the old values would "the unrestrained violence of a Beulah Annan wearing fawn-colored hose" be "relegated to the shambles of a terrible nightmare."[1]

In subsequent decades, almost every one of the occasional news stories that mentioned Beulah took her guilt for granted. "Few female killers ever go to prison," wrote Peter Levins, citing Beulah as a notable example of a murderer to whom a gentle jury said, "Go, little one, and sin no more." Another of Levins's examples was Olympia Macri, who had been tried in 1925 for killing John Bagnano, "father of her nameless child." Both women were acquitted, Levins wrote, which was true; and both went on to pursue movie careers, he added, which was not true but may have been a variation on an old reporters' joke. Just over a decade prior, a New York sportswriter had observed that a Michigan jury had "convicted a female killer of second-degree murder instead of sentencing her to the vaudeville stage." Or perhaps Levins was thinking of Roxie Hart's declaration that she intended to become an actress or of claims after Beulah's trial that she had the same intention. As for Olympia Macri, she was a Yale opera student who shot a man *in front of* a movie theater. There is no evidence that she ever became a movie actress.[2]

In 1932, Beulah was mentioned in a widely published news-service article about Dorothy Pollak, who was accused of murdering her husband, Joseph Pollak, the "bootleg king." Pollak had been dubbed "Chicago's prettiest killer" by other papers, and the news-service article declared that "not since a succession of susceptible juries exonerated such shooting sirens as Beulah Mae Annan and Belva Gaertner and Cora May Orthwein of shooting their sweethearts has Chicago beheld such a combination of screen beauty and ability." In fact, the original news coverage had not described Gaertner or Orthwein as women of "screen beauty." But the idea that screen-worthy beauty guaranteed trial success was irresistible. The article also mentioned how Maurine Watkins had made Beulah the basis for a play, and it repeated the fiction that Beulah had gone to Hollywood after her trial.[3]

Two years later, Peter Levins returned to the topic of jury softness on women murderers by writing a feature article on the reluctance of Cook County to execute them. In this article, Levins reported that in the past hundred years, 119 men had been sentenced to hang and only three women. This was surprising to hear since the Chicago police logs and court documents for the first third of those hundred years had been destroyed in the Great Chicago Fire. Moreover, while it was true that Cook County juries rarely sentenced women to death, the raw numbers were misleading, since they failed to reflect the fact that comparatively few women had been tried for murder compared to men. For example, in the 1920s, women made up only about 6 percent of the capital cases that were brought to trial.[4]

Levins's lengthy article also included retellings of some of the Chicago trials from the 1920s, including those of Sabella Nitti, Cora Orthwein, Belva Gaertner, and Beulah Annan, who, "for four hours," Levins damningly but erroneously declared, had watched Harry Kalsted slowly die. There were also photographs of a number of the defendants, as well as one of Francine Larrimore playing the role of Roxie in *Chicago*. Levins repeated his claim that "some" of the murderesses had "made a nice profit through stage contracts and stories of their exciting lives," but the only example he gave, a mistaken one, was Beulah. In fact, Dorothy Pollak, not mentioned in Levins's piece, was the only woman who received such an entertainment contract. It was for a brief vaudeville stint, probably a theater's effort to capitalize on her notoriety.[5]

The year 1935 saw two widely circulated articles on the topic of jury "chivalry" shown to female killers. Both traced out a history of women favored by "knightly" rescue, beginning with the trial of Beulah Annan, whose "famous murder case," it was noted, "supplied a great deal of the background for Maurine Watkins's satirical drama Chicago." Just over a decade later, in 1947, Levins composed still another widely published feature story about Beulah, this time with artist's illustrations instead of photographs. "She was to become known as the most beautiful woman ever housed in Chicago's Murderess' Row," Levins wrote, and "she was to become the prototype of Roxie Hart, in the play 'Chicago,' which was written by Maurine Watkins." According to Levins, it was not Beulah but her attorney who came up with the idea that she and Kalsted "both reached for the gun." But that attorney was actually Roxie's lawyer in the play, not O'Brien in the Annan case.[6]

One of Beulah's younger cousins recalled her parents saying that Beulah "crossed her legs and pulled up her dress" when testifying in front of the all-male jury. "That's all in the movie," she added. In fact, it was *only* in the movie and the play. For those who had seen the play or the 1927 De Mille film or the 1942 movie *Roxie Hart*, it must have been difficult to separate the fictional Roxie from the real Beulah. It was difficult even for reporters who had ready access to press files on the Annan case. This was well illustrated by an article in a 1951 *Chicago Tribune* series titled "Famous Chicago Crimes." In "Beulah, the Beautiful Killer," Charles Collins told his readers that Maurine Watkins's *Chicago* was "fantastic yet close to the truth." Among the minor details Collins recited about the Annan case were that Beulah received offers of marriage during her incarceration and that she wore a kneecap skirt at her trial. Neither detail was true, but they were both in the 1926 play and the 1927 movie.[7]

In 1954, thirty years after Beulah's trial, her case was described in a *Newsday* article titled "A Banner Season for High Class Crime." The author, Virginia Pasley, surveyed several murder cases from the 1954 headlines to illustrate the public's fascination with murders that featured either mystery or passion, especially when they involved "class," a very elastic category as

THE FLASHLIGHTS SNAP and Roxy is the heroine of the applauding throng.

Artist's sketch of a scene from the play *Chicago*. *San Francisco Examiner*, April 10, 1927, p. 42. Newspapers.com.

Pasley defined it. Along with descriptions of four contemporary cases, Pasley also reached back to 1924 for the story of Beulah, beginning and ending with her and not failing to mention that her "story was paraphrased into a play two years later." Like the journalists who preceded her, Pasley took for granted that Beulah was guilty. And like the other journalists, it was primarily from Maurine Watkins's reporting and play that Pasley drew that conclusion. "After three days on the witness stand, with downcast eye, crossed leg, and handsome wardrobe, [Beulah] was acquitted," Pasley wrote. "She dated every man on the jury" and "divorced her husband who had paid for the trial." The seductively "crossed legs" were actually Roxie's. The idea that Beulah "dated every man on the jury" was perhaps inspired by Roxie's mid-trial remark to Flynn about how attentive she had been to the jurors: "I've done everything but give them my phone number." The "husband who paid for her trial" was the silent film's Amos Hart, who scraped together every cent he could, including cashing in his life insurance policy to pay Roxie's attorney.[8]

That same year, 1954, actor-dancer Gwen Verdon saw a television rerun of the 1942 movie *Roxie Hart*. This iteration of *Chicago*, starring Ginger Rogers as a burlesque dancer, kindled an interest in Verdon to play Roxie in a musical. Verdon discussed the idea with dancer-director Bob Fosse, and in 1956, Fosse, Verdon, and the producer Robert Fryer sought to secure rights from Maurine Watkins, with the aid of Sheldon Abend, the new president of the American Play Company. When they approached Watkins, she refused. She would keep on refusing all such requests until her death in 1969. It was only then that the rights to *Chicago* were released, by her estate, and the musical version of *Chicago* was finally produced.[9]

Few details are known about Watkins's latter years. After spending the 1930s collaborating on movie scripts and typing out a steady stream of short stories and articles, she vanished from public view in the early 1940s, having retired from her writing career. Her father died in 1941; her mother eventually moved to Jacksonville, Florida; and at some point, Watkins moved to Jacksonville to be near her mother.[10]

In 1955, around the time when Verdon, Fosse, and their producer made their first efforts to secure the rights to turn *Chicago* into a musical, Watkins became seriously ill. When she recovered, she composed a will. This testament contained many bequests that reflected Watkins's twin interests in historical biblical studies and classical antiquity, the same set of interests that had led her, many years earlier, to consider pursuing a PhD degree in classics at Radcliffe.[11]

Those interested in the rights to Watkins's play had difficulty contacting her directly from the mid-fifties through the sixties. Sheldon Abend is said to have hired a retired FBI detective to track her down. There were reports that she wore a black veil to cover a disfiguration caused by face cancer. The American Play Company "received yearly checks and thank-you notes from her for keeping interested producers away." She "turned to religion," it was claimed, then took up astrology and became "a virtual recluse." She and her mother supposedly supplemented their income by "writing greeting cards for Hallmark."[12]

The speculations grew in a vacuum, and most were implausible. Watkins, who was quite wealthy, did not need to earn money by writing for Hallmark, and it is hard to imagine the author of *Chicago* doing that for fun. Nor did she "turn to religion" late in life. Watkins had been a devout Christian since her childhood, having grown up in the home of a minister; she composed *Chicago* to express a moral message based on her Christian religious commitments; and her will reflected her lifelong dedication to her faith. Whether she incorporated astrology into her belief system is possible but doubtful. Sheldon Abend and Gwen Verdon claimed that her study of astrology charts told her that it was too risky to let *Chicago* be produced again. If Watkins said that, it was probably tongue-in-cheek.[13]

According to Bob Fosse, "she wouldn't let us have the show because the world was in a bad state, with the bomb and everything. She thought we shouldn't do a show that had so many despicable characters in it." According to a thirdhand report of something one of Watkins's aunts said, "Over the years Maurine became disturbed that she had assisted in getting an acquittal for a murderer" because "her reporting set a positive tone and gained sympathy" for Beulah Annan. Whether the aunt believed this or not, it is surely mistaken, since Watkins's articles about Beulah were not calculated to win sympathy for her, much less exonerate her.[14]

A more likely reason for Watkins's reluctance to release the rights to her play is suggested by what one of her *Tribune* colleagues wrote under the byline Mae Tinée when the first film version of *Chicago* was produced by Cecil B. De Mille in 1927. In a review titled "Our Maurine's Fine Play is Film-Flammed," the anonymous drama critic wrote, "Well, they have slaughtered Maurine Watkins's play to make a De Mille holiday." Watkins's "clever, satiric, diabolically human, uproariously funny play that could well have been made into just such a picture has had all its fine parts ironed out. It has been fluted and tucked and dyed ala De Mille and the result is just a fussy, ordinary melodrama that is rather funny in spots." Watkins cannot have been happy about those changes, and she was probably even more annoyed by the 1942 movie version, *Roxie Hart* (starring Ginger Rogers), which portrayed Roxie as a frustrated dancer who was *innocent* of the murder and confessed to it only in hopes of winning publicity to launch her career.[15]

Watkins died of lung cancer on August 10, 1969. The only public notice of her passing was a short obituary in the *Florida Times-Union*. The obituary stated that she had been a playwright. It did not mention any of her plays, not even *Chicago*.[16]

16. BOB FOSSE'S MUSICAL REMAKE OF MAURINE WATKINS'S PLAY

Watkins's death may not have been publicly noted outside Jacksonville, Florida, but it did not go unnoticed by producers interested in *Chicago*. "A number of people came out of the woodwork, wanting to acquire rights," recalled C. R. Leonard, who managed the trust that held Watkins's estate. Bob Fosse obtained the rights in the early 1970s and remade Chicago as a musical. The musical was produced in 1975 and subsequently revived in the 1990s.[1]

The publicity around the revival made Watkins herself a subject of interest, and biographical curiosity about her and the original *Chicago* only increased with the debut of the extraordinarily successful movie version of the musical in 2002. This in turn sparked curiosity about the play's historical background, which led to a rediscovery of Beulah, thanks to the availability of a recent reprinting of Watkins's *Tribune* articles in an appendix to a new edition of her play.[2]

Beulah was occasionally mentioned in reviews of the various new iterations of *Chicago*, and she also began appearing as a topic in books ranging from light historical treatments to more serious ones. Authors typically followed an interpretation of Beulah that matched Watkins's portrayal of her, whether they relied solely on Watkins's articles for their information or supplemented her accounts with additional bits of the original reporting. Once the connection between Roxie Hart and Beulah Annan was rediscovered, there was a tendency to assume that Beulah was a cheap, vain, vile creature just like Roxie.[3]

The most scathing characterizations of Beulah have been penned by two recent analyzers of the play who conclude that Watkins wrote *Chicago* as a trenchant attack on women like Beulah and the systems that coddled them or were fooled by them. Ethan Mordden, an expert on American theater, sees *Chicago* as an exposé of the "wanton killer" of 1920s Chicago, who acts not from "self-defense, passion, revenge, or for gain" but merely because "I feel like it," examples being the thrill killers Nathan Leopold and Richard Loeb, various cruel persons of the era who murdered for seemingly trivial reasons (as described by Ben Hecht), and the "anti-heroine, Roxie Hart," who "kills because her will has been thwarted. Or she's offended. Or something." Since Roxie was a fictional character, Mordden immediately clarifies that "there actually was a Roxie, one Beulah Annan, and Watkins . . . could tell that Annan was guilty of sheer senseless murder."[4]

Zsófia Tóth develops a similar equation between Beulah and Roxie. In an interdisciplinary book titled *Merry Murderers*, Tóth interprets *Chicago* as the story of a fictional vampire, Roxie Hart, based on the real-life vampire Beulah Annan. As Tóth describes the vampire of old silent films, she was a type of femme fatale, a beautiful woman who used her looks and seductive skills to pursue selfish and nefarious interests, usually leading to the ruin or death of her victims. She often masqueraded as an innocent, good-hearted woman to deceive her unsuspecting victims. Born in fiction, the celluloid vampire, or "vamp," did not remain there, according to Tóth. Type characters in silent films represented possibilities to be performed in life, and the vamp/femme fatale of movies and literature was one of the cultural identities that some significant number of young women adopted and performed in their own lives. Moreover, one supposedly can identify a real-life femme fatale by correlating known facts about her with the surface indicators of her looks, words, and manner that betray her as a dissembling vampire, so long as one is able to read the signs. Hence, Tóth regards the fictional vamps as templates for recognizing vamps in real life, and she contends that Maurine Watkins—although Watkins did not call Beulah a vampire or femme fatale—recognized that Beulah cleverly performed the vamp type, with its disguises, to get what she wanted and that Beulah was also a cavalier destroyer of the men she exploited, one of whom she murdered.[5]

There were certainly many dangerous and deceptive men and women in the 1920s, just as there are today, but there is no reason to think that some significant number of dangerous women took their cues from movie vamps. Moreover, even at their most dangerous, silent-film vamps did not shoot, stab, poison, or otherwise murder their men. And when the term *vamp* was applied to real people, it typically carried a watered-down sense. One of the most frequent real-life applications was to call an adolescent girl a vamp if she "wore Theda Bara headdresses and practiced the sinuous slithery sliding gait of Theda, and made eyes and paid many nickels to see the queen of the vamps and all the other vamps in the films." Another common application was to call any young woman a vamp if she used her looks and manner to attract young men and get something from them, such as persuading a man to spend money on her or simply give her a ride in his car. And when a pretty female criminal defendant was acquitted, cynics sometimes said that she must have "vamped" the jury, meaning that her good looks had swayed them. Hence, when the jurors who were selected for the famous 1922 murder trial of Madelynne Obenchain swore that they would *not* be influenced by a pretty face, observers called the resultant jury "vamp proof," which was analogous to calling Beulah's jury "beauty proof." The *Chicago American* asked in a caption to a photo of Beulah, "Will the Red Head Vamp the Jury?"[6]

None of these colloquial uses of the word *vamp* contained the elements of the movie-world's vampire, who pretends to be all sweetness and light while cunningly exploiting the men she ruins. Everyone understood this, and people sometimes joked about there being no vamps in real life. The film star Richard Barthelmess, who had played opposite one of the most famous film vamps, declared that he had never met a vamp outside a film; so did Theda Bara herself, and so did the writer Upton Sinclair, who added, tongue in cheek, that "from the movies I know how these dangerous animals behave and if I ever meet one I'll know just what to do." There was also the occasional one-line joke about the subject: "The only place we've ever seen a real vamp was in a shoe" (a vamp being a part of a shoe). One newspaper supplied a joking rejoinder, remarking that people who say they have never seen a vamp have "never lived in a boarding house." This snide quip traded on the application of the term *vamp* to working-class girls who powdered their noses, acted flirtatiously, accepted rides to work from men they did not know, and sometimes rewarded a date with a kiss or a bit of petting if he spent money on them. In Chicago, there was a spate of public discussion about "boulevard vamps," working girls who lined up along certain thoroughfares each morning to get rides to work and thus save streetcar fare or who accepted rides after work, sometimes going with the driver to some amusement, which was a form of casual dating.[7]

To whatever degree that the vivacious, pretty, and sometimes flirtatious Beulah might have fit someone's colloquial use of the word *vamp*, she was nothing like the cunning men-ruining vampires of the silent films. And no one in her own day claimed that she was, not even Maurine Watkins. In fact, Watkins did not even cast the fictional Roxie Hart as a vampire. *Chicago's* Roxie is callous and self-centered, but she is also naïve, not cunning, and has to be tutored by her lawyer, the matron, and Jake in the ways of deception.

Those who knew Beulah personally are long dead, but a few reports suggest that they retained an affection for her, even if some of them engaged in a good deal of frowning and eye-rolling over the course of their acquaintance with her. Her first cousin Emma Marksberry recalled her fondly and also with sympathy "for the kind of life she had got into." Perry Stephens refused to be interviewed about Beulah but always "carried a torch" for her. When an amateur Owensboro historian named Stan LeMaster gave a talk on Beulah at the Daviess County historical society in 1982, an elderly woman came up to him and whispered, "Beulah didn't have a chance." Whatever that meant exactly—LeMaster was unable to follow up—it was an expression of sympathy from someone who had known her. Years earlier, LeMaster had tried to gather information about Beulah for a story regarding unusual tombstones. He had placed a request for information in an Owensboro newspaper but had received no help, only several phone calls, usually late in the evening, "from angry persons who demanded to know exactly what I wanted to know." LeMaster never learned their identities. By all accounts, they were not family members, either from Beulah's side or Perry's. They must have been friends of Beulah who objected to the damning stories about her that showed up periodically in the Owensboro newspapers.[8]

The public image of Beulah, now a hundred years old, does not cry out for rehabilitation in fairness to her memory. The single historically significant moment of her life was at best a tragic event caused by a split-second, drunken judgment, and it will never be known whether she acted out of fear that she was in immediate danger from an enraged lover or gave in to an angry impulse, which she immediately regretted. She deserves, at most, no more than the benefit of the doubt about what happened during those deadly seconds in her bedroom on the afternoon of April 3, 1924.

Beulah became historically significant only because Maurine Watkins regarded her case as a prime example of justice miscarried in 1920s Chicago and because the theater critics and other commentators interested in the "true crime" history behind *Chicago* have immortalized her by making her infamous. But she was almost forgotten. Both Beulah and Watkins, who were somewhat regularly mentioned in the press from the late 1920s through the 1930s, were much less frequently named in the years following the 1942 movie *Roxie Hart*. Watkins's retreat from Hollywood and from professional writing altogether might have spelled the end of public interest in her and in Beulah, had not Gwen Verdon seen a rerun of *Roxie Hart* in the mid-1950s.[9]

Although Verdon's and Fosse's initial efforts to acquire the rights to *Chicago* failed, Fosse, ever hopeful, began looking into the history behind the play and paid researchers, including Al Friendly, who worked at *Newsweek's* Chicago bureau, to gather information. This was done through mediators. Fosse's attorney Jack Perlman communicated with a senior editor at *Newsweek* named Lester Bernstein, who in turn put Friendly to work. In correspondence, Friendly refers to Perlman's and Bernstein's client only as "your friend," which suggests that he was not given a name, no doubt because Fosse did not want outsiders to know about his interest in the material. In 1963, Friendly provided Bernstein with photocopies of Watkins's *Tribune* articles about Beulah and other women who had been tried for murder in the 1920s. Friendly also worked out correlations between characters in the play and these historical women. And he identified certain living persons who had known Beulah, in case the client wished to speak with them.[10]

A decade later, having finally secured rights to *Chicago* from Watkins's estate, Fosse went to work with lyricist Fred Ebb and melodist John Kander. According to Verdon, Fosse "adapted the original play, along with transcripts of the original trial." That was not quite true. Fosse did not have the original trial transcripts, only summaries and transcriptions in newspaper accounts. He was also less interested in Beulah than in Watkins and her play.[11]

Fosse's version of *Chicago* was meant to hew closely to the spirit of the original play, unlike the De Mille film and the 1942 *Roxie Hart*. The musical staging was very different from the 1926 play, however, and not simply because Fosse's *Chicago* had songs and dancing. The 1970s *Chicago* was a "concept" musical. Instead of presenting a realistic set and chronology, it blurred time and space, kept the dialogue spare, and let the musical numbers carry the play's emotion and message. In form it was a throwback to musical vaudeville, a series of period-styled musical acts, satirical in tone. The satire was dark, biting, and cynical. *Chicago* was "Bob's response to Watergate," Verdon explained.[12]

When the musical was previewed in Philadelphia in April of 1975, with Verdon as Roxie Hart and Chita Rivera as Velma, it was a "disaster." It may have been too cynical even for the post-Watergate 1970s. In the face of bad reviews, the show underwent extensive revision before finally heading to Broadway, where it received better reviews but was overshadowed by *A Chorus Line* and went on to a somewhat bumpy two-year run. Twenty years later, however, and nearly a decade after Fosse's death, *Chicago* the musical was revived to glowing reviews.[13]

Scene from the 1975 Broadway production of the musical *Chicago* by Bob Fosse (with John Kander and Fred Ebb). Martha Swope photo, Lincoln Center Library for the Performing Arts, New York Public Library.

The 1975 *Chicago* was no flop; it received fourteen Tony nominations. But the critics liked the 1990s version much better and attributed its strength at the box office to the times. Fosse's *Chicago* was "so prescient about '90s justice, the press, and celebrity," wrote Linda Winer in *Newsday*, "that it's almost eerie." Richard Zoglin commented in *Time* magazine that "what seemed cynical in 1975 is now au courant. *Chicago* hasn't merely aged well; it has come of age." The reason, wrote A. R. Gurney of the *New York Times*, was that "after the trials of O. J. Simpson and the Menendez brothers, today's audiences understand very well the theatrical ploys of media-conscious trial lawyers and the connections that link crime and celebrity and money." This was the common view. When the revival was being prepared, the director Walter Bobbie recalled, "I was reading *Chicago* and watching the O. J. trials at the same time, and I thought, 'Oh, my God, this satire has turned into a documentary. . . . The manipulation of the courts, the abuse of celebrity, everybody having a press agent—all that seemed to be newly minted." Cynicism was no longer regarded as a fault; it was just realism. In the words of Gurney, *Chicago* told audiences that "we live in a tough, materialistic, violent society and that show business is the best revenge," which means that "crime leads to celebrity leads to money, and you'd better look good if you want to survive."[14]

Another reason for the revival's greater success was that audiences in the nineties were more accustomed to entertainment where the production values were the primary draw, not a clear story line. "With the multichanneled ubiquity of television in the 1990s," wrote Vincent Canby of the *New York Times*, "we have become an avid audience for a world more often concerned with presentation than content. As our world plays to us, we observe it with detachment, demanding only that it entertain us so we can accept it as showbiz." In a similar vein, his *Times* colleague Ben Brantley opined that the public was won over by the sheer entertainment power of *Chicago* and by characters who broke the fourth wall and mocked the audience for taking such pleasure in their dark romp. If the musical had a message, it was the idea that everything had become show business: "all the world's a con game and show business is the biggest scam of all." Velma makes the latter point when she greets the *audience* with the words "Hello, suckers" at the beginning of act II.[15]

Some of the drama critics of the 1990s had also written reviews of the original production and were in a position to make comparisons. Howard Kissel had found the 1970s *Chicago* "trashy." When he saw the revival, he loved it and concluded that the trashiness was deliberate. Times had changed. "*Chicago* is about the way we make celebrities of criminals, a theme more pertinent today than in 1975," he wrote. Clive Barnes had also been an active theater critic in the 1970s. Back then, when he had reviewed the original run, he had concluded that perhaps "never in the history of Broadway has so much been done for so many for so few final results." The music had been fabulous, he had granted; the stars had performed the songs and steps magnificently; costumes and atmospherics had been impressive. Barnes had also praised the way the musical commented on its own genre and legacy with "wry, at times even cynical objectivity." But for all these virtues and despite being "easily one of the best musicals of the season," *Chicago* had disappointed because its subject matter was not worth the effort, deriving as it did from an only moderately amusing comedy melodrama of the 1920s. Yet when Barnes viewed essentially the same show twenty years later, he showered it with undiluted praise, explaining that the 1970s version had been "over-produced and over-pretentious."[16]

Did Barnes engage in "revisionist history"? Little was changed in the book and musical numbers for the 1996 revival. But Joel Grey, who played Amos in the revival, remembered the original production as "awfully, awfully dark, and also over-produced." This is exactly what Barnes recalled. And according to Terry Teachout, who compared the revival to that of the original-cast album (no substantial film footage having survived), the 1975 numbers were performed "with a detached and chilly slickness consistent with Grey's memory." Members of the 1975 production had felt the same way during rehearsals. Fosse had demanded not simply a cynical edge, as they remembered it, but an angry, gloomy tone. The dances were *so* slow, the dancers' expressions blank, zombie-like. "It was creepy," one of Fosse's assistants recalled.[17]

The differences of opinion about the character and reception of the 1970s *Chicago* and its 1990s revival did not entail any dispute about the *message* of the musical. It was agreed that *Chicago* held up a mirror to contemporary American culture and proclaimed that there is no real difference between fame and infamy; that courts, the supposed guardians of justice, are little different from entertainment venues; and that all of modern life is more show than sincerity. The reviewers did not question the depiction of the justice system, probably because they tended to treat high-profile murder trials as emblematic of the justice system generally, just as critics and audiences of Watkins's play did in the 1920s. High-profile, media-saturated criminal cases galvanize opposing blocs of public opinion and inevitably infuriate one side when the verdict does not go their way, precipitating misguided generalizations about stupid or corrupt juries and the failure of the criminal-justice system as a whole.[18]

But Fosse's point was not so much about the criminal-justice system; it was chiefly about American life. For Fosse, the media-hyped trial in his *Chicago* was a cipher for American culture as show business, "razzle dazzle," an extension of the entertainment industry. By contrast, the original play was much more focused on the role of newspapers in turning criminal trials into circuses. It would have undercut Watkins's and the 1920s critics' notion of good satire to have suggested that all of life was such a show, the case of Roxie being a mere symptom and metaphor for that. The classical notion of satire with which Watkins, her teacher George Baker, and the era's commentators operated assumed that the audience occupies a position outside the show and possesses full agency to be informed by the lesson of a play and to take action. Fosse's idea was that the audience is *inside* the show, lacks agency, and can only laugh. In the end, it laughs at itself.

"In some genres—historical fiction, science fiction of certain kinds, even political satire—departures from fact based on mistakes can seriously affect the overall achievement." So writes Peter Lamarque, a modern philosopher of art and literature. Truth claims in satire take many different forms. Not all concern a satire's external targets, and those that do vary in focus. Some concern specific persons, others *types* of people, as well as social conditions and institutions.[19]

I have referred to the claims that a satire makes about its external targets as its "message." In some periods of antiquity and early-modern Europe, theatrical entertainments that ridiculed real persons made authors and actors vulnerable to state punishment or civil penalties. Thankfully, that is no longer the case in most modern societies, where judgments about the truth of a satire's message are matters for public debate, not legal adjudication, or else for analysis by critics and historians.[20]

To the extent that a satire carries a serious social message, assessing its truth is not a question of whether it mirrors real-life events, since it is typical of satire to invent a fresh story. Nor does a serious-minded satire fail the truth test simply because it exaggerates or distorts, since satire typically conveys its message through caricature. The targets—contemporary persons, types of person, institutions, other social entities—need only be sufficiently recognizable to prompt identification by audiences. To the extent that audiences are able to see through the veil of caricature to what they know in real life, they can also judge the degree of a caricature's hyperbole. If a satire's claims are obviously untrue and made merely for the sake of laughs, audiences can often recognize that, too. Satires that deal mostly in the latter are perhaps better termed *spoofs*.

Hecht and MacArthur's dramatic comedy *The Front Page*, whose subject matter significantly overlaps with that of *Chicago*, offers a useful example and point of comparison. *The Front Page* was produced in 1928 as a comedy about Chicago's crime reporters and their interactions with their bosses and city politicians. The authors modeled the play's main press boss, Walter Burns, on a Chicago city editor named Walter Howey. It was not necessary for audiences to know who Howey was. To the extent that the Burns character seemed believable as a type, the play succeeded in making its point about the press as a power broker. On the other hand, playgoers who assumed that there were *no* city editors like Burns, that he was merely a farcical character, would have found him funny but not revealing as a vehicle for social comment.[21]

As it happens, many of the first reviewers of *The Front Page* were newspaper men who had firsthand experience of the news-gathering culture of the crime reporters portrayed in the play. Walter Whitworth declared that "the great thing about this play is its faithfulness to the life it portrays." That did not mean that the drama mirrored actual events. While the story may have included a few moments that reflected small real-life incidents, it completely transformed others (notably a jailbreak and an arrest on a train); and it featured plenty of inventing. What made *The Front Page* true to life was the faithfulness with which it reflected the *character* of persons and institutions. Although two theater critics who worked for Hearst newspapers protested that the reporters depicted in *The Front Page* were unrealistic, the consensus was that Hecht and MacArthur presented accurate epitomes of the era's big-city crime reporters. Onetime Chicago journalist Vincent Starrett remarked that those "who believe the play to be exaggerated know nothing of the newspaper world . . . especially the Hearst newspaper world." Robert Tucker told readers of the *Indianapolis Star* that "what we like most about *The Front Page* is its sheer honesty, its penetrating and unerring satire in dealing with life as their police reporters found it." New York's Burns Mantle called it "the true stuff of life." And Chicago's Fanny Butcher praised the play's verisimilitude, comparing its characters to the soldiers in *What Price Glory*—"unsentimental, factual, actual, and blasphemous."[22]

Hecht and MacArthur described *The Front Page* as "a Valentine" to the grunts of the Chicago newspaper world, to whose fraternity the playwrights themselves had recently belonged. The play's point of view is that of its reporter characters, which is similar to Jake the reporter's role in *Chicago*. Manifestly, *The Front Page* is designed to encourage the playwrights' own chuckling fondness for the reporters and to induce audiences to root for the principal reporter character Hildy Johnson. But the play is also a searing commentary on the ruthless and Machiavellian Walter Howey, city editor of the *Chicago Herald and Examiner*, and on two-time Chicago mayor William Hale Thompson and his political allies. The play was no Valentine to them.[23]

The genre question posed about Watkins's *Chicago* was also at issue in the critical reception of *The Front Page*. Was it a satire? The play achieved its commentary on Howey and Mayor Thompson by depicting them through representative characters and by having the reporters wisecrack about those characters. There was a consensus that the play did not grossly exaggerate or distort in limning its targets, which probably explains why most reviewers did not call *The Front Page* a satire but judged it to be realistic drama with some farcical elements. The bits of farce appeared in the action (for instance, an escaped criminal popping back in through a courtroom pressroom window to be captured by a reporter), not in the character portraits.

When Watkins claimed that her play was "all straight, without any idea of exaggeration," she may have meant that, like *The Front Page*, most of its humor arose from realistic mimicry, which was the main conveyer of its message. Since she subtitled it a satirical comedy but subsequently claimed that it was *not* meant to be a satire, she must have felt ambivalent about the label. Perhaps in her mind, if *Chicago* was to be called satire, it was the sort of satire that credibly imitated rather than grossly exaggerated and that if satire meant hyperbole from beginning to end, then *Chicago* was not a satire. The same could be said of *The Front Page*. According to Hecht, the play's depiction of the relationship between editor Walter Burns (real-world Howey) and reporter Hildy Johnson (based in part on Charles MacArthur, who had once worked for Howey) was no exaggeration. In fact, Hecht later wrote, "we watered it down" because "the Howey and MacArthur relationship in the *Examiner* office of 1919 would have been too eerie a tale for any theatre."[24]

Unlike *Chicago*, where the plot drivers and significant elements of the play's social message depended to a large extent on things that Watkins had not witnessed—conversations between defendants and lawyers, conversations between inmates and matrons outside the ears of reporters, and jury deliberations—the whole substance of *The Front Page* was well known to the two seasoned reporters who authored that play: the pressroom, the city editor, the Chicago mayor and his political allies, whom both authors had covered and whose lawlessness in pursuing and maintaining political power was well documented.

The one subject that Watkins knew as an insider was the newspaper business, and her play achieved verisimilitude in showing the tendency of the press to turn murder trials into entertainment events. As both a newspaper reader and a press insider, Watkins was familiar with this phenomenon, which had long been a target of critics of the tabloid press and was generally known to the public as well. Her portrait of the methods of the press included staged photo scenes, stolen letters, invented diaries, a sob sister who oozed calculated sympathy for accused women, and a hard-boiled reporter who traded publicity for scoops.

Watkins had no inside knowledge about which women tried for murder were guilty, whether their defense attorneys routinely coached them to lie, and whether juries routinely ignored evidence and based their verdicts on chivalry or sympathy or beauty. She did not have accurate knowledge of conviction rates either. In all these matters, she relied on prevailing opinions or at least on opinions held in certain quarters.

Another difference between *The Front Page* and *Chicago* is that Hecht and MacArthur targeted powerful men who wielded significant influence over the City of Chicago, while Watkins, except for her pillory of the tabloid press, targeted the impotent—insignificant women, whose social influence was nil, and ordinary citizens who answered the call to jury duty.

The Front Page would have been funny even if it were not realistic and even if the arrows it sent at real-world targets missed their mark. But it would not have been the great newspaper play it was hailed to be and remains still, "the best known critique and cliché of American journalism," as one student of the subject has written. Watkins's *Chicago* was very funny in its day, and it has held up well as comedy. Yet the play's realism fell short, and its social message was misleading.[25]

POSTSCRIPT

When Beulah died in 1928, Al did not attend her funeral. He was living in Louisville at the time with his sister Elizabeth and her husband, Floyd. At some point after 1930, he returned to Chicago and worked at the only employment for which he had any special skill: auto repair. Around 1932, he met a woman named Othelia Griffin, a onetime hospital nurse who had begun providing medical services of some sort out of her apartment on the south side, operating under the name Othelia Schaefer. One suspects that she conducted abortions and that for a share of the fees, doctors and druggists sent Othelia patients. Al moved into Othelia's flat as "Mr. Schaefer," and they lived off the money she earned.[1]

The relationship was tumultuous. Al fell into a pattern of drinking and physically abusing Othelia. After one of these episodes, Othelia collapsed and died. Al was arrested, charged, and eventually convicted of manslaughter. A week later, the judge in the case rescinded the verdict, citing the state's failure "to establish certain salient facts." According to the final report of the coroner's physician, it was unclear whether Othelia had died from blows or from the effects of her own chronic drinking. Al's history with Othelia raises the question of whether Al physically abused Beulah. It is unusual for a man to become a wife beater only late in life. And although there is no hint in Beulah's 1923 diary that he ever struck her, the diary is not a comprehensive account of their life together.[2]

Following his release from jail, Al went to Louisville to live with his sister Ruth; later he moved back to Chicago. The fall of 1940 found him in a cheap hotel on South State Street. He was fifty-five by then, suffered from poor eyesight and varicose veins, and wore a full set of dentures. Alone and jobless, Al enlisted in the Illinois National Guard as a mechanic. His health declined further, and in March of 1945 he was transferred to an army hospital at Fort Knox. Shortly thereafter, the army gave him a disability discharge because he no longer had the physical stamina to carry out his daily work as the supervisor of a motor pool. The army awarded him a small pension, and he returned to Chicago's south side. Eventually, he was too incapacitated to manage on his own and went to live with Ruth again. He died not many years later, exactly when and where are unknown.[3]

After Beulah's death, her mother, Mary Neel, remained in Chicago and earned a living as a supervisor in a dry goods store. To bring in a bit of extra money, she rented a room to a boarder. Beulah's passing had taken the bottom out of her life. She went to work every day, tended to Beulah's cats and canaries, and fought against depression and ill health. For some years she had suffered from a vaguely diagnosed heart condition. Now she developed a persistent cough and began to lose weight. A doctor diagnosed her condition as pulmonary tuberculosis. She could not afford a sanitarium and ended up in Cook County Hospital. Three months later, in March of 1931, she died there, at the age of fifty-two. Her body was transported back to Kentucky, where her stepdaughter Anice Bartlett received it and held a private funeral. John Sheriff and his wife, Sue-Mal, attended the brief ceremony in the front room of the Bartlett home; a Baptist minister presided. Anice had Mary buried in Elmwood Cemetery. The grave remains unmarked.[4]

Perry Stephens eventually moved back to Chicago and took a job with the *Chicago Sun Times*. He and Alice and their son, John Lloyd, lived in Rogers Park on Chicago's north side, not far from the sanitarium where Beulah had spent her final days. In his later years, Perry was even more of a homebody than ever. His only leisure interest was cards, bridge in particular. When he died in 1972, his family buried him with a pack of playing cards in his pocket.[5]

Beulah's son, P. W., graduated from Owensboro High School in 1934, then went to work in his aunt Willie Lee's floral shop. In 1941 he joined the army as an infantryman and served in the Pacific from 1942 to 1945, earning several non-combat medals and ribbons as a competent and faithful clerk. After the war, he joined the research laboratory of General Electric in Owensboro and earned a reputation as a man of considerable technical acumen. His grandmother Margaret Stephens died in August of 1947; his grandfather William died four months later. At William's funeral, an elderly man approached P. W., who now went by Perry, and said, "I'm your grandfather." For more than thirty years—out of respect and, in the beginning, humiliation—John Sheriff had honored Margaret and William Stephens's ban on any Sheriff family contact with Perry. Now that Margaret and William were dead, John interpreted the ban as ended and went to William's funeral to meet his grandson. By this time, John had sold his farm and was living with Sue-Mal in a modest house in Owensboro. Perry began visiting him there and in the course of time came to know various cousins. One was a first cousin once removed named Ruth. Perry and Ruth married in 1950.[6]

Perry had a photograph of his mother, given to him by his father. The small, faded picture, kept for too many years in Perry's wallet, shows a teen-aged Beulah around the time she married his father. Perry died in 1999, liked by everyone and remembered by all as a kind, unselfish man. According to one Owensboroan who knew him, he was the one good thing to come from Beulah's life.[7]

NOTES
BIBLIOGRAPHY
INDEX

NOTES

Introduction

1. Bettman, "Criminal Justice Surveys Analysis," 63–65 (the quotation).
2. Mayor Thompson as quoted in Pauly, *Chicago by Maurine Watkins*, xxvii (emphasis added), citing *CEP*, September 12, 1927 (clipping, New York Public Library). "We were a real hanging paper, out for conviction always," Watkins said in a 1927 interview (Merrill, "Pistol Fire Lights Up 'Chicago,'" M1).

1. Beulah Mae

1. Beulah's birth year: 1899 on her gravestone; November 17, 1896, on her Indiana marriage license (where she lied about her age) (Spencer County, Indiana, Marriage Records, Book 6, p. 177).
2. Personal interviews with Beulah's cousins Bevie Marksberry and Anna Price; Field, "Country Church and the Country Girl" (1916), 86.
3. Personal interviews with Beulah's cousins.
4. Mary Sheriff v. John R. Sheriff, No. 9233, Daviess County, KY. The filings, from the petition to the judgment, date from May 13, 1907, to the December court term in 1911, when the case was dropped due to inactivity on the part of the plaintiff.
5. Carroll, *Kentucky Statutes* (1903 and 1915 eds.), ch. 66 § 2123 with annotation.
6. Mary Sheriff ("hat trimmer" for a "milliner") and her daughter "Buhla" in the April enumeration of the 1910 federal census for Owensboro, KY; Heflin, "Life on Mulberry Street," 50–56; Van Kleeck, *Seasonal Industry*, 70, 81, 104–12.
7. The 1910 federal census (listing Mary as a widow); the 1911–1912 Owensboro city directory (listing Mary as a widow and a "solicitor," a period name for a peddler); Davis, *Age of Indiscretion*, 143–45 (the social status of the divorced or separated woman, some of whom presented themselves as widows); Hamilton, "Errors of Society," 83 (the minister's comment); Fine, *Psychoanalytic Vision*, 458 (a man's recollection about his mother); additional period examples of divorced or separated women representing themselves as widows.
8. Personal interview with Beulah's cousin Mary Rafferty; Beulah's cousin Thelma Marksberry Thompson as quoted in Davis, "True Roots of 'Chicago'

Story Lie with Two Kentucky Women," K1; a friend quoted in an AP story published in *OI*, March 14, 1928, p. 2.

9. *OM*, April 17, 1912, p. 8 (John Sheriff's remarriage). Local news implies that Beulah lived with her father from May of 1912 (*Twice-A-Week Messenger*, May 22, 1912, p. 6) through August 1914 (*OM*, August 29, 1914, p. 8) and made periodic visits to her mother in Owensboro (twelve additional references to her in Handyville news for 1913 and 1914). Beulah's mother is still "Mary Sheriff" when Beulah visits her in July of 1913 (*Twice-A-Week Messenger*, July 19, 1913, p. 8); she is "Mrs. Neal" [*sic*] when Beulah visits her in August of 1914 (*OM*, April 28, p. 5). In 1918, Beulah, recently divorced and therefore back in the custody of her father, sued to have her mother made her legal guardian (*OM*, February 20, 1918, p. 6).

10. Personal interview with Ruth Stephens; a letter from Perry to Beulah published in *CA*, April 4, 1924, p. 1 (expressing his great love for her).

11. 1900 federal census; marriage affidavit for John Sheriff and Mary Stone attesting the age of Mary Stone (Spencer County, Indiana, Marriage Affidavits, Book 2, p. 119, Indiana State Library, Indianapolis). Since Mary could read and write (1910 census), the X must have been Baumgaertner's doing.

12. Beulah's and Perry's marriage license, Spencer County, Indiana, Marriage Records, Book 6, p. 177. Secrecy is implied by the fact that Beulah was underage and eloped to Rockport. According to *OM* (February 12, 1915, p. 5), the marriage was a surprise to Beulah's and Perry's friends. Maintaining secrecy and the Rounds Bros. packet schedule required an early-morning departure from the farm.

13. Descriptions of the flood in this and the following paragraphs are based on reporting in the *OM* and the *OI*, January 31 through February 11, 1915.

14. *OM*, February 7, sec. 2, p. 1 (normal conditions return to Panther Creek neighborhoods); *OM*, February 11, p. 2 and February 12, p. 3 (stranded steamers).

15. Mary Neel as quoted in *OI*, April 6, 1924, p. 1.

16. Beulah's and Perry's marriage license, Spencer County, Indiana, Marriage Records, Book 6, p. 177; *OM*, February 12, 1915, p. 5; staff photo of the *Inquirer* printers circa 1915, showing Ray Hicks as well as Perry (p. 12); *OM*, February 12, 1915, p. 3 and February 11, p. 1.

17. *OM*, February 12, 1915, p. 3 (Ohio River "five miles wide"); *OM*, February 11, p. 1 (landings submerged); Blake and Edds, *Owensboro*, 9 (photo); Dew and Dew, *Owensboro*, 130 (photo).

18. Marriage license, Spencer County, Indiana, Marriage Records, Book 6, p. 177.

19. Marriage license, Spencer County, Indiana, Marriage Records, Book 6, p. 177 (signed by L. N. Varble, minister of the Christian Church of Rockport).

20. *OM*, February 12, 1915, p. 5 (the elopement surprised the couple's friends); deposition of W. L. Stephens (November 21, 1917), Perry Stephens vs. Beulah Stephens in Equity, No. 1157. In his deposition, William Stephens states that Perry and Beulah were married in February of 1915 and that he himself first met Beulah about two and a half years prior to November 1917, hence around June or July of 1915, which would have been several months after the elopement. Perry's father must have been speaking roughly.
21. Personal interviews with Beulah's cousins Mary Rafferty and Mildred Jenkins; Beulah's cousin Thelma Marksberry Thompson as quoted in Davis, "True Roots of 'Chicago' Story Lie with Two Kentucky Women," K1.
22. Personal interview with Ruth Stephens.
23. Owensboro 1918 city directory (Mary as factory worker); personal interview with Ruth Stephens; Perry Stephens vs. Beulah Stephens in Equity, No. 1157 (quotations from the deposition of Margaret Stephens). Perry, who had legal custody of P. W., stated in his divorce petition that he put the child in the care of his mother. This agrees with what Beulah's cousin Thelma Marksberry Thompson heard, as quoted in Davis, "True Roots of 'Chicago' Story Lie with Two Kentucky Women," K1.
24. Perry's ultimatum letter to Beulah, *CA*, April 4, 1924, p. 1. When asked by Perry's attorney whether Beulah was leading a "dissolute" life, Perry's father answered, "according to all reports" (Perry Stephens vs. Beulah Stephens in Equity, No. 1157). The word *dissolute* was often associated with wasting one's life through drinking and idle recreations. The expression *straight life* often meant having "purity" in one's habits such as abstaining from alcoholic beverages. See, for example, Hall, "Why a Boy Should Sign a Pledge," 77.
25. *OM*, January 8, 1916, p. 3; August 22, 1916, p. 4; July 16, 1918, p. 5; *OI*, July 29, 1918, p. 8; November 1, 1918, p. 3.
26. Beulah's 1923 diary, various entries. These are described at the end of the present chapter.
27. Perry letter to Beulah, *CA*, April 4, 1924, p. 1.
28. *OM*, November 25, 1917, p. 1 and November 26, 1917, p. 3.
29. *OM*, February 20, 1918, p. 6.
30. Beulah as quoted or paraphrased in *CHE*, April 7, 1924, p. 3; Mary as quoted in *CDJ*, April 5, 1924, p. 1.
31. Personal interview with Ruth Stephens; *OM*, May 25, 1924, p. 4; *CDT*, April 5, 1924, p. 1; Owen, "Woman Too Pretty to Hang," 6C; *OM*, Oct. 17, 1920, p. 13 (Perry living in Evansville) and May 13, 1924, p. 5 (Perry living in Chicago).
32. Perry Stephens (P. W.) as quoted in Owen, "Woman Too Pretty to Hang," 6C.
33. Personal interview with Ruth Stephens.

34. *OM*, May 12, 1918, p. 2; and May 13, 1918, p. 2.

35. Mrs. Mary Neel v. Green River Distilling Co.; Thelma Marksberry Thompson as quoted in Davis, "True Roots of 'Chicago' Story Lie with Two Kentucky Women," K1; Caron's Louisville city directory for 1919 (Mary took in sewing).

36. Caron's Louisville city directory; personal interview with Ruth Stephens (Mary once managed a boardinghouse); Beulah's relationship to car thief Jack Thorpe, as reported in the *Louisville Courier-Journal*, May 6, 1919, p. 4 and *OM*, May 3, 1919, p. 3; further reporting on Thorpe, his fellow car thieves, and their methods in the *Louisville Courier-Journal*, May 1, 1919, p. 11; May 3, 1919, p. 14; August 15, 1921, p. 12; August 16, 1921, p. 7.

37. *Louisville Courier-Journal*, May 6, 1919, p. 4; *OM*, May 3, 1919, p. 3.

38. Personal interview with Josephine Kolaya (Anice's daughter); Kentucky Marriage Certificate for Alfred Lee Bartlett and Anice Neel, March 13, 1920.

39. NEA story, published in *Tuscaloosa News and Times Gazette*, July 11, 1926, Society sec., p. 1; *CA*, April 5, 1924, p. 2; Albert Annan and Beulah Stephens, Cook County Marriage License No. 860858.

40. *CDJ*, April 4, 1924, p. 1 (Al's self-description). Beulah's 1923 diary reveals her affection for Al.

41. Klein, *Burden of Unemployment*, 225–27 (depressed employment conditions in Chicago, 1920–1922); *CEP*, April 5, 1924, p. 1; *CDJ*, April 5, 1924, p. 1; Beulah's 1923 diary.

42. *CDJ*, April 4, 1924, p. 1; Beulah's diary.

43. *CDJ*, April 5, 1924, p. 1; on the twin resort towns of St. Joseph and Benton Harbor as a destination for Chicagoans in the 1920s, see Hilton, *Lake Michigan Passenger Steamers*, 113, 125.

44. Personal interview with Mary Rafferty about how John Sheriff typically dressed.

45. Beulah's diary entry for August 21, 1923; *CDN*, May 24, p. 1 (had worked at Tennent's since August 1923).

46. Beulah's diary entries for September 30 and October 6–10, 1923.

47. *CDN*, May 24, p. 1. (the Annans moved into the flat at 817 East Forty-Sixth on December 1, 1923).

48. Beulah as quoted or paraphrased in *CHE*, April 7, 1924, p. 3.

2. A Shooting

1. Statement of Albert Annan (dated April 4, 1923) in MHK; *CA*, April 5, 1924, p. 2 (Al's place of employment); Sanborn map of southeast corner of Forty-Sixth and Cottage Grove Avenue; James D. Johnson et al., *Century of Chicago Street Cars*, 26.

2. *CEP*, April 5, 1924, p. 2; help-wanted ads for bookkeepers in *CDT*, August 1923 through April 1924; Al's statement in MHK.

3. *CA*, April 5, 1924, p. 2; *CHE*, April 5, 1924, p. 3.
4. Wilcox's inquest testimony in CIHK; Maybelle Bergman's trial testimony as quoted in *CDJ*, May 24, 1924, p. 1; Beulah in her after-midnight statement, p. 28 (using the name "Anna" when quoting Harry addressing her).
5. The affair is detailed in Beulah's after-midnight statement. She expressed guilt about the affair retrospectively (e.g., *CHE*, April 7, 1924, p. 3; *CA*, April 5, 1924, pp. 1–2).
6. Beulah's after-midnight statement, pp. 27, 28.
7. Beulah's after-midnight statement, p. 31; CIHK (William Wilcox's inquest testimony).
8. *CDN* photos of Beulah in custody, held by the Chicago History Museum; Beulah's diary entry for September 18, 1923.
9. Beulah's after-midnight statement, p. 25.
10. Regarding Beulah's attire, chapter 10, n. 3; *CDT*, April 5, 1924, p. 1 (the ring).
11. *CDT*, April 5, 1924, p. 1; MHK (police report mentioning unmade bed, which was also noted in the *Daily Calumet*, April 4, 1924, p. 1). Regarding the gun and its location, see chapters 2 and 5.
12. See chapter 1, n. 43 (the thefts in Michigan); officer Thomas Torpy's testimony about the gun (CIHK); serial number of the gun, implying that it was a used weapon (CIHK); Crowe's efforts to restrict licensing of handguns (*CDT*, August 30, 1923, p. 5; September 21, 1923, p. 3; October 23, 1923, p. 1); the *Tribune*'s anti-handgun crusade (*CDT*, February 11, 1924, p. 8).
13. Wilcox quoting Beulah (CIHK); *Fresno Morning Republican*, May 2, 1919, p. 4 (child getting hold of a gun under a pillow). The search phrase "gun under a pillow" turns up in at least twenty-two articles in newspapers from 1900 through 1924, according to a search of newspapers.com Additional examples resulted from a search with the expression "revolver under a pillow." The question regarding the gun's location just prior to the shooting is discussed in chapters 5 and 10.
14. The Sanborn map for 4228–30 Cottage Grove Avenue; photographs and information about steam laundries in Mohun, *Steam Laundries*; *CA*, May 24, 1924 (Betty Bergman's request for the key).
15. Beulah's after-midnight statement, p. 31.
16. AP story in *OM*, May 25, 1924, p. 4; *CDJ*, May 23, 1924, p. 4 (call from Billy was at "10:30 o'clock"); Beulah's after-midnight statement, pp. 26–27.
17. Beulah's after-midnight statement, p. 27.
18. Beulah's after-midnight statement, p. 26 (the rumor about Harry); evidence inventory of Homicide Bureau in MHK (house dress).
19. Harry Kalsted's biography as reconstructed from the following: federal census records; Kalsted's 1918 draft card; State of Minnesota (Isanti County) v. Harry

Kalsted, case no. 1877 (bastardy); State of Minnesota (Isanti County) v. Harry Kalsted, case no. 2208 (criminal); Lydia Kalsted v. Harry T. Kalsted, Isanti County, case no. 2217 (divorce); personal correspondence from Leo Wiley (criminal court supervisor, Fourth Judicial Circuit, State of Minnesota); testimony of William Wilcox in CIHK; Beulah's after-midnight statement.

20. Reconstruction based on sources listed in n. 19.
21. Court documents in n. 19; William Wilcox's testimony in CIHK and his typed statement in MHK; Beulah's after-midnight statement.
22. Beulah's after-midnight statement, p. 28; Officer Torpy's statement in MHK.
23. Beulah's after-midnight statement, pp. 26, 31.
24. Beulah's account in her after-midnight statement, pp. 27–28. Where the transcript gives a dash, I have inferred that Beulah used the word *whore* (in quoting Harry); the *Daily Journal* used the euphemism "inmate of a disorderly house" in reporting the police's account of Beulah's statement (*CDJ*, April 4, 1924, p. 1).
25. Autopsy report of coroner's physician Joseph Springer (attached to CIHK); Springer's testimony at Beulah's trial as paraphrased in an AP story ("death had been instantaneous"—*OM*, May 25, 1924, p. 4); Albert Annan's April 4 statement in MHK and his testimony in CIHK; officer Thomas Torpy's April 6 statement in MHK (Kalsted's hat and coat on unmade bed); the statement of Dr. Clifford Oliver regarding position of the body (p. 45); Officer Torpy's testimony regarding the position of the body (in CIHK); report of officers Michael Collins and James McLaughlin, mentioning Beulah's blood-stained clothing (in MHK); her "house dress" and "stockings" were collected as evidence (evidence inventory of Homicide Bureau in MHK).
26. Beulah's after-midnight statement, pp. 28–29; report of officers Collins and McLaughlin in MHK (mentioning that there was blood on Beulah's dress and stockings).
27. Report of officers Michael Collins and James McLaughlin in MHK (James McLaughlin not to be confused with the assistant state's attorney in the case, William McLaughlin); Malachi Murphy's testimony at the trial (as referenced in CA, May 24, 1924); testimony of William Wilcox in CIHK.
28. CIHK; April 4 statement of Albert Annan in MHK.
29. CA, April 5, 1924, p. 2.
30. Beulah's after-midnight statement, p. 28 (an idiomatically unlikely "you have" changed to a contraction). Details about the moment when she pulled the trigger are mentioned by William Wilcox in his description of what she had said *earlier*, at the flat, when she gave a different and mostly false account of the killing. Although that account was largely false, it appears to have included a distinct and accurate description of certain physical elements of the moment of the shooting—how she "closed her eyes and pulled the trigger, and she remembers of seeing a flash, and jerked the gun from the

front" (Wilcox in CIHK, p. 20). Since she saw the flash, she must have only partly closed her eyes.

31. Beulah's after-midnight statement, p. 29.
32. Beulah's after-midnight statement, p. 29; testimony of Springer, the coroner's physician (see n. 25). A comparison of passages on pages 29 and 30 of the after-midnight statement shows that Beulah's interrogator, Roy Woods, recognized that Beulah had "found he was dead," based on Kalsted's appearance and by checking his eyes, meaning that she correctly established that fact right away.
33. Beulah's after-midnight statement, pp. 29–30.
34. Bureau of Homicide evidence list in MHK and references to evidence introduced at the trial (CDN, May 23, 1924, p. 3; CA, May 24, 1924). The recording of "Hula Lou" was either the December 1923 version with Margaret Young (Youngblood) or the January 1924 version with Sophie Tucker.
35. Beulah's after-midnight statement, pp. 24, 30.
36. The reconstruction of Beulah's actions in this and the following paragraphs (about a failed plan to move the body) is based on inferences from the following facts: (1) that she was asked at the trial about whether she tried to get rid of the body (CA, May 24, 1924); (2) that she called the laundry around 4:10 p.m. to ask Betty Bergman where Harry was (CDJ, May 24, 1924, p. 1; AP story in OM, May 25, 1924, p. 4); (3) that by the time police arrived, the empty wine quart bottles had been put away in the kitchen (CIHK); (4) that when she finally called for help, she telephoned Al, not the police.
37. CA, May 24, 1924 and AP story in OM, May 25, 1924, p. 4.
38. See n. 36.
39. Al's April 4 statement in MHK.
40. Beulah's after-midnight statement, p. 24; Al's statement in MHK and his testimony in CIHK; the report of officers Collins and McLaughlin in MHK.
41. Beulah's account of what Al told her (after-midnight statement, p. 24; substantially the same in Al's statement in MHK); the police's account of what Beulah said on the phone (CDT, April 4, 1924, p. 1; cf. Daily Calumet, April 4, 1924, p. 1).

3. An Alleged Confession

1. Officer Torpy's April 3rd statement in MHK; Torpy's testimony in CIHK; report of officers Collins and McLaughlin in MHK.
2. Report of Collins and McLaughlin in MHK.
3. Report of Collins and McLaughlin. When Beulah changed her clothes, her attire was probably not a suit coat over a *night dress*, as Perry claims in *Girls of Murder City*, 91–92. The outfit appears in a photograph of Beulah in police custody (p. 40) and again in photos of her at the inquest (p. 84), at a meeting with her attorney (p. 98), and in Cook County Jail (p. 76).

4. Report of Collins and McLaughlin in MHK; Beulah's trial testimony (AP story in *OM*, May 25, 1924, p. 4; *CA*, May 24, 1924); Wilcox's testimony at trial (*CDN*, May 3, 1924, p. 3).
5. Report of Collins and McLaughlin in MHK; court reporter Elbert Allen as quoted in *CEP*, May 23, 1924, p. 1. The newspapers called the court reporter "Albert" Allen. His first name was in fact Elbert (G.J. no. 138, The People of the State of Illinois vs. Beulah Annan).
6. Beulah's trial testimony, as quoted in *CDT*, May 24, 1924, p. 1. The reporting in the *Daily News* is nearly identical (*CDN*, May 23, 1924, p. 3 and May 24, p. 1). For Wilcox's testimony, see *CDN*, May 23, 1924, p. 3.
7. Prosecution witness Wilcox, quoting Beulah and Woods's response, according to *CDT*, May 24, 1924, p. 1 (also *OM*, May 25, 1924, p. 4; *CA*, May 23, 1924, p. 1); police report in MHK; Woods, as quoted in CIHK.
8. The "kitchen" statement is quoted and paraphrased in the following: *CEP*, May 23, 1924, p. 1 and in an AP story in *OM*, May 25, 1924, p. 4. At the time of the inquest, the kitchen statement had not yet been transcribed from the shorthand version. It was later used at Beulah's trial and read into the trial transcript, but neither the trial transcript nor the original document has survived in county records. Attorneys kept personal copies of trial transcripts, but in 1963, when Al Friendly approached Beulah's attorney William Scott Stewart about getting a copy, Stewart could not find it (letter of Al Friendly to Lester Bernstein, April 9 [1963], in the Bob Fosse/Gwen Verdon collection at the Library of Congress).
9. *CEP*, April 4, 1924, p. 1; Springer's autopsy report (attached to CIHK) about the path of the bullet.
10. Wilcox as quoted in *CDJ*, May 23, 1924, p. 4 (poorly preserved microfilm wording completed based on obvious meaning); *OM*, May 25, 1924, p. 4 ("true account"). The after-midnight statement is wholly extant in two copies, one in CIHK and the other in MHK.
11. Roy C. Woods's passport application (May 29, 1923); the federal census enumerations for Woods in 1880, 1900, and 1920; Woods's World War I draft card.
12. Kenneth Roberts's 1922–1923 diary for July 16–20 and November 15, 1923; his 1926 diary entry for February 1, 1926 (Special Collections, Rauner Library, Dartmouth College); Roberts, *I Wanted to Write*, 156–60; Richards, *Rescue of the Romanovs*, 185–86; Woods as quoted in Dean, "Valley Lawyer Takes Secret of Romanovs' Fate to the Grave," 1, 11.
13. Roy C. Woods's 1923 passport application (May 29, 1923); the sources in n. 12.
14. Roberts, *I Wanted to Write*, 158 and 160.
15. The authoritative account is Massie, *Romanovs*.
16. Roberts, *I Wanted to Write*, 159.

17. In what follows, unless otherwise indicated, all the descriptions of the interrogation and the quotations are taken from Beulah's after-midnight statement.
18. Beulah, as quoted in *CDN*, April 4, 1924, p. 1. On the general reliability of this *CDN* story, see chapter 4.
19. *CDN*, April 4, 1924, p. 1. This edition of the *Daily News* was published in the afternoon. It is uncertain whether Beulah saw a morning paper or only heard from her jailers what the prosecutors were saying about her.

4. Police and Prosecutors Shape the Narrative

1. See Dornfeld, *Behind the Front Page*, 9, 13, 98.
2. Joseph Springer's dated report attached to CIHK; Officer Torpy's April 3rd statement in MHK; Clifford Oliver's handwritten note in MHK (p. 45); Matthew 14:1–12 (story of Salome's dance); *CDT*, April 4, 1924, p. 1; *CDN*, April 4, 1924, p. 1.
3. The accounts in the *Daily News* and *Herald and Examiner* are described below.
4. *CEP*, April 4, 1924, p. 1; *CDJ*, April 4, 1924, p. 1; *CA*, April 4, 1924, p. 1. On "rewrite men," see Terrett, "Taking It off the Phone," n.p.
5. *CDN*, April 4, 1924, p. 1; "Chicago Police Stations," 83–84.
6. *CHE*, April 5, 1924, p. 1.
7. *CDN*, April 4, 1924, p. 1. On the press's routine presentation of paraphrase as quotation, see chapter 6.
8. *CHE*, April 5, 1924, p. 1; the *Journal, Post,* and *American* as cited in n. 4.
9. *CDT*, May 14, 1926, p. 1 and case no. 8388 in the Chicago police logs (Kowalkowski); *CDT*, April 6, 1924, p. 4 (Beulah to Maurine Watkins). A search of newspapers.com reveals quite a few instances in the 1920s and 1930s where someone was quoted as saying, "I'm glad I did it," in admitting to a homicide. Usually, police are the source of the quotation.
10. Book summary in *Outlook* [British] 20 (November 16, 1907): 651; *CDT*, May 9, 1924, p. 6 (Unkafer corrected to Uncapher); Watkins, *Chicago*, 17.
11. *CDT*, April 5, 1924, p. 1.

5. Inquest into the Death of Harry Kalsted

1. April 3rd statement of officer Thomas Torpy in MHK. Unless otherwise indicated, all descriptions of the inquest's official proceedings, including its reports and testimony, are from CIHK and MHK.
2. *CDT*, April 5, 1924, p. 1.
3. See chapter 3, n. 8 regarding the kitchen statement.

6. Finding Beulah behind the Press's Tropes and Paraquotations

1. Preble and Miller, "Medical and Health Conditions in the Cook County Jail," 94, 97.

2. *CA*, April 5, 1924, p. 1 (cell number); Rich, "Detention of the Woman Offender,"112; image on p. 58.
3. Rich, "Detention of the Woman Offender," 112–14, 123; image on p. 59; *CA*, April 5, 1924, p. 2 (mentioning the radio).
4. *CA*, April 4, 1924, p. 1.
5. Hearst (in his *New York Daily Mirror*) as quoted in Bessie, *Jazz Journalism*, 139; Murray, *Madhouse on Madison Street*, 72, 35. For an informative description of tabloid sensationalism in the 1920s, see Tucher, *Not Exactly Lying*, 150–57.
6. Murray, *Madhouse on Madison Street*, 57–58, 309; cf. "Animated Journalism," 13477.
7. *CHE*, April 7, 1924, p. 3.
8. *City Club Bulletin* (Chicago), March 7, 1921, p. 44; Ross, "Suppression of Important News," 303; Yarros, "Journalism, Ethics, and Common Sense," 411. See further Marzolf, *Civilizing Voices*, 25–31, 34–40, 76–78, and passim.
9. *CEP*, April 4, 1924, p. 1; *CDN*, April 4, 1924, p. 1; *CDT*, April 4, 1024, p. 1.
10. *CA*, April 4, 1924, p. 1.
11. On the complex musical and cultural relationships between white and Black jazz in Chicago in the 1920s, see William Kenney's classic study, *Chicago Jazz*.
12. *Sullivan's Englewood Times*, March 23, 1923, p. 5 and February 16, 1923, p. 8.
13. *Salina (KS) Evening Journal*, August 17, 1921, p. 4 (emphasis added); *Muncie (IN) Evening Press*, May 14, 1920, p. 4 (just one of many associations of "jazz life" with speed, the hectic modern pace, etc.).
14. *Eagle* (Bryan, TX), June 16, 1920, p. 5; *South Bend (IN) News-Times*, April 1, 1922, p. 6; *Brooklyn Standard Union*, July 20, 1922, p. 2; Maurine Watkins, *CDT*, June 1, 1924, p. 5; Watkins, *Chicago*, 69 (emphasis added).
15. UP story in, for example, *Cincinnati Post*, April 4, 1924, p. 1.
16. On "rewrite men," see Terrett, "Taking It off the Phone," n.p.; on the origin of the interview, a distinctly American custom invented in the 1830s, see Tucher, *Not Exactly Lying*, 55.
17. Arthur, "Reporting, Practical and Theoretical," 37; Shuman, *Steps into Journalism*, 70, 71. I owe these two examples to Tucher, *Not Exactly Lying*, 61, 59.
18. Hyde, *Newspaper Reporting and Correspondence*, 256.
19. Fishkin, *From Fact to Fiction*, 138 (quoting the style sheet of the *Kansas City Star*); Sandwick, *Junior High School English*, 128 (when to use quotation marks); William Rockhill Nelson as quoted (or perhaps paraphrased) in Bleyer, *Main Currents in the History of American Journalism*, 316. On commitment to facts in early-twentieth-century journalism, including period debates about objectivity, interpretation, and point of view, see Ward, *Invention of Journalism Ethics*, 236–58.

20. Olin, *Journalism*, 17; Bleyer, *Newspaper Writing and Editing*, 46; "Newspaper Accuracy," *New Outlook* 95 (1910): 606 (606–7); Maurine Watkins, "Charles A. Bickford Makes a Hit with Maurine Watkins," *New York Herald Tribune*, January 16, 1927, E5.
21. CDN, April 4, 1924, p. 1.
22. CEP, April 4, 1924, p. 1.
23. CA, April 5, 1924, pp. 1–2.
24. CA, April 5, 1924, p. 2.
25. Sonia Lee, CA, April 5, 1924, pp. 1, 2 (Sabelle corrected to Sabella). The various characterizations of Beulah's good looks can be found in *CEP*, April 4, 1924, p. 1; *CDJ*, April 5, 1924, p. 1 (in heading); *CHE*, April 6, 1924, p. 1 (headline); *CDN*, April 4, 1924, p. 1, May 23, p. 3 and May 24, 1924, p. 1; *CDT*, April 5, 1924, p. 1 (headline) and May 23, 1924, p. 6; *OM*, April 6, p. 1 (heading) and May 24, 1924, p. 1.
26. Ethnic labeling in articles by Genevieve Forbes and Maurine Watkins: CDT, July 10, 1923, p. 1 and July 12, 1923, p. 3 (Nitti); *CDT*, April 1, 1923, p. 6 (Klimek); June 7, 1924, p. 10 (Foster and Epps).
27. UP story from Chicago published in various papers, including *Indianapolis Times*, July 10, 1923, p. 2; Lee, CA, April 5, 1924, p. 2; Forbes, CDT, July 10, 1923, p. 1.
28. CDN, April 5, 1924, p. 3. The article mentions that Beulah's reflections took place after "a prison breakfast."
29. CEP, April 5, 1924, p. 1 (Quinby, describing an interview that took place "today" but rehearsing, at one point, what Beulah had said "in the county jail last night," whether that was based on Quinby's own interview or another source); *CEP*, April 4, 1924, p. 1 (the *Post's* initial reporting). None of the *Post* stories about Beulah are signed, but the jacket for Quinby's *Murder for Love* (1931) says that when Quinby worked for the *Post*, she covered all women accused of murder.
30. CEP, April 5, 1924, p. 1; *CDJ*, April 5, 1924, p. 1.
31. Approximations, based on census data for 1920 in table 1 of DeVault, "'Everybody Works but Father,'" 372. See also Goldin, "Marriage Bars," 511–36.
32. Advice columnist as quoted in Deutsch, "From Ballots to Breadlines," 425.
33. Goodsell, *Problems of the Family*, 153.
34. CHE, April 5, 1924, p. 1 (the paper's words, paraphrasing Al).
35. On companionate marriage, see Simmons, *Making Marriage Modern*, 121–34.
36. Zeitz, *Flapper*, 5–10 (summarizing ways in which "the flapper" represented ideas of the New Woman and was also a consumerist fad); Faderman, *Woman*, 198–223 (on the New Woman), 229–35 (on "working girls"); pp. 40, 76, 84, and 98 (the fawn-colored suit dress); Thelma Marksberry Thompson (born

January 6, 1912) as quoted in Bartholomy "Even without 'Chicago,' Roxie Remains in Relatives' Hearts," 1C, 3C; *CDT*, April 5, 1924, p. 1 ("the prettiest woman").

37. *CEP*, April 5, 1924, p. 1 (Kostedt corrected to Kalsted).

38. *CDJ*, April 5, 1924, p. 1.

39. *CDJ*, April 5, 1924, p. 1.

40. *CDJ*, April 5, 1924, p. 1.

41. *CHE*, April 6, 1924, p. 1. At her trial, Beulah claimed that Kalsted tried to rape her. This idea was probably planted in her head by O'Brien. The claim appeared nowhere in her Saturday interviews, which stood much closer to the account in her after-midnight statement.

7. Maurine Watkins's News with Wit

1. Details about Watkins's childhood and education can be found in "The Author of 'Chicago,'" *New York Times*, January 2, 1927, X1; Mary Bostwick, *Indianapolis Star*, January 6, 1928, pp. 1–2; Lillian Genn, *Baltimore Evening Sun*, August 8, 1928, p. 16; "Chicago: Transy Student Started It All," 15. A short biography of Maurine Watkins is given in Rumore and Mather, *He Had It Coming*, 180–217.

2. 1923 letter (undated) from Watkins to Baker, regarding her efforts with Dietrichstein, as quoted in Rumore and Mather, *He Had It Coming*, 191.

3. *Brooklyn Daily Eagle*, March 24, 1912, sec. 4, p. 4 (Baker's advice); "The Author of 'Chicago,'" *New York Times*, January 2, 1927, X1; *Indianapolis Star*, March 11, 1928, p. 32; Watkins as quoted in Merrill, "Pistol Fire Lights Up 'Chicago,'" M1.

4. "The Author of 'Chicago,'" *New York Times*, January 2, 1927, X1; *Baltimore Evening Sun*, August 8, 1928, p. 16. The *Chicago Tribune*'s March (1924) articles about Belva Gaertner are unsigned, but their *style*, together with their subject-matter association with Watkins's play *Chicago*, makes it almost certain that Watkins authored them. This is also the judgment of Pauly, *Chicago by Maurine Watkins*, xiii, 115–22.

5. Watkins as quoted in Merrill, "Pistol Fire Lights Up 'Chicago,'" M1; Lutes, *Front-Page Girls*, 65–93; *Spectator* 90 (1903): 21 (an early use of the expression "sob sister").

6. On debates about the new "objective" style and whether it lacked sufficient point of view and interpretation, which is what the muckrakers argued, see Ward, *Invention of Journalism Ethics*, 254–55. Generally speaking, the muckrakers were highly committed to factual accuracy, but they also claimed that a neutral style, together with an absence of interpretation, could be misleading. Their genre, however, was typically the magazine article, not "straight news."

7. See Forbes's articles in *CDT*, March 7, 1923, p. 3; March 10, 1923, p. 3; March 14, p. 1; June 8, 1923, p. 7; June 13, 1923, p. 2; June 17, 1923, p. 2; *CDT*, February 19, 1924, p. 7.

8. See Kaszuba, "'Mob Sisters,'" (the quoted words are from the abstract). Kaszuba does not happen to mention the earliest examples of the style in Forbes's 1923 coverage of homicide trials. Nor does she include the rare crime reporting of *Tribune* reporter Maude Martin Evers. For an Evers crime story, see *CDT*, February 12, 1919, p. 11.

9. *CDT*, March 12, 1924, pp. 1–2. On the authorship of this *Tribune* story, see n. 4.

10. *CDN*, March 12, 1924, p. 1; Merrill, "Pistol Fire Lights Up 'Chicago,'" M1.

11. *CDT*, April 4, 1924, p. 1. When Watkins characterized her crime reporting in Chicago, she listed "murder trials, inquests, the county jail and things like that" but not night shifts at police stations (*Indianapolis Star*, January 8, 1928, p. 1).

12. *CDT*, April 5, 1924, p. 1.

13. *CDT*, April 5, 1924, p. 1 (Watkins's account of O'Brien's questioning of Wilcox at the inquest); CIHK (the transcript of O'Brien's questioning); Beulah's after-midnight statement, p. 28.

14. *CDT*, April 5, 1924, p. 1.

15. *CDT*, March 10, 1923, p. 3; June 13, 1923, p. 2; June 17, 1923, p. 2.

16. *CDJ*, April 5, 1924, p. 1.

17. *CDT*, April 6, 1924, p. 4.

18. *CDT*, April 6, 1924, p. 4 (with correction of "here" to "her").

19. *CDT*, April 6, 1924, p. 4.

20. *CDT*, April 6, 1924, p. 6.

21. *CDT*, April 7, 1924, p. 14.

8. Back in Owensboro

1. *OI*, April 9, 1924, p. 1 (reporting about Mary's trip, based on information obtained from "L. Allard," who is described as "a friend").

2. *Scranton Times*, April 4, 1924, p. 28; *Sapulpa (OK) Herald*, April 4, 1924, p. 1; *Buffalo Evening Times*, April 4, 1924, p. 1; *OM*, April 5, 1924, p. 1.

3. LeMaster, "Beulah Sheriff," 2; *OM*, May 13, 1924, p. 5 (Perry's marriage and residence). Perry appears in the Chicago city directories for 1924/25 and 1925/26; he is absent from the Owensboro directory for 1922–1923 (none survive for adjacent years). He returned to Owensboro in the late 1920s.

4. Owen, "Woman Too Pretty to Hang," 6C; personal interview with Ruth Stephens.

5. In Watkins's play *Chicago*, Billy Flynn demands a fee of $5,000 (Watkins, *Chicago*, 27, 40).

6. *OI*, April 9, 1924, p. 1; article by Allard in an "Owensboro special" to the *Buffalo Times*, May 1, 1924, p. 3; article by Allard in *CHE*, April 20, 1924, p. 4. The *Buffalo Times* article is unsigned, but since the author writes "as we drove away," it can only have been Allard. Its contents are closely related to the signed Allard article in *CHE*.
7. *Buffalo Times*, May 1, 1924, p. 3; also Allard's shorter account of this conversation in *CHE*, April 20, 1924, p. 4. On the meaning of the word *folly*, see Grundy, "Polite Society," 609.
8. *CHE*, April 6, 1924, p. 1 and *CDJ*, April 5, 1924, p. 1 (reports that Beulah's father was a wealthy farmer). According to Bobby Sherriff, John Sheriff's nephew, John was "land-rich" but not otherwise wealthy.
9. Leola Allard, "Beulah Melts Father's Heart," *CHE*, April 20, 1924, p. 4.

9. Popular Opinions about Jury Bias in Favor of Women

1. *CDT*, May 9, 1924, p. 6 and *CDT*, May 8, 1924, p. 1. On the trope, see chapter 4.
2. The Illinois Supreme Court reversed the decision in the Nitti case and remanded it for retrial (*CDT*, April 24, 1924, p. 10). According to "Homicide in Chicago 1870–1930," a database hosted by Northwestern University containing transcriptions of the Chicago police's homicide logs (https://homicide.northwestern.edu/), Epps and Foster were "colored." The database does not give the race of Nichols, but the shooting took place at the home of the victim, an African American woman living in a predominantly Black neighborhood, and Watkins mentions that Nichols was "colored" (*CDT*, June 7, 1924, p. 10). On white newspaper coverage of African Americans in this period, see Gist, "Negro in the Daily Press," 405–11. Gist notes that in a randomly selected sixty-day period, sometime between 1920 and 1932, the *Chicago Tribune* devoted almost four times the space to "anti-social" activities by African Americans than anti-social activities by white people.
3. *CA*, April 18, 1924, pp. 1–2; *CHE*, April 18, 1924, p. 4; Cheatwood, "Capital Punishment for the Crime of Homicide in Chicago: 1870–1930," 857–58.
4. *CHE*, April 18, 1924, p. 4 (sound of hammers).
5. *CDT*, May 9, 1924, p. 6 (Beulah's pregnancy); *CDJ*, April 4, 1924, p. 1 and *CHE*, April 6, 1924, p. 1 (prosecutors' intention to seek the death penalty in Beulah's case).
6. INS story in the Mattoon, Illinois, *Daily Journal-Gazette*, February 21, 1924, p. 1 (Malm jury); *CDT*, July 10, 1923, pp. 1–2; Lucchesi, *Ugly Prey*, 35 (Nitti's youngest children).
7. "Women Executed in the US: 1900–2021" (based on the "Epsy File" made available through the Inter-University Consortium for Political and Social Research). On the limitations of the report and transcription, see Blackman

and McLaughlin, "Epsy File on American Executions." The database lists five executions of women for the period 1900–1924. Two were white women in their twenties, and three were African American women of various ages. In view of the limitations of the database, I infer that the totals were probably "fewer than ten."

8. *CDT*, May 9, 1924, p. 6; Watkins, *Chicago*, 13.
9. *CDT*, June 25, 1921, p. 2 (quoting Heth); June 24, 1923, A, pt. 1, p. 5 (quoting Jonas); Nitti's attorney as quoted by Forbes, *CDT*, July 11, 1923, p. 1.
10. Gunnell and Ceci, "When Emotionality Trumps Reason," 852; Devine, *Jury Decision Making*, 95.
11. Genevieve Forbes Herrick, "Lady Murderesses: The Orthwein Case," *CDT*, February 6, 1927, S10.
12. Lloyd Heth in *CDT*, June 24, 1921, p. 3; state's attorney as quoted in UP story from Chicago in the *Daily Telegram* (Long Beach, CA), June 25, 1921, p. 1; "Can a Beauty Be Convicted?" (INS story) in the *Dayton (OH) Herald*, July 16, 1923, p. 2; Forbes describing Orthwein in *CDT*, February 6, 1927, S10; an article about Bernice Zalimas in *CDT*, May 10, 1925, p. 1.
13. Forbes, *CDT*, November 29, 1923, p. 2; Watkins, *CDT*, May 9, p. 6.
14. Sabella Nitti's story is told in Lucchesi, *Ugly Prey*.
15. *CDT*, July 7, 1923, p. 2 and July 10, pp. 1–2 (verdict); Lucchesi, *Ugly Prey*, 81–86, 93–95, 97–99, 169–73.
16. *CDT*, July 11, 1923, p. 1 (quoting jury foreman's wife and Stone); July 16, 1923, p. 8 (the quoted citizen's opinion, together with other letters, for and against the verdict, in Voice of the People, a selection of letters to the editor).
17. *CDT*, July 12, 1923, p. 3 (Forbes quoting letter of Nitti's jail mates who defended Nitti against Forbes's characterizations of her).
18. Lucchesi, *Ugly Prey*, 215–17, 285–86, 78.
19. Watkins in *CDT*, June 7, 1924, p. 10; Lucchesi, *Ugly Prey*, 61–65, 203–17, 257–58, 261–62, 279–82, 286.

10. Beulah Annan Goes to Trial

1. In June 1925, a year after defending Beulah, Stewart and O'Brien's win-to-loss ratio was said to be 28:0 (McConnell, *Fatal Fortune*, 62).
2. Stewart, *Stewart on Trial Strategy*, 7. On over-prosecution of women by state's attorney Robert Crowe in 1924, see chapter 13.
3. *CHE*, May 23, p. 1; *CDJ*, May 23, 1924, p. 4.
4. *CDT* May 23, 1924, p. 6 (fresh marcel, curls). Photographs and references to Beulah's attire during the period from her arrest through the close of her trial permit a reconstruction of her wardrobe: *CDT*, April 5, 1924, p. 1; May 23, 1924, p. 6; a photograph in *CDN*, May 23, 1924, p. 4; *Tribune* photograph published in Rumore and Mather, *He Had It Coming*, 8; photo and

description in *CDJ*, April 4, 1924, p. 1; *CEA*, April 21, 1924, p. 2; *CDT*, April 22, 1924, back page; a description of the dresses that Al brought to the jail, in *CDT*, April 7, 1924, p. 14. Images on pp. 40, 76, 84, and 98.

5. *CDT*, May 23, 1924, p. 6; *CHE*, May 23, 1924, p. 1; *CDJ*, May 23, 1924, p. 4.

6. *CDT*, June 8, 1923, p. 7.

7. *CDT*, June 4, 1924, p. 4 (Gaertner jury selection); *CHE*, May 23, 1924, p. 1 (Annan jury selection). The expression "beauty proof jury" is used of Beulah's jury in *CEP*, May 23, 1923, p. 1; *OM*, May 24, 1924, p. 1 and May 25, p. 1; Watkins in *CDT*, May 25, 1924, p. 1.

8. *CDT*, May 24, 1924, p. 1.

9. *CA*, May 23, 1924, p. 1; *CDN*, May 23, 1924, p. 3; *CDT*, May 24, 1924, p. 1; *CEP*, May 23, 1924, p. 1.

10. *CDN*, May 23, 1924, p. 3; *CEP*, May 23, 1924, p. 1; cf. Stewart's closing argument as summarized in *CDJ*, May 24, 1924, p. 1.

11. Regarding Kalsted spotting the gun on the bed, see the description of Beulah's trial testimony below. In view of Beulah's after-midnight statement, it is almost certain that Kalsted did not try to rape her. That she interpreted his reach for the gun as threatening is plausible, although impossible to prove.

12. AP story in *OM*, May 25, 1924, p. 4 (testimony of Springer, Wilcox, and Allen); *CDT*, May 24, 1924, p. 1 (testimony of Wilcox and Woods); *CA*, May 24, 1924 (reference to what Murphy testified).

13. *CDJ*, May 24, 1924, p. 1; cf. *CA*, May 24, 1924 (substantially the same).

14. Reconstruction of Beulah's trial testimony based on the transcription in *CDJ*, May 24, 1924, p. 1 and *CA*, May 24, 1924.

15. Reconstruction based on the trial transcriptions in *CDJ*, May 24, 1924, p. 1; *CA*, May 24, 1924; and a UP article in Chicago's *Daily Calumet*, May 1924, p. 1.

16. See chapters 2 and 5 for discussions about the location of the gun.

17. *CA*, May 24, 1924.

18. *CA*, May 24, 1924.

19. *CA*, May 24, 1924.

20. *CDT*, May 25, 1924, p. 1.

21. *CDJ*, May 26, 1924, p. 8.

22. *CDT*, May 25, 1924, p. 5 (photo caption identifying Harry Dunham as the jury foreman; further particulars about him in the 1923 city directory and the *Economist*, April 1, 1922, p. 743).

23. Two papers reported the bare facts of jury ballot-taking with a small disagreement about the number of ballots: *CDT*, May 25, 1924, p. 1 (two hours of deliberation, three ballots); AP story in *OM*, May 25, 1924, p. 1 (hour and a half of deliberation, four ballots).

24. *CDJ*, May 26, 1923, p. 8; *CDT*, May 25, 1924, p. 1.

25. The quoted definition of reasonable doubt (emphasis added) was affirmed by the Illinois Supreme Court in 1866 in Miller v. People, 39 Ill. 457 and reaffirmed in subsequent opinions over the next sixty years in May v. People, 60 Ill. 119; Connaghen v. People, 88 Ill. 460; Dunn v. People, 109 Ill. 635; Little v. People, 157 Ill., 158; and the 1930 case People v. Lenhardt, 340 Ill., 538.

11. Watkins's Tendentious Reporting on the Annan Trial

1. Maurine Watkins as quoted in Merrill, "Pistol Fire Lights Up 'Chicago,'" M1.
2. CDT, May 23, 1924, p. 6; May 24, 1924, p. 1.
3. CDT, May 25, 1924, p. 1.
4. CA, May 24, 1924; CHE, May 25, 1924, p. 1.
5. Washington Post, April 15, 1907, p. 4 and Lexington Herald, February 11, 1907, p. 4 (Nesbit's "histrionic ability"); Philadelphia Inquirer, January 6, 1909, p. 1 (Catharine Beisel); New York Sun, June 7, 1914, p. 10 (Mellen); CDT, March 14, 1922, p. 1 (prosecutor's question to Obenchain); CDT, March 10, 1922, p. 1 (Trib correspondent Doherty's description of Obenchain).
6. People v. Munday (1917), 280 Ill. 32, 67; CDN, May 24, 1924, p. 1 (misprinted "I" corrected to "they," and a few words guessed at, the obvious choices, where the microfilm has gaps or is hard to read).
7. CDN, May 24, 1924, p. 1; Watkins, CDT, May 25, 1924, p. 1 (emphasis added).
8. CDT, May 25, 1924, p. 1.
9. CDT, June 5, 1924, p. 12; CDT, June 6, 1924, p. 1.
10. Ogden, "Ex-reporter, Now Playwright, Tells of High Spots in Career."
11. Jake the reporter in Watkins, Chicago, 15; Watkins as quoted in Merrill, "Pistol Fire Lights Up 'Chicago,'" M1, M7 (similar remarks quoted by Ogden, "Ex-reporter, Now Playwright, Tells of High Spots in Career"); Watkins responding to Archer in the New York American (undated clipping in Watkins/Chicago collection, New York Public Library of the Performing Arts); Watkins quoting and responding to Archer in the Hartford Courant, December 30, 1926, p. 20.
12. Merrill, "Pistol Fire Lights Up 'Chicago,'" M1; CDT, March 13, 1924, p. 1.
13. On the muckrakers' devotion to factual accuracy, see Ward, Invention of Journalism Ethics, 254–5; Filler, Muckrakers, xix, 5, 86, and passim. On Ida Tarbell, see the introduction to Kochersberger, More Than a Muckraker, xix–l.

12. A Play Is Born

1. CDT, June 11, 1924, p. 6; June 12, 1924, p. 9; July 9, 1924, p. 15; July 12, 1924, p. 4; August 7, 1924, p. 2; Watkins as quoted in Baltimore Evening Sun,

August 8, 1928, p. 16 ("had my fill"); Watkins as quoted in Ogden, "Ex-reporter, Now Playwright, Tells of High Spots in Career" ("murder-story complex"). Watkins's string of film reviews at the *Tribune* appeared in *CDT* from July 15 through August 4, 1924. She worked about eight months for the *Tribune*, circa February to September (*Indianapolis Star*, January 6, 1928, p. 1).

2. *New York Herald Tribune*, January 2, 1927, E7.
3. Rumore and Mather, *He Had It Coming*, 193–94; "The Author of 'Chicago,'" *New York Times*, January 2, 1927, X1.
4. Baker letter to a reporter, dated February 22, 1929 (George Pierce Baker Papers, Houghton Library, Harvard University), as quoted in Rumore and Mather, *He Had It Coming*, 194; Maurine Watkins as quoted by Joseph Mulvaney, US story, *El Paso Times*, January 9, 1927, p. 14; Watkins, as quoted in the *Indianapolis Star*, January 6, 1928, p. 1; Belva Gaertner as quoted in Pauly, *Chicago by Maurine Watkins*, xxvi, citing *CHE*, September 19, 1927 (clipping, New York Public Library); Forbes Herrick in *CDT*, October 16, 1927, pt. 7, p. 1 (letter printed in Frederick Donaghey's column). On the inspiration for the *name* "Roxie Hart," see Griffin Winfrey, "Maurine Watkins Makes Satire Out of Murder."
5. My deductions based on close comparisons of the play's characters with the reporting about the various real-life defendants. See also n. 6.
6. Genevieve Forbes provided a key to each character's connection to a real person (*CDT*, October 16, 1927, pt. 7, p. 1). Forbes was correct that Moonshine Maggie resembled Sabella Nitti. But Maggie's *case* was based on the conviction of "Moonshine Mary" Wazeniak (*CDT*, April 6, 1924, A1, p. 3), and Watkins had originally given Maggie the name Mary. Wazeniak ran a saloon in Brookfield, Illinois, where a patron drank some bad "hootch" and died shortly thereafter. Roxie complains about "the *Ledger* woman" after reading a newspaper article that mentions Roxie's nose-powdering in a tone that resembles Watkins's April 5 (1924) article about Beulah (Watkins, *Chicago*, 28–29).
7. Watkins, *Chicago*, 4–5.
8. C. C. Nicolet, *Yonker's (NY) Herald*, September 17, 1927, p. 4. See the similar observations about the plot structure in Mordden, *All That Jazz*, 45, 49.
9. Freeman, *Singing Bone Detective Stories* (1911).
10. Watkins, *Chicago*, 12.
11. Watkins, *Chicago*, 25–26 (Roxie's admission), 66 (Kitty's admission), 62–63 (Maggie's guilt), 33 (Liz's speech).
12. Watkins, *Chicago*, 26, 41–42.
13. Maurine Watkins, "Charles A. Bickford Makes a Hit with Maurine Watkins," *New York Herald Tribune*, January 16, 1927, E5.
14. Watkins, *Chicago*, 8.

15. Watkins, *Chicago*, 15 ("nice, juicy murder," free publicity), 13 (odds of acquittal), 18 ("you gotta play ball").
16. Percy Hammond in the *New York Herald Tribune*, January 9, 1927, E1; *CDT*, September 12, 1927, p. 31; Watkins, *Chicago*, 14, 29, 41; Watkins, "Chicago," *New York World*, January 16, 1927, M2 (describing the role of the press in her play).
17. Watkins, *Chicago*, 42, 109–11.
18. Watkins, *Chicago*, 13 (Jake's statistic), 30–31, compared to Yale manuscript "Chicago," p. 1-12.
19. Watkins, *Chicago*, 31 (Lucia convicted but granted a new trial), 56 (Liz's conviction and the matron's explanation), 56, 63 (implying that Maggie has been convicted, although p. 61 has her awaiting trial); 30–31 (Lucia as Velma's servant), 61–63 (the Maggie scene); Robert Coleman, *New York Daily Mirror*, January 1, 1927 (Maurine Watkins/Chicago: clippings 1920–1935, New York Public Library of the Performing Arts) (criticizing the Maggie scene); see also Lutes, "Tears on Trial in the 1920s," 355–56 (discussing Watkins's treatment of Maggie in the play); Yale manuscript "Chicago," 3–16.
20. Watkins, *Chicago*, 37 (cf. the reference to a restaurant dinner at p. 40).
21. Watkins, *Chicago*, 14, 64, 56. On a woman's whiteness being as influential as her gender in diminishing her chances of conviction in the 1920s, see chapter 13.
22. Watkins, *Chicago*, 82, 87, 88–89.
23. Watkins, *Chicago*, 16 (Harrison) and 104 (Flynn).
24. "Flynn" in Watkins, *Chicago*, 74; amended title page (p. 130); date and title in the play's copyright registration (p. 123); Watkins, letter to the dramatic editor, *New York World*, January 16, 1927, p. M2.
25. Images on pp. 123 and 126; *Webster's New International Dictionary of the English Language*, vol. 2, 1882. The traditional definition of satire is still common. Nevertheless, many students of satire reasonably prefer a wider definition. See Greenberg, *Cambridge Introduction to Satire*, 11–26.
26. Summary of *What the Public Wants* in *St. Louis Post-Dispatch*, May 2, 1922, p. 15.
27. Watkins as quoted in Joseph Mulvaney, US story, *El Paso Times*, January 9, 1927, p. 14.
28. *Baltimore Sun*, January 17, 1928, p. 11.
29. John Daly, "'Chicago' Comes to Town," *Washington Post*, January 23, 1928, p. 16; J. Brooks Atkinson in the *New York Times*, December 31, 1926, p. 11; *Boston Daily Globe*, April 10, 1928, p. 10.
30. Rupert Hughes, *San Francisco Examiner*, April 10, 1927, K6; Marquis Busby in the *Los Angeles Times*, March 20, 1927, C25.
31. Frank Vreeland, *New York Telegram*, December 31, 1926, p. 6.

32. George Baker letter to the Theatre Guild, as quoted in Kinne, *George Pierce Baker and the American Theatre*, 267.

33. Baker to Watkins, January 3, 1927, in Kinne, *George Pierce Baker and the American Theatre*, 267.

34. Watkins, "Chicago" (a letter to the dramatic editor), *New York World*, January 16, 1927, M2 ("conditions," "pass for realism"); Watkins as quoted in Joseph Mulvaney, US story, *El Paso Times*, January 9, 1927, p. 14 (Sam Harris, "real, all through," "all straight"); Watkins as quoted in Mantle, *American Playwrights of Today*, 204 ("an honest attempt").

35. *Asbury Park (NJ) Evening Press*, August 7, 1928, p. 3 (drama); Brooks Atkinson, *New York Times*, August 26, 1928, p. 95; Burns Mantle, *Minneapolis Journal*, August 26, 1928, amusement sec., p. 1; *CDT*, December 8, 1928, p. 27 (a melodrama "overlaid with a satire"); Fanny Butcher, *CDT*, November 25, 1928, pt. 7, p. 5; Frederick Donaghey (F. D.), *CDT*, November 26, 1928, p. 35; Michael Blakemore as quoted in Barry Norman, "Michael Blakemore," *Times* (London), June 17, 1972, p. 11 (as cited in Hilton, *Front Page*, 28 n. 63).

36. Rupert Hughes, *Arizona Republic*, March 17, 1927, sec. 6, p. 7; Burns Mantle, *CDT*, January 9, 1927, pt. 7, p. 1 (emphasis added) and *CDT*, June 5, 1927, pt. 7, p. 1; *CDT*, May 18, 1927, p. 10; Armchair Playgoer, *CDT*, October 29, 1927, p. 16; Frederick Donaghey, *CDT*, September 18, 1927, pt. 7, p. 1; *CDT*, December 31, 1926, p. 11; Alexander Woolcott, *Baltimore Sun*, January 9, 1927, pt. 2, sec. 1, p. 1; *Indianapolis Star*, April 29, 1928, magazine sec., n.p.; *South Bend (IN) Tribune*, March 14, 1928, p. 14 ("almost identical"); UP story (Chicago), *St. Louis Star*, September 12, 1927, p. 3 ("straight stuff"); *OM*, June 5, 1927, sec. 2, p. 2 ("a photograph").

37. Burns Mantle, *New York Daily News*, December 16, 1925, p. 42 and December 31, 1926, p. 19.

38. Mantle, *New York Daily News*, December 16, 1925, p. 42 (on *Chivalry*) and December 31, 1926, p. 19 (comparing *Chivalry* and *Chicago*).

39. *Miami Herald*, February 14, 1927, p. 4; Watkins as quoted by Joseph Mulvaney in a US article, *El Paso Times*, January 9, 1927, p. 14; Watkins as quoted in the *Indianapolis Star*, January 6, 1928, p. 2; International Feature Service story about Beulah Annan in, for example, the *Indianapolis Star*, April 29, 1928, magazine sec., n.p.

40. Percy Hammond in the *New York Herald Tribune*, December 31, 1926, E10 and January 9, 1927, E1.

13. The Truth about Chicago's Criminal-Justice System

1. Watkins as quoted in Mantle, *American Playwrights of Today*, 204. The 1922 report on race relations is discussed later in this chapter.

2. *CDT*, October 3, 1912, p. 13; *Chicago Inter Ocean*, September 1, 1912, p. 21.

3. *CDT*, January 13, 1922, p. 11; March 14, 1923, pp. 1, 6; an article from a Chicago news service in *OM*, July 6, 1924, p. 3.

4. Adler, *First in Violence, Deepest in Dirt*, 108–9.

5. *Chicago Inter-Ocean*, January 10, 1906, p. 1; *CDT*, December 28, 1912, pp. 1–2; *CEP*, March 16, 1914; *CDT*, November 21, 1914, p. 1. These examples are cited in Adler, *First in Violence, Deepest in Dirt*, 107, 112, 115.

6. Oscar Hewitt, "13 'Lady Killers' Sent to Prison in Crowe Term," *CDT*, March 26, 1924, p. 5.

7. These numbers and percentages are based on my analysis of the Chicago police homicide logs transcribed in "Homicide in Chicago 1870–1930" (https://homicide.northwestern.edu/), supplemented by newspaper reports. My homicide totals here and elsewhere exclude instances of the following: deaths by automobile accident (which almost never led to charges), murder-suicides, abortions, and infanticides (which were probably often carried out by mothers but the perpetrators were almost never known). Hewitt reported thirteen convictions of women as of the date of his article.

8. These numbers and percentages are based on the analysis described in n. 7. The fifty-two women known to have been tried by Cook County juries in these years are the following. Convicted in 1920: Martha Domeneous, Lillie Dell Saunders. Acquitted: none. Convicted in 1921: Dora Waterman, Jennie (Jeanette) Wilkerson. Acquitted: Cora Orthwein, Contella DelGindice. Convicted in 1922: Elizabeth Talley (Wilson), Grace Pearl, Rose Abrahamson, Ida Raymond, Iola Clay. Acquitted: Mary/Marie/Maria Carbonara, Lucy Alice Clark, Bertha Jones, Mrs. Henry Jennings, Lillian Thomas. Convicted in 1923: Sabelle(a) Nitti-Crudelle (granted new trial in 1924), Stella Rouse, Levisa/Levina Thortone (alias Tylo), Hazel Cox, Tillie Klimek. Acquitted: Antonia Warwosiynia, Caroline Hall, Lucille Kavanaugh, Anna McGinnis, Myna Pioch, Tennie or Jennie McFarland/McMarland, Theresa (Florence) Contursi or Contoursi. Convicted in 1924: Estelle Edwards, Elizabeth Uncapher, Katherine Malm, Tillie Evans (Tilley Lacey), Mary Waseniak/Wazeniak, Shirley Jones, Annie Peciulis (found guilty, committed to an asylum). Acquitted: Minnie Bernatowicz, Blanche Marin, Beulah Annan, Minnie Nichols, Leila Foster, Eleanora Mack, Mabel Feelow, Lillie White, Anna Valamis, Lucille Marshall, Rose Epp/Epps, Rosena Montana, Madelina Montana, Maggie Taylor, Belva Gaertner, Emily Strutynski (not guilty by reason of insanity, committed to an asylum), Sylvia Vorac (not guilty by reason of insanity, committed to an asylum).

9. See n. 8. Odds converted to percentage: 47:1 = 47 ÷ (47 + 1) = 0.979.

10. Rorabaugh, *Prohibition*, 88.

11. Bettman, "Criminal Justice Surveys Analysis," 63–65.

12. Fischer, "Juries in Felony Cases, in Cook County," 239 (of 13,000 felony cases, about 500, or 3.8 percent, were handled by juries in 1926), 239–40 (quotation, emphasis original).

13. Lashly, "Homicide (in Cook County)," 612.

14. These percentages are based on analysis of the Chicago police homicide logs transcribed in "Homicide in Chicago 1870–1930" (https://homicide .northwestern.edu/).

15. The analysis is based on the transcribed police logs in "Homicide in Chicago 1870–1930." The percentages could be slightly off due to a few cases of uncertainty about race. Period estimates of the number of African Americans in Chicago in 1923 ranged from 135,000 to as many as 200,000, according to Arthur Evans, writing in the *Chicago Tribune* about the continuing Great Migration (*CDT*, September 20, 1923, p. 13). Evans thought a better estimate was 135,000 to 150,000, the latter figure being 5 percent of the estimated population of Chicago in July in mid-1923, (the population being 2,886,121, according to a federal estimate reported in *CDT*, April 6, 1923, p. 3). Lashly's report in *The Illinois Crime Survey* also gives 5 percent for the years 1926 and 1927 ("Homicide," 628). In 1926, Lashly notes, 108 Black men were charged with murder and 187 white men. "This," he wrote, "is all out of proportion to the ratio of population of the respective races, is 5% colored and 95% white." By "charged with murder" Lashly meant arrested for murder, not tried for murder (see p. 625). He also showed that in 1926 and 1927 the conviction rate for Black people was much higher than for white people, his numbers being comparable with my findings for trial convictions in 1920 through 1924 (p. 628). Although Lashly's comparisons are for convictions of those charged, not the subset thereof brought to trial, it is not surprising that both data pools show essentially the same thing.

16. Chicago Commission on Race Relations, *Negro in Chicago*, 641.

17. On the history of the third degree, see Thomas and Leo, *Confessions of Guilt*, 112–40; Chafee, Pollak, and Stern, "Third Degree," 13–262 (for various cities), 171 (Chicago's goldfish room); Stewart, *Stewart on Trial Strategy*, 113–14 (referring to an early 1920s case, where investigators beat a defendant and wrung a false confession from his alleged accomplice, an innocent man).

18. Chafee, Pollak, and Stern, "Third Degree," 136 (95 percent); 131 ("best lie detector"); "'Third Degree' Talked into Senate Discard," *CDT*, May 14, 1923, p. 12 ("too much sentiment").

19. *Chicago Inter Ocean*, September 1, 1912, M1 (an argument for permitting women to serve on juries); *CDT*, July 15, 1924, p. 8 (women jurors would not be swayed by a defendant's looks); *CDT*, January 17, 1926, p. 8 (an editorial noting, although not agreeing with, the claim that women would not hand

out as many "mawkish" acquittals as men do). On jury-service avoidance, see below with n. 20.

20. Drake Hotel case: *CDT*, September 9, 1925, p. 11 and September 10, 1925, pp. 1–2; real reasons for jury avoidance, a judge's proposal: "Report of the Committee on Juries," 28–29 and *CDT*, March 8, 1923, p. 13.

21. *CDT*, March 17, 1922, p. 5; *CDT*, September 10, 1925, p. 1; *CDT*, April 28, 1921, p. 17; *CDT*, March 10, 1922, p. 8; "Advocates Change in Selection of Jurors in Criminal Cases," 24 (riff-raff); *CDT*, March 8, 1923, p. 13 (complaints about excuses by prospective jurors in the Drake Hotel case); *CDT*, September 10, 1925, p. 1 (the jurors seated in the Drake Hotel case, giving their occupations).

22. William Blackstone's ratio was frequently quoted in slightly different wordings but always with the ten-to-one ratio. The principle was often quoted in American newspapers, always as a well-known and accepted commonplace. An examination of books and articles on the law in the early decades of the twentieth century shows that the reasonable-doubt principle was deeply embedded in criminal jurisprudence.

23. "Jury Held 'Stupid' Seeks Vindication," *New York Times*, March 2, 1932, p. 40. Reporting on the judge's instructions, the *Times* referred simply to "doubt," but the judge would have used the standard formulation "reasonable doubt."

24. Hadley, "Criminal Justice in America," 676.

25. The 1922 publication of the report of the Chicago Commission on Race Relations, which investigated the 1919 race riots and the racial factors in the criminal-justice system more generally, was reported and even discussed in papers outside Chicago, but the *Tribune* made no mention of it in any of its news or opinion stories (although the publisher, the University of Chicago, ran an ad for the book in the *Tribune*). The report was published the second week of October 1922, and even the *Daily News* seems to have ignored it. I could not find any reference to the report in *CDN*'s primary news pages, typically pages 1–6 of the paper, for all of October that year.

26. Watkins, "Chicago" (a letter to the dramatic editor), *New York World*, January 16, 1927, M2; see the discussion of conviction/acquittal statistics in chapter 13.

27. On Watkins's coverage of the Snyder trial, see chapter 14 with n. 2.

28. Mayor Thompson's response to *Chicago* as quoted in Pauly, *Chicago by Maurine Watkins*, xxvii (emphasis added). Pauly cites *CEP*, September 12, 1927 as a clipping held by the New York Public Library. As of the present writing, the library cannot locate this clipping, nor have I been able to find the article in the microform version of *CEP*. I have no doubt, however, that Pauly did indeed find the Thompson quotation in one of the sources he examined.

14. The Unhappy Finish to Beulah's Short Life

1. *CDT*, December 30, 1951, pt. 6, p. 12 (172 performances in New York); *Brooklyn Daily Eagle*, January 10, 1927, 8A; *Lexington (KY) Leader*, January 9, 1927, p. 16 (still enrolled in Baker's class); *Indianapolis Times*, March 22, 1927, p. 7 (visit to Washington, DC); *New York Daily News*, February 4, 1927, p. 40 (visit to Atlantic City).

2. Maurine Watkins in the *New York Telegram*, April 20, 1927, p. 3, as quoted in Lutes, "Tears on Trial in the 1920s," 358–59; Watkins as quoted in the *Indianapolis Times*, April 27, 1927, p. 2 (liars or eccentrics).

3. *Philadelphia Inquirer*, September 7, 1927, p. 2 and September 16, p. 12; *Brooklyn Daily Eagle*, September 13, 1927, 12A; *Montclair (NJ) Times*, October 29, 1927, p. 11.

4. *Indianapolis Star*, March 11, 1928, p. 32 (March 10 interview in New Orleans).

5. Certificate of Evidence in Beulah Annan vs. Albert Annan, Superior Court of Cook County, no. 440102. Conflicting accounts of Beulah's and Al's relationship after the trial: a widely published article in, for example, the *Baltimore Sun*, July 13, 1924, pt. 2, sec. 4, p. 3 and the *Washington Post*, July 13, 1924, SM5; a story out of Chicago in *OM*, June 24, 1924, p. 2; a more believable article by Chicago reporter H. H. Robertson, dated May 25 and published in the *Atlanta Constitution*, May 26, 1924, p. 1; additional versions, which do not contradict Robertson, in *CDN*, May 25, 1924, p. 7 and *CEJ*, May 26, 1924, p. 8. At the time of her divorce from Albert Annan, comments by Beulah about her marriage to Al were paraquoted, in rather implausible words that resemble some of the foregoing accounts, in an article by the Chicago office of the NEA, published in *OI*, July 4, 1926, p. 3.

6. *CDT*, January 18, 1927, pp. 1, 38; January 19, 1927, p. 3; *Barrington Courier-Review*, January 20, 1927, p. 8; Certificate of Evidence in Beulah Annan Harlib vs. Edward Harlib, no. 456459, May 11, 1927.

7. Testimony of Beulah and two witnesses who saw her injuries (the bruised chin, bandaged ribs, and a blackened eye) in Certificate of Evidence in Beulah Annan Harlib vs. Edward Harlib, no. 456459, May 11, 1927.

8. Al Friendly, quoting Harlib, in a letter to Lester Bernstein, March 21, 1963 (Bob Fosse/Gwen Verdon Collection, Music Division, Library of Congress).

9. The judge's comments in Certificate of Evidence in Beulah Annan Harlib vs. Edward Harlib, no. 456459, May 11, 1927; *Washington Post*, May 8, 1927, p. 18; *CDT*, May 8, 1927, A, pt. 1, p. 22.

10. Beulah's Cook County death certificate. For information about typical symptoms of peritoneal tuberculosis, I have relied on Lobue, Perry, and Cantanzaro, "Diagnosis of Tuberculosis," 355; Kapoor, "Abdominal Tuberculosis," 459–67; and other sources. Her death certificate gives her address as 2478 N. Albany.

11. *OI*, March 14, 1928, p. 2 (Beulah and Abel Marcus had planned to marry).
12. *CDT*, January 19, 1927, p. 3; Pauly, *Chicago by Maurine Watkins*, xxvi, citing *CHE*, September 19, 1927 (clipping, New York Public Library).
13. Beulah's death certificate; personal interview with Ruth Stephens; *Illinois Health Quarterly* 1 (1929): 9.
14. Beulah's death certificate reads "Stevens"; newspaper notices of her death gave her pseudonym as "Stephens."
15. Personal interview with Bill Marksberry (Bill's father, Hense Marksberry, went to Chicago with John Sheriff to accompany Beulah's body home to Kentucky); *OI*, March 13, 1928, p. 10 (John Sheriff went to Beulah's bedside); the funeral sermon as summarized in *OM*, March 15, 1928, p. 4 and *OI*, March 14, 1928, p. 1; *OI*, March 14, 1928, p. 2 ("thin and faded"); personal interview with Ruth Stephens; death certificate.
16. Beulah's death certificate; *OI*, March 14, 1928, p. 1.
17. *OI*, March 14, 1928, pp. 1–2; Bryan Schrock of the James H. Davis Funeral Home.
18. Personal interview with Ruth Stephens for information in this and the following paragraphs. Mary Rafferty heard from family members that Beulah was buried with a diamond tiara.

15. Beulah Remembered as Roxie

1. *Evansville (IN) Journal*, March 16, 1928, p. 6.
2. Peter Levins, *Atlanta Constitution*, March 9, 1930, magazine sec., p. 10; *Hartford Courant*, April 19, 1925, 6D (describing the Olympia Macri case); *Brooklyn Daily Eagle*, May 30, 1918, p. 10 (reporter's joke).
3. Peter Levins, NEA story, *Austin American-Statesman*, August 21, 1932, p. 6; UP story, *Decatur (IL) Review*, August 7, 1932, p. 2 ("Chicago's prettiest killer").
4. Peter Levins, NS story published in, for example, the *New York Daily News*, February 25, 1934, pp. 50–51. The estimate that women constituted about 6 percent of the homicide cases brought to trial in the 1920s is an extrapolation from the enormous data set of the Chicago police homicide logs ("Homicide in Chicago 1870–1930," a database hosted by Northwestern University), which I analyzed for the five-year span from 1920 through 1924.
5. *New York Daily News*, February 25, 1934, p. 51 (stage contracts); *Tulare (CA) Daily Times*, September 22, 1932, p. 7 (Pollak's stage contract).
6. UP story (Chicago), "Knighthood Flowering with Chicago Juries," *Wisconsin State Journal*, March 31, 1935, p. 20; "Again Chivalrous Chicago Frees a Beauty," *Atlanta Constitution*, May 12, 1935, magazine sec., p. 2. Levins's story was widely published and can be found in, for example, the magazine section of the Sunday *San Francisco Examiner*, December 21, 1927, pp. 22–23.

7. Anna Howard, as quoted in Bartholomy, "Even without 'Chicago,' Roxie Remains in Relatives' Hearts," 3C; Charles Collins, "Beulah the Beautiful Killer," *CDT*, December 30, 1951, pp. 3, 12. Compare the image on pg. 102, showing Beulah on the witness stand wearing an ankle-length dress, with the one on pg. 155 of an artist's sketch of Roxie testifying, which more or less jibes with a photograph of a scene from the play, where actress Francine Larrimore crosses her legs to show her knees (New York ad in a newspaper clipping in Maurine Watkins/Chicago: clippings 1920–1935, New York Public Library of the Performing Arts).

8. *Newsday* (Nassau ed., Hempstead, NY), July 24, 1954, 4R.

9. Gwen Verdon interview with Mary Daniels, *CDT*, April 14, 1978, sec. 2, p. 3; Lewis Funke (*New York Times*), *Cincinnati Enquirer*, February 4, 1973, 2H.

10. Rumore and Mather, *He Had It Coming*, 212.

11. The first page of the will and a photograph of a letter of instructions, from Maurine to her mother, is published in Rumore and Mather, *He Had It Coming*, 213–14. Rumore and Mather also describe the bequests to institutions (*He Had It Coming*, 215–16).

12. Funke, *Cincinnati Enquirer*, February 4, 1973, 2H.

13. Funke, *Cincinnati Enquirer*, February 4, 1973, 2H; cf. Kiernan, "Murder, She Wrote," 7.

14. Funke, *Cincinnati Enquirer*, February 4, 1973, 2H; Fosse as quoted in Linda Winer, *CDT*, February 19, 1978, sec. 2, p. 6; Margaret Brown, Watkins's aunt, as quoted by C. R. Leonard, as quoted in Charlie Patton, "Author of Original 'Chicago' Lived and Died in Jacksonville," *Florida Times-Union*, May 17, 2018, https://www.jacksonville.com/story/news/2018/05/17/author-of-original-chicago-lived-died-in-jacksonville/12194557007/.

15. Mae Tinée, *CDT*, March 20, 1928, p. 31. The 1942 movie *Roxie Hart* was written by Nunnaly Johnson, with the assistance of Ben Hecht; it was directed by William Wellman.

16. *Florida Times-Union*, August 12, 1969, p. C8 (obituary). Photographs of the death notice and the obituary are printed in Rumore and Mather, *He Had It Coming*, 218, 222.

16. Bob Fosse's Musical Remake of Maurine Watkins's Play

1. C. R. Leonard as quoted by Charlie Patton in the *Florida Times-Union*, May 17, 2018, https://www.jacksonville.com/story/news/2018/05/17/author-of-original-chicago-lived-died-in-jacksonville/12194557007/. Fosse and Fred Ebb cowrote the musical's script; Ebb and John Kander composed the musical numbers.

2. Pauly, *Chicago by Maurine Watkins*.

3. Portrayals of Beulah that agree with the picture of her set forth in the *Tribune* articles include the Wikipedia entry for Beulah Annan as of the present writing and the following publications (whether the authors relied primarily on Watkins or not): Pauly, *Chicago by Maurine Watkins*, xvi; Lesy, *Murder City*, 203 and passim; Lucchesi, *Ugly Prey*, 252, 257, 286; Mordden, *All That Jazz*, 37 (see further below); Tóth, *Merry Murderers*, 162–63 (see further below); Lutes, "Tears on Trial in the 1920s," 352; Holland, *Weird Kentucky*, 96; Perry, *Girls of Murder City*, 93 (quoting as fact the misleading paraquotation of the "confession," *CDT*, April 4, 1924, p. 1; elsewhere writing in a tone that encourages trust in Watkins's accounts); Rumore and Mather, *He Had It Coming*, 19–20 (and the book's subtitle: "Four Murderous Women").

4. Mordden, *All That Jazz*, 37.

5. Tóth, *Merry Murderers*, 11 (see also p. 162).

6. C. Nario, "What's a Vamp?" *Oakland Tribune*, February 2, 1919, magazine sec., p. 3; applications of the term *vamp* to girls' casual dating or ride-seeking in Chicago (*Decatur (IL) Herald*, June 25, 1921, p. 6; *CDT*, January 12, 1922, p. 17); various 1920s newspaper references to "jury vamping" (e.g., "Women Killers Vamp Juries in New York No Longer," *Wisconsin State Journal*, March 11, 1923, p. 25); *CDT*, March 20, 1922, p. 1 (Madelynne Obenchain's "vamp proof" jury); references in *CDN*, May 25, 1924, p. 1 and *CHE*, May 23, 1924, p. 1 to Beulah's "beauty proof" jury; *CA*, April 4, 1924, p. 3. Robert Klepper's summaries of hundreds of silent films in *Silent Films, 1877–1996* contain no references to a femme fatale or vampire engaging in murder.

7. *Nashville Tennessean*, January 1, 1922, p. 21 and other papers quoting Richard Barthelmess; Theda Bara, quoted in the *Sioux City Journal*, May 9, 1920, p. 32 (on movie vampires: "there's no such thing in real life") and in the *St. Louis Globe-Democrat*, October 14, 1920, p. 6 ("the vampire that you see on the screen could never succeed in real life"); Upton Sinclair as quoted in the *Sacramento Bee*, February 7, 1925, p. 6; the vamp joke in *Twin City Review* (Champaign, IL), June 24, 1921, p. 6 and other papers; rejoinder to the joke in the *Ironwood (MI) Daily Globe*, October 19, 1921, p. 2; *Decatur (IL) Herald*, June 25, 1921, p. 6 (in Chicago, "thousands" of boulevard vamps get rides downtown every morning); *CDT*, January 12, 1922, p. 17 (after-work "boulevard vamps" looking for amusement).

8. Personal interviews with Anna Howard (daughter of Emma Marksberry) and Ruth Stephens (Perry carried a torch for Beulah); LeMaster, "Beulah Sheriff," 2 (Perry refused to be interviewed, always carried a torch for Beulah); Owen, "Woman Too Pretty to Hang," 6C (angry phone calls that LeMaster received). According to personal interviews with many Sheriff family relatives, including Perry Jr.'s wife, Ruth, none ever heard their parents or other family members speak in anger about LeMaster's request for information;

nor did they have any sense that family members wanted to keep Beulah a secret. The one exception was Beulah's first husband, Perry Stephens. Perry Jr. was confident that his father was not one of the callers.

9. Lewis Funke (*New York Times*), *Cincinnati Enquirer*, February 4, 1973, 2H; Gwen Verdon interview with Mary Daniels, *CDT*, April 14, 1978, sec. 2, p. 3; Wasson, *Fosse*, 188.

10. Letters from Al Friendly to Lester Bernstein, a letter from Bernstein to Jack Perlman, and handwritten notes, in the Bob Fosse/Gwen Verdon Collection, Music Division, Library of Congress.

11. Wasson, *Fosse*, 347; Gwen Verdon as quoted by Daniels, *CDT*, April 14, 1978, sec. 2, p. 3. A letter from Lester Bernstein to Jack Perlman (March 23, 1963) shows that Fosse was primarily interested in Maurine Watkins, not Beulah Annan (Bob Fosse/Gwen Verdon Collection).

12. Verdon as quoted in Wasson, *Fosse*, 413.

13. Wasson, *Fosse*, 413 ("a disaster").

14. Linda Winer, *Newsday* (NY ed.), November 15, 1996, B3; Richard Zoglin, *Time*, November 25, 1996, https://content.time.com/time/subscriber/article /0,33009,985604,00.html; A. R. Gurney, "Coming Home to a Musical That Sounds Like America," *New York Times*, September 8, 1996, H11, H26 ("after the trials" and "we live in a tough"); Walter Bobbie as quoted in Terry Teachout, "'Chicago': An American Selfie," *Commentary* (March 2008), https://www.commentary.org/articles/terry-teachout/chicago-american-selfie/.

15. Vincent Canby, *New York Times*, November 24, 1996, H4; Ben Brantley, *New York Times*, November 15, 1996, A1.

16. Howard Kissel, *New York Daily News*, May 4, 1996, p. 18 and November 15, 1996, p. 51; Clive Barnes, *New York Times*, June 4, 1975, p. 23 and *New York Post*, November 15, 1996 (as cited without a page number in Winkler, *Big Deal*, 207).

17. Joel Grey as quoted in Teachout, "'Chicago': An American Selfie," along with Teachout's observation; Wasson, *Fosse*, 407–10 (including assistant Tony Stevens's observation, p. 408).

18. The expression "a fractured justice system" is used by Brantley in summarizing the majority view of the musical's main idea as it resonated with 1990s cultural experience (Brantley, *New York Times*, November 15, 1996, A1).

19. Lamarque, *Opacity of Narrative*, 131.

20. Atkinson, "Curbing the Comedians," 56–64 (comedic playwrights brought before the Athenian Assembly on charges of slander); Beacham, *Spectacle Entertainments of Early Imperial Rome*, 158, 164–65 (imperial punishment of actors for maligning the emperor or magistrates); Bricker, "Libel and Satire," 889–921.

21. The real-world models for *The Front Page* are identified in detail in Hilton, *Front Page by Ben Hecht and Charles MacArthur*, 39–52. On Walter Howey

as a *target*, see below, together with the citations to Cardullo in n. 23 and to Hecht's memoir about Charles MacArthur in n. 24.

22. Hilton, *Front Page by Ben Hecht and Charles MacArthur*, 18–19. Hilton rehearses the original assessments of *The Front Page* by the two Hearst reporters and by others (including Walter Whitworth, *Indianapolis News*, November 23, 1928, p. 20; Starrett, *Born in a Bookshop*, 97; and Robert Tucker, *Indianapolis Star*, November 23, 1928, p. 7); Burns Mantle's New York review in *CDT*, August 26, 1928, sec. 7, p. 1; Fanny Butcher, *CDT*, September 16, 1928, sec. 7, p. 10.

23. Hilton, *Front Page by Ben Hecht and Charles MacArthur*, 12–13; Cardullo, *Play Analysis*, 135; epilogue appended by Hecht and MacArthur to the third Covici-Friede printing of *The Front Page*, reproduced in Hilton, *Front Page by Ben Hecht and Charles MacArthur*, 187–88.

24. Hecht, *Charlie*, 49. On Watkins's remarks about whether her play was a satire, see chapter 12.

25. Cardullo, *Play Analysis*, 133.

Postscript

1. Albert Annan's application under the World War Adjusted Compensation Act (application no. 3674032, August 17, 1925); the 1930 federal census; Coroner's Inquest on the Body of Othelia Griffin, October 17, 1934; *Southtown Economist* (Chicago), October 18, 1934, pp. 1, 13; December 13, 1934, p. 1; *Louisville Courier-Journal* October 17, 1934, pp. 1, 12.

2. The events described in this paragraph are based on sources mentioned in n. 1, together with *CDT*, October 17, 1934, p. 2; *Syracuse Herald*, October 17, 1934; *Helena Independent*, October 18, 1934, p. 1; *CDT*, December 12, 1934, p. 7; December 18, p. 2; December 29, p. 1.

3. Albert Annan's Application [to the United States Army] for Certificate in Lieu of Lost or Destroyed Discharge Certificate, August 3, 1935; Caron's Louisville city directory; his Army Service Record, p. 2; Enlistment Record, National Guard of Illinois, September 9, 1940; enlistment card, dated September 16, 1940; Physical Examination, Enlistment Record, National Guard of Illinois, September 9, 1940; Service Record, p. 28 (transferred to Regional Hospital, Fort Knox, KY, in March, 1945); Army Separation Qualification Record (undated), Certificate of Disability for Discharge (March 15, 1945), Enlisted Record and Report of Separation (March 17, 1945). That he received a pension is an assumption. Part of his army records were destroyed by fire, perhaps pages containing information about his pension and his death.

4. 1930 federal census; Mary Neel's Cook County death certificate; *OM*, April 3, 1932. In testimony to the judge when she divorced Al, Beulah mentioned that her mother had some kind of illness. Beulah's cats and canaries are

mentioned in an AP story out of Chicago published at the time of Beulah's death (*Cincinnati Enquirer*, March 15, 1928, p. 4).

5. Ruth Stephens; obituary for Perry Waller Stephens, *CDT*, November 23, 1972, sec. 2, p. 29.

6. Perry W. Stephens's Enlisted Record and Report of Separation, Honorable Discharge (April 4, 1947); Kentucky death index entries for Margaret Stephens and William L. Stephens. Other particulars are based on information from those who knew him, including his wife, Ruth Stephens.

7. Personal conversations with various people who had known Perry Stephens personally, both family members and coworkers at General Electric.

BIBLIOGRAPHY

Abbreviations and shorthand references

Beulah's after-midnight statement. This statement is preserved in the transcript of the coroner's inquest (CIHK, pp. 23–31).

Beulah's 1923 diary. This diary was collected by the police and published in the *Chicago American*, April 4, 1924, p. 3.

CIHK. Coroner's Inquest on the Body of Harry Kalsted. See under Documents.

MHK. "Murder of Harry Kalstedt" (a report). See under Documents.

Yale manuscript "Chicago." See "Chicago" under Documents.

Newspapers

CA	*Chicago American*
CDJ	*Chicago Daily Journal*
CDN	*Chicago Daily News*
CDT	*Chicago Daily Tribune*
CEP	*Chicago Evening Post*
CHE	*Chicago Herald and Examiner*
OI	*Owensboro Inquirer*
OM	*Owensboro Messenger*

News services

AP	Associated Press
INS	International News Service
NEA	Newspaper Enterprise Association
NS	News Syndicate
UP	United Press
US	Universal Service

Documents and Published Court Cases

Albert Annan and Beulah Stephens. Cook County Marriage License No. 860858. Cook County Clerk's Office.

Certificate of Evidence in Beulah Annan Harlib vs. Edward Harlib, no. 456459, May 11, 1927.

Certificate of Evidence in Beulah Annan vs. Albert Annan, Superior Court of Cook County, no. 440102.

"Chicago" by Maurine Watkins. Typed and hand-revised manuscript, Beinecke Rare Book Room and Manuscript Library, Yale University.

Coroner's inquest, transcript of (CIHK). "Inquest No. 114647 on the body of Harry Kalstedt [Kalsted], April 4th, 1924, at 4227 Cottage Grove and 4th District Police Station." Office of the Cook County Medical Examiner. A copy is also part of MHK report in the Bob Fosse/Gwen Verdon Collection in the Music Division of the Library of Congress.

Kenneth Roberts's 1923 diary in Special Collections, Rauner Library, Dartmouth College.

Lydia Kalsted v. Harry T. Kalsted, Isanti County, case no. 2217, August 10 and 11, September 6, 1921.

Mary Sheriff v. John R. Sheriff. No. 9233, Daviess County, KY, Petition in Equity, Daviess County Circuit Court. Kentucky Department for Libraries and Archives, Frankfort, KY.

Mrs. Mary Neel v. Green River Distilling Co. in *Workmen's Compensation Board of the Commonwealth of Kentucky, Third Report of Leading Decisions January 22, 1919 to March 16, 1920, 124–135*. Frankfort, KY: Workmen's Compensation Board, 1920.

"Murder of Harry Kalstedt [sic] by Mrs. Beulah Annan," containing the following: a handwritten report by Dr. Clifford Oliver (April 3); the Chicago police "Accident Report"; two inventories of physical evidence; a report by officers Michael Collins and James McLaughlin (April 14, 1924); another evidence inventory (Homicide Bureau, April 14); "Statement of Mrs. Beulah Annan Made at the Hyde Park Police Station on Friday, April 4, 1924, at 12:30 a.m." (which is also in CIHK); two statements given by officer Thomas Torpy (dated April 3 and April 6); statement of Albert Annan (April 4); statement of R. M. Love, Albert Annan's boss (dated April 4); statement of William Wilcox (April 8); typed statement of Dr. Clifford Oliver's report (April 3); statement of patrolman Patrick Houlihan (April 5). This state's evidence report was collected by researchers hired by Bob Fosse in the 1960s; it is preserved in the Bob Fosse/Gwen Verdon Collection in the Music Division of the Library of Congress.

Perry Stephens and Beulah Sheriff marriage license. Spencer County, Indiana, Marriage Records, Book 6, p. 177.

Perry Stephens vs. Beulah Stephens in Equity, No. 1157. Kentucky Department for Libraries and Archives, Frankfort, KY.

State of Minnesota (Isanti County) v. Harry Kalsted, case no. 1877, October 9, 1916.

State of Minnesota (Isanti County) v. Harry Kalsted, case no. 2208, July 27 and 28, 1921.

Works Cited

Adler, Jeffery S. *First in Violence, Deepest in Dirt: Homicide in Chicago, 1870–1920.* Cambridge, MA: Harvard University Press, 2006.

"Advocates Change in Selection of Jurors in Criminal Cases." *Bulletin of the Chicago Crime Commission* 44 (October 12, 1926): 24.

"Animated Journalism." *World's Work* 20 (1910): 13466–77.

Arthur, John. "Reporting, Practical and Theoretical." *Writer* 3 (February 1889): 37.

Atkinson, J. E. "Curbing the Comedians: Cleon versus Aristophanes and Syracosius' Decree." *Classical Quarterly* 42 (1992): 56–64.

Bartholomy, Suzi. "Even without 'Chicago,' Roxie Remains in Relatives' Hearts." *Messenger-Inquirer* (Owensboro), February 12, 2003, 1C, 3C.

Beacham, Richard C. *Spectacle Entertainments of Early Imperial Rome.* New Haven, CT: Yale University Press, 1999.

Bessie, Simon M. *Jazz Journalism: The Story of the Tabloid Newspapers.* New York: Dutton, 1938.

Bettman, Alfred. "Criminal Justice Surveys Analysis." In *Report on Prosecution,* by National Commission of Law Observance and Law Enforcement, 39–221. Washington, DC: Government Printing Office, 1931.

Blackman, Paul H., and Vance McLaughlin. "The Epsy File on American Executions: User Beware." *Homicide Studies* 15 (2011): 209–27.

Blake, Terry, and David Edds Jr. *Owensboro.* Charleston, SC: Arcadia, 2007.

Bleyer, Willard G. *Main Currents in the History of American Journalism.* Boston: Houghton Mifflin, 1927.

———. *Newspaper Writing and Editing.* Boston: Houghton Mifflin, 1913.

Bricker, Andrew B. "Libel and Satire: The Problem with Naming." *ELH* 81 (2014): 889–921.

Cardullo, R. J. *Play Analysis: A Casebook on Modern Western Drama.* Rotterdam: Sense, 2015.

Carroll, John D., ed. *The Kentucky Statutes.* Louisville: Baldwin Law Book Company, 1903 (3rd ed.), 1915 (5th ed.), 1922 (6th ed.).

Chafee, Zechariah, Walter H. Pollak, and Carl S. Stern. "The Third Degree." In idem, *Report on Lawlessness in Law Enforcement,* 13–262. National Commission on Law Observance and Law Enforcement no. 11; Washington, DC: U.S. Government Printing Office, 1931.

Chamberlin, H. B. "The Chicago Crime Commission: How the Business Men of Chicago Are Fighting Crime." *Journal of the American Institute of Criminal Law and Criminology* 11 (1920): 386–97.

———. "Report of the Operating Director." *Bulletin of the Chicago Crime Commission* 17 (January 31, 1921): 5–7.

Cheatwood, Derral. "Capital Punishment for the Crime of Homicide in Chicago: 1870–1930." *Journal of Criminal Law and Criminology* 92 (2002): 843–66.

Chicago Commission on Race Relations. *The Negro in Chicago: A Study of Race Relations and a Race Riot*. Chicago: University of Chicago Press, 1922.

"Chicago Police Stations." *Institution Quarterly* 7, no. 1 (1916): 82–96.

"Chicago's Jails from a New Angle." *Institution Quarterly* 6, no. 4 (1915): 53.

"Chicago: Transy Student Started It All." *Transylvania University Magazine* 20, no. 3 (2003): 15. https://www.transy.edu/sites/default/files/downloads/magazine/2003-summer.pdf.

Courtney, Edward. *A Commentary on the Satires of Juvenal*. 1980. Reprint, Berkeley: California Classical Studies, 2013.

Davis, Clyde B. *The Age of Indiscretion*. Philadelphia: J. B. Lippincott, 1950.

Davis, Merlene. "True Roots of 'Chicago' Story Lie with Two Kentucky Women." *Lexington Herald-Leader*, April 23, 2000, K1.

Dean, Paul. "Valley Lawyer Takes Secret of Romanovs' Fate to the Grave." *Arizona Republic*, December 11, 1977, B1, B11.

Deutsch, Sarah J. "From Ballots to Breadlines, 1920–1940." In *No Small Courage: A History of Women in the United States*, ed. Nancy F. Cott, 413–72. Oxford: Oxford University Press, 2000.

DeVault, Ileen A. "'Everybody Works but Father': Why the Census Misdirected Historians of Women's Employment." *Social Science History* 40 (2016): 369–83.

Devine, Dennis J. *Jury Decision Making: The State of the Science*. New York: New York University Press, 2012.

Dew, Lee A., and Aloma W. Dew. *Owensboro: The City on the Yellow Banks*. Bowling Green, KY: Rivendell, 1988.

Dornfeld, Arnold A. *Behind the Front Page: The Story of the City News Bureau of Chicago*. Chicago: Academy Chicago Publishers, 1983.

Elliott, John. "Tearing Up the Pages." *Portland Review* 29, no. 1 (1983): 51–56.

Erickson, Hal. *Any Resemblance to Actual Persons: The Real People behind 400+ Movie Characters*. Jefferson, NC: McFarland, 2017.

Faderman, Lillian. *Woman: The American History of an Idea*. New Haven, CT: Yale University Press, 2022.

Field, Jessie. "The Country Church and the Country Girl." In *The Church and Country Life*, ed. Paul L. Vogt, 86–88. New York: Missionary Education Movement of the United States and Canada, 1916.

Filler, Louis. *The Muckrakers*, rev. ed. with a new preface by the author. Stanford, CA: Stanford University Press, 1993.

Fine, Reuben. *The Psychoanalytic Vision*. New York: Free Press, 1981.

Fischer, Gustave F. "The Juries, in Felony Cases, in Cook County." In *The Illinois Crime Survey*, ed. John H. Wigmore, 221–43. Chicago: Illinois Association for Criminal Justice, 1929.

Fishkin, Shelley Fisher. *From Fact to Fiction: Journalism and Imaginative Writing in America*. Baltimore: Johns Hopkins University Press, 1985.

Freeman, R. Austin. *The Singing Bone: Detective Stories*. London: Hodder & Stoughton, 1911.

Gist, Noel P. "The Negro in the Daily Press." *Social Forces* 10 (1932): 405–11.

Goldin, Claudia. "Marriage Bars: Discrimination against Married Woman Workers from the 1920s to the 1950s." In *Favorites of Fortune: Technology, Growth, and Economic Development since the Industrial Revolution*, ed. Patrice Higonnet, David S. Landes, and Henry Rosovsky, 511–36. Cambridge, MA: Harvard University Press, 1991.

Goodsell, Willystine. *Problems of the Family*. New York: Century, 1928.

Greenberg, Jonathan. *The Cambridge Introduction to Satire*. Cambridge: Cambridge University Press, 2018.

Griffin Winfrey, Emily. "Maurine Watkins Makes Satire Out of Murder." In Jodie Steelman Wilson, Emily Griffin Winfrey, and Rebecca McDole, *Hidden History of Montgomery County, Indiana*, 67–72. Charleston, SC: History Press, 2012.

Grundy, Mr. [pen name]. "Polite Society." *Atlantic Monthly* 125 (1920): 610.

Gunnell, Justin J., and Stephan J. Ceci. "When Emotionality Trumps Reason: A Study of Individual Processing Style and Juror Bias." *Behavioral Sciences and the Law* 28 (2010): 850–77.

Gurney, A. R. "Coming Home to a Musical That Sounds Like America." *New York Times*, September 8, 1996, H11.

Hadley, Herbert S. "Criminal Justice in America: Present Conditions Historically Considered." *American Bar Association Journal* 11 (1925): 674–79.

Hall, Edith S. "Why a Boy Should Sign a Pledge." *Christian Advocate* (January 18, 1912): 76–77.

Hamilton, Braddin. "The Errors of Society." *Smart Set* 2, no. 4 (October–November 1900): 81–86.

Hecht, Ben. *Charlie: The Improbable Life and Times of Charles MacArthur*. New York: Harper, 1957.

Hecht, Ben, and Charles MacArthur. *The Front Page*. New York: Covici-Friede, 1928.

Heflin, Shelia Brown. "Life on Mulberry Street." *Daviess County Historical Society Quarterly* 10, no. 3 (1992): 50–61.

Hilton, George W., ed. *The Front Page by Ben Hecht and Charles MacArthur: From Theater to Reality*. Hanover, NH: Smith and Kraus, 2002.

———. *Lake Michigan Passenger Steamers*. Stanford, CA: Stanford University Press, 2002.

Holden, C. R. "Report of the Committee on Origin of Crime." *Bulletin of the Chicago Crime Commission* 10 (January 19, 1920): 12–13.

Holland, Jeffrey S. *Weird Kentucky: Your Travel Guide to Kentucky's Local Legends and Best Kept Secrets*, ed. Marc Sceurman and Marc Moran. New York: Sterling, 2009.

Hyde, Grant M. *Newspaper Reporting and Correspondence: A Manual for Reporters, Correspondents, and Students of Newspaper Writing*. New York: D. Appleton, 1916.

Johnson, James D. *A Century of Chicago Street Cars, 1858–1958*. Wheaton, IL: Traction Orange Company, 1964.

Kapoor, V. K. "Abdominal Tuberculosis." *Postgraduate Medical Journal* 74 (1998): 459–67.

Kaszuba, Beth Fantaskey. "'Mob Sisters': Women Reporting on Crime Prohibition-Age Chicago." PhD diss., Pennsylvania State University, 2013.

Kenney, William H. *Chicago Jazz: A Cultural History, 1904–1930*. Oxford: Oxford University Press, 1993.

Kiernan, Louise. "Murder, She Wrote." *Chicago Daily Tribune*, July 16, 1997, sec. 5 (Tempo), p. 7.

Kinne, Wisner P. *George Pierce Baker and the American Theatre*. Cambridge, MA: Harvard University Press, 1954.

Klein, Philip. *The Burden of Unemployment: A Study of Unemployment Relief Measures in Fifteen American Cities, 1921–1922*. New York: Russell Sage Foundation, 1923.

Klepper, Robert K. *Silent Films, 1877–1996: A Critical Guide to 646 Movies*. Jefferson, NC: McFarland, 1999.

Kochersberger, Robert C., ed. *More Than a Muckraker: Ida Tarbell's Lifetime in Journalism*. Knoxville: University of Tennessee Press, 1994.

Lamarque, Peter. *The Opacity of Narrative*. London: Rowman & Littlefield, 2014.

Lashley, Arthur V. "Homicide (in Cook County)." In *The Illinois Crime Survey*, ed. John H. Wigmore, 589–640. Chicago: Illinois Association for Criminal Justice, 1929.

LeMaster, Stan. "Beulah Sheriff—The Girl Who Was Too Pretty to Hang." Unpublished paper delivered to the Daviess County Historical Society, September 17, 1982; typescript in the Kentucky Room of the Daviess County Public Library.

Lesy, Michael. *Murder City: The Bloody History of Chicago in the Twenties*. New York: W. W. Norton, 2007.

Lobue, Philip A., Sharon Perry, and Antonio Cantanzaro. "Diagnosis of Tuberculosis." In *Tuberculosis: A Comprehensive International Approach*, 2nd ed., ed. Lee B. Reichman and Earl S. Herschfield, 342–76. New York: Dekker, 2000.

Lucchesi, Emilie Le Beau. *Ugly Prey: An Innocent Woman and the Death Sentence That Scandalized Jazz Age Chicago*. Chicago: Chicago Review Press, 2017.

Lutes, Jean Marie. *Front-Page Girls: Women Journalists in American Culture and Fiction, 1880–1930*. Ithaca, NY: Cornell University Press, 2006.

———. "Tears on Trial in the 1920s: Female Emotion and Style in 'Chicago' and 'Machinal.'" *Tulsa Studies in Women's Literature* 30 (2011): 343–69.

Mantle, Burns. *American Playwrights of Today*. New York: Dodd, Mead, 1929.

Marzolf, Marion Tuttle. *Civilizing Voices: American Press Criticism, 1880–1950*. New York: Longman, 1991.

Massie, Robert K. *The Romanovs: The Final Chapter*. New York: Random House, 1995.

McConnell, Virginia A. *Fatal Fortune: The Death of Chicago's Millionaire Orphan*. Westport, CT: Praeger, 2005.

Merrill, Flora. "Pistol Fire Lights Up 'Chicago': Or Telling It to the Maurine." *New York World*, January 16, 1927, M1.

Meyerowitz, Joanne J. *Women Adrift: Independent Wage Earners in Chicago, 1880–1930*. Chicago: University of Chicago Press, 1988.

Mohun, Arwen P. *Steam Laundries: Gender, Technology, and Work in the United States and Great Britain, 1880–1940*. Baltimore: Johns Hopkins University Press, 1999.

Mordden, Ethan. *All That Jazz: The Life and Times of the Musical* Chicago. Oxford University Press, 2018.

Murray, George. *The Madhouse on Madison Street*. Chicago: Follett, 1965.

Nathan, George J. Preface to *Chicago*, by Maurine Watkins. Edited by George J. Nathan. New York: Knopf, 1927.

"Newspaper Accuracy." *New Outlook* 95 (1910): 606–7.

Ogden, Clare. "Ex-reporter, Now Playwright, Tells of High Spots in Career." *New York Telegraph*, January 9, 1927. New York Public Library for the Performing Arts, Chicago/Maurine Watkins: Clippings, 1920–1935.

Olin, Charles H. *Journalism: Explains the Workings of a Modern Newspaper Office and Gives Full Directions for Those Who Desire to Enter the Field of Journalism*. Philadelphia: Penn Publishing, 1906.

Owen, Karen. "The Woman Too Pretty to Hang." *Messenger-Inquirer* (Owensboro), December 7, 1992, 6C.

Pauly, Thomas A., ed. *Chicago by Maurine Watkins with the Tribune Articles That Inspired It*. Carbondale: Southern Illinois University Press, 1997. Same pagination of play as 1927 edition.

Perry, Douglas. *The Girls of Murder City: Fame, Lust, and the Beautiful Killers Who Inspired* Chicago. New York: Viking, 2010.

Preble, R. B., and Joseph L. Miller. "Medical and Health Conditions in the Cook County Jail." In *Reports Comprising the Survey of the Cook County Jail*, 93–102. Chicago: Chicago Community Trust, 1922.

Quinby, Ione. *Murder for Love*. New York: Civici, Friede, 1931.

"Report of the Committee on Juries." *Bulletin of the Chicago Crime Commission* 31 (March 1, 1924): 27–31.

Report on Lawlessness in Law Enforcement. National Commission on Law Observance and Law Enforcement no. 11; Washington, DC: U.S. Government Printing Office, 1931.

Report on Prosecution. National Commission on Law Observance and Law Enforcement no. 4. Washington, DC: U.S. Government Printing Office, 1931.

Reports Comprising the Survey of the Cook County Jail. Chicago: Chicago Community Trust, 1922.

Rich, Mrs. Kenneth F. [Adena Miller Rich]. "Detention of the Woman Offender." In *Reports Comprising the Survey of the Cook County Jail*, 110–50. Chicago: Chicago Community Trust, 1922.

Richards, Guy. *The Rescue of the Romanovs.* Old Greenwich, CT: Devin-Adair, 1975.

Roberts, Kenneth. *I Wanted to Write.* Garden City, NY: Doubleday, 1949.

Rorabaugh, W. J. *Prohibition: A Concise History.* Oxford: Oxford University Press, 2018.

Ross, Edward A. "The Suppression of Important News." *Atlantic Monthly* (March 1910), 303–11.

Rumore, Kori, and Marianne Mather. *He Had It Coming: Four Murderous Women and the Reporter Who Immortalized Their Stories.* Chicago: Midway, 2019.

Sandwick, Richard L. *Junior High School English*, vol. 2. Boston: Heath, 1920.

Shuman, Edwin L. *Steps into Journalism: Helps and Hints for Young Writers.* Evanston, IL: Evanston Press, 1894.

Simmons, Christina. *Making Marriage Modern: Women's Sexuality from the Progressive Era to World War II.* Oxford: Oxford University Press, 2009.

Sims, E. "Fighting Crime in Chicago: The Crime Commission." *Journal of the American Institute of Criminal Law and Criminology* 11 (1920): 21–28.

Starrett, Vincent. *Born in a Bookshop: Chapters from the Chicago Renascence.* Norman: University of Oklahoma Press, 1965.

Stewart, William S. *Stewart on Trial Strategy: Practical Suggestions to the Young Lawyer on How to Obtain and Hold Clients, How to Prepare Cases and Try Lawsuits.* Chicago: Flood, 1940.

Teachout, Terry. "'Chicago': An American Selfie." *Commentary*, March 2008. https://www.commentary.org/articles/terry-teachout/chicagoamerican-selfie/.

Terrett, Courtenay. "Taking It off the Phone: The Hidden Cog in the Newspaper Machine." Appendix to *The Reporter's Handbook*, by Carrol B. Dotson. New York: Newspaper Institute of America, 1926.

Thomas, George C., and Richard A. Leo. *Confessions of Guilt: From Torture to Miranda and Beyond.* Oxford: Oxford University Press, 2012.

Tóth, Zsófia A. *Merry Murderers: The Farcical (Re)Figuration of the Femme Fatale in Maurine Dallas Watkins' Chicago (1927) and Its Various Adaptations.* Newcastle upon Tyne, UK: Cambridge Publishing, 2011.

Tucher, Andie. *Not Exactly Lying: Fake News and Fake Journalism in American History.* New York: Columbia University Press, 2022.

Van Kleeck, Mary. *A Seasonal Industry: A Study of the Millinery Trade in New York.* New York: Russell Sage Foundation, 1917.

Ward, Stephen J. A. *The Invention of Journalism Ethics: The Path to Objectivity and Beyond*, 2nd ed. Montreal: McGill-Queen's University Press, 2015.

Wasson, Sam. *Fosse.* New York: Houghton Mifflin Harcourt, 2013.

Watkins, Maurine. *Chicago.* Edited by George J. Nathan. New York: Knopf, 1927. Reprinted with same pagination in *Chicago by Maurine Watkins with the Tribune Articles That Inspired It*, ed. with an introduction by Thomas H. Pauly. Carbondale: Southern Illinois University Press, 1997.

Webster's New International Dictionary of the English Language, vol. 2. Edited by W. T. Harris and F. Sturgis Allen. Springfield, MA: G. & C. Merriam, 1909.

Winkler, Kevin. *Big Deal: Bob Fosse and Dance in the American Musical* (Oxford: Oxford University Press, 2018.

"Women Executed in the US: 1900–2021." Death Penalty Information Center. https://deathpenaltyinfo.org/stories/women-executed-in-the-us-1900-2015.

Yarros, Victor S. "Journalism, Ethics, and Common Sense." *International Journal of Ethics* 32 (1922): 410–19.

Zeitz, Joshua. *Flapper: A Madcap Story of Sex, Style, Celebrity, and the Women Who Made America Modern.* New York: Three Rivers Press, 2006.

INDEX

Italicized page numbers indicate illustrations.

Charles H. Cosgrove is an emeritus professor of early Christian literature at Garrett Seminary in Evanston, Illinois. He is the author of numerous books and articles in a wide range of fields, ranging from early Christian life and ethics to ancient music and American history. Recent examples include *Fortune and Faith in Old Chicago: A Dual Biography of Mayor Augustus Garrett and Seminary Founder Eliza Clark Garrett* (Southern Illinois University Press, 2020) and *Music at Social Meals in Greek and Roman Antiquity.*